CHEATING IN COLLEGE

Cheating in College

Why Students Do It and
What Educators Can Do about It

DONALD L. MCCABE
KENNETH D. BUTTERFIELD
and LINDA K. TREVIÑO

The Johns Hopkins University Press

Baltimore

© 2012 The Johns Hopkins University Press
All rights reserved. Published 2012
Printed in the United States of America on acid-free paper
9 8 7 6 5 4 3 2 1

The Johns Hopkins University Press
2715 North Charles Street
Baltimore, Maryland 21218-4363
www.press.jhu.edu

Library of Congress Cataloging-in-Publication Data

McCabe, Donald L.
    Cheating in college : why students do it and what educators can do about it /
Donald L. McCabe, Kenneth D. Butterfield, and Linda K. Treviño.
        pages cm
    Includes bibliographical references and index.
    ISBN 978-1-4214-0716-6 (hdbk. : alk. paper) — ISBN 978-1-4214-0756-2 (electronic) —
ISBN 1-4214-0716-7 (hdbk. : alk. paper) — ISBN 1-4214-0756-6 (electronic)
    1. Education, Higher—Moral and ethical aspects.   2. Cheating (Education)—United
States.   3. College students—United States—Conduct of life.   I. Treviño, Linda
Klebe.   II. Butterfield, Kenneth D.   III. Title.
    LB3609.M27 2012
    378.001—dc23   2012007935

A catalog record for this book is available from the British Library.

*Special discounts are available for bulk purchases of this book. For more information,
please contact Special Sales at 410-516-6936 or specialsales@press.jhu.edu.*

The Johns Hopkins University Press uses environmentally friendly book materials,
including recycled text paper that is composed of at least 30 percent post-consumer
waste, whenever possible.

CONTENTS

CHEATING IN COLLEGE

CHAPTER ONE

A Journey and a Commitment to Action

This book is the history of a two-decade-long journey that dominated our research and often our lives during that time. When we began this project in early 1990, no one would have predicted that it would last more than a year or two, the time it would take to conduct a replication of the groundbreaking work of Bill Bowers in the early 1960s (the original goal of our project) and to disseminate the results to those schools that elected to participate in the original survey—31 schools from across the country: big and small, coed and all female, liberal arts colleges and some of our best universities, and representing a truly eclectic mix of majors. The unifying theme of that original sample was that all but two schools were small to medium in size (typically fewer than ten thousand students, and many fewer than five thousand) and all were highly selective in their admissions policies and highly residential in character. These were and still are some of our nation's best schools, educating many of its future leaders. Yet, here we are, still at it after all these years.

Since this first project, we have moved on to survey students and faculty at larger institutions, public and private, those with honor codes of varying types and strengths and those with relatively weak academic integrity policies. Over the years, we have amassed a dataset that, we believe, is unmatched and has allowed us to study the incidence of cheating and its effects on academic integrity over time. Bill Bowers's generosity in sharing his data from the 1960s has allowed us to evaluate how these phenomena have changed (or remained the same) over a fifty-year period. The key findings and conclusions discussed in this book include:

- Cheating habits among college students probably develop long before they get to college. Most college-bound students are exposed to significant cheating cultures during their high school years.

- More than two-thirds of college students report that they engaged in some form of academic dishonesty in the previous year. Some shifts appear to be occurring, as certain types of self-reported cheating seem to be increasing (e.g., collaborative cheating) and some seem to be decreasing (e.g., plagiarizing written work, as this practice is displaced by Internet plagiarism).
- Cheating is also rampant in graduate and professional schools. Data suggest that cheating may be lower in certain professional schools (e.g., law schools) and higher in others (e.g., business, pharmacy, dentistry).
- A major shift has occurred in cheating-related attitudes and definitions among students. This may help to explain the reported decreases in certain types of self-reported cheating.
- Both individual and contextual factors influence academic integrity and cheating behavior. Among the most powerful contextual influences are peer disapproval, peer behavior, and a strong ethical environment.
- A deeply embedded and well-run honor code can play a key role in creating a strong ethical environment. However, a strong ethical environment can also be created in the absence of an honor code.

At the end of the book (chapter 9), we will share our overall assessment of student cheating and academic integrity in higher education today, recognizing the significance of the problem and offering recommendations about what we think can and should be done to create campus cultures of integrity. Indeed, we believe that administrators and faculty have an opportunity as well as an obligation to play a part in creating a strong ethical culture and reducing cheating on their campuses.

We use the term *cheating* extensively throughout the book, so we should clearly state our definition of cheating at the outset. One of the challenges of reviewing research in this domain is that different researchers have used different definitions of cheating and measured it differently (and students may have their own definitions as well). In our survey research, we use a standard measure of cheating (based in part on Bowers's earlier measure) that asks respondents to answer questions about whether they have engaged, in the past year, in a set of very specific behaviors. Included in the measure used in the research reported in this book (unless explicitly stated otherwise) are the following nine behaviors: copying a few sentences of material without footnoting them in a paper; "padding" a few items on a bibliography (i.e., adding citations not actually used in the paper); plagiarizing from public material in preparing a paper; getting exam questions or answers (ahead of time) from someone who has already taken the same exam; copying from another student on a test or exam (two measures consolidated into one here: with and without the other student's knowledge); working on the same homework with several students when the teacher does not allow it; turning in a paper done entirely or in part by another student(s); giving answers to other students during an exam; and using (unpermitted or unauthorized) crib notes (or cheat notes) during an exam. At least half the students in our initial surveys indicated that at least seven of these measures constituted cheating in their minds. The remaining two items—working on the same homework with several students when the teacher does not allow it (unpermitted collaboration) and getting questions or answers (ahead of time) from someone who has already taken the same exam—have also been named by a large number of respondents as cheating and were included in the Bowers surveys, as well as in each of ours. Thus, when we refer to cheating, we are describing the behavior of a student who has self-reported engaging in at least one of these nine behaviors in the past year.

Why Should We Care about Academic Integrity?

When people ask us, which many have, why we care so much about academic integrity when the world is gripped by bigger problems, we find this question perplexing. It challenges a view that we take for granted: that academic integrity matters a lot, especially when viewed as a barometer of the general ethical inclinations of the rising generation. We view academic integrity as a harbinger of things to come, a reflection of the general mores that society is passing on to the next generation.

We can think of at least six reasons why we should care about academic integrity: (1) integrity is the cornerstone of academia, (2) cheating is widespread and on the rise, (3) the college years are a critical period for ethical development, (4) college students face significant pressures to cheat, (5) students are being taught that cheating is acceptable, and (6) today's college students represent tomorrow's leaders.

Integrity Is the Cornerstone of Academia

In our two decades of work, we have come to believe that a failure to address academic dishonesty devalues the educational process and leaves colleges and universities vulnerable to questions about the quality of the product they produce—the future leaders of society. Almost every societal sector, from sports to business to politics, has recently been plagued by questionable integrity of some sort. Some would even go so far as to suggest that the failure of many of our leading universities to cultivate positive values has contributed to the problem we face as a nation and as a larger society. Even Bowers shared this concern, almost fifty years ago: "The tendency to develop a disposition in one social context and to carry it into another suggests that academic dishonesty in college may lead to dishonesty and deceit in other areas of social life" (1964, 4).

We should care about academic integrity because we believe it is one of the issues that students face in college for which colleges and universities can make a difference, providing society's future leaders with an experience of living within a community of integrity—a touchstone for their future. That's why we continue to work on academic integrity and why we hope this book will encourage many faculty members and administrators to think more carefully about the importance of their role in supporting academic integrity.

Cheating Is Widespread and on the Rise

I think that the problem of academic dishonesty runs rampant throughout the campus. Although some professors make an effort to prosecute offenders, the general attitude seems to be that everyone cheats. Since everyone does it, it's okay (student at a large state school in the Midwest).

As this comment suggests, cheating in colleges and universities is a widespread problem (something we elaborate on in chapter 3). In his early 1960s survey of more than five thousand students at 99 college campuses, Bowers found that more than half of the students he surveyed reported engaging in some form of academic dishonesty since coming to their current college. Using data from the Bowers study as a baseline, subsequent research has reported even higher levels of some kinds of cheating, even though some of this research, including our own, has asked students to report only cheating in which they have been engaged in the past year. For example, a study we conducted in 1993 at nine large public universities from the original Bowers sample showed significant increases in the rate of self-reported cheating on tests and exams over the 30-year period, as well as in collaborative cheating—for example, collaborating on written assignments when the instructor explicitly asked for individual work (McCabe and Treviño 1997).

These findings are underscored by a number of cheating scandals. For example, in 2005, 119 prospective Harvard MBA students' applications were rejected because the applicants allegedly hacked into the school's admissions website (Lindsay 2005). Another notable example occurred in 2001 at the University of Virginia, a school with a long-standing honor code tradition, when a physics professor found evidence of plagiarism in as many as 60 papers submitted by students (Schemo 2001). If we choose not to care about academic integrity, student cheating may well continue to grow unabated. This is likely to have many unfortunate consequences, such as calling into question the legitimacy of the degrees and other credentials that we bestow on our students.

The College Years Are a Critical Period for Ethical Development

Academic integrity and dishonesty also matter because most college students are at a developmental level where their approach to ethical decision making is being formed. Research has long demonstrated that the college years represent a period of significant moral development. For example, in their classic study spanning the 1930s, 1960s, and 1990s, Newcomb and his colleagues investigated the social and political attitudes of students enrolled at Bennington College. Their findings supported a thesis of "stability and change": students' attitudes change in college, and these attitudes tend to persist later in life (Feldman and Newcomb 1969, 332). Tomlinson's (1974) work supports this view, indicating that the college years typically represent a period of moral development and growth as students question their beliefs and, one hopes, advance in terms of moral maturity. Other longitudinal research has further established a significant correlation between adult cognitive moral development and years of formal education, supporting the notion that higher education contributes to moral development (Rest and Thoma 1986).

Our own research has extended this tradition by demonstrating that students' ethics-related attitudes and behaviors are influenced by particular kinds of educational communities (McCabe and Treviño 1993; McCabe, Treviño, and Butterfield 1996). This includes students who attend college full-time at a residential campus, but is particularly true for students who experience a collegiate honor code environment. According to Melendez (1985), an honor code environment is one that involves certain procedures (a peer judiciary), benefits (unproctored examinations), and requirements (students pledge that they will not engage in unethical conduct and, in some cases, that they will report students who do). In such environments, students typically learn a great deal about living in a community where individuals are trusted and where people who violate community norms are sanctioned. This has the potential to affect their ethical attitudes, beliefs, and development. Our research has also demonstrated that involvement in such a community can influence ethics-related behaviors and reduce academic dishonesty (McCabe and Treviño 1993).

Just as an honor code can promote ethical attitudes and behavior, a strong peer cheating culture can have the opposite effect. At this life stage, most students look to others for cues about appropriate behavior, and peers play a powerful role in shaping attitudes and behavior. As discussed by Sanford (1964), the college experience marks a crucial turning point, when adolescents abandon their own beliefs in favor of their fellow students' opinions and values. Students require guidance during these formative years, and academic institutions can play a central role in this developmental process.

College Students Feel Significant Pressure to Cheat

So much pressure and stress is put on getting ahead that we will take any advantage we can get (male student majoring in education).

Another reason we should care about academic integrity is that today's students say they feel growing pressures to demonstrate high academic achievement. As our qualitative work has shown (McCabe, Treviño, and Butterfield 1999), this pressure comes from many sources, including societal expectations, family expectations, and peer pressure. Many students also place enormous pressure on themselves to excel academically, to obtain a good job, and to gain admission to a prestigious graduate school.

Research indicates that peer influence may be the strongest of these pressures. Our research has consistently shown that observed peer behavior is among the most important influences on student cheating (McCabe, Butterfield, and Treviño 2006; McCabe and Treviño 1993, 1997; McCabe, Treviño, and Butterfield 2002). Peer cheating provides a kind of normative support or license for cheating. When peers are seen cheating, cheating may come to be viewed as an acceptable way of behaving and getting ahead. Peer cheating can also create competitive pressure. If students see others getting ahead by cheating, they may feel compelled to do the same in order to preserve their place in the pecking order. Students often report feelings of frustration due to perceived unfairness when other students are cheating, and some conclude that they have no choice but to cheat to "level the playing field" and avoid falling behind their peers.

College Students Are Being Taught That Cheating Is Acceptable

We should also care about academic integrity because many influences, both inside and outside academic institutions, are prompting students to question whether cheating is wrong or even undesirable. This is reflected in the following student comments:

The world is a cutthroat place, and cheating, or getting the advantage is an unspoken result of our capitalist society, it is a taboo but at the same time it has earned its way into our way of life (male student at a private university).

In today's world and culture and climate, [ethics] has become a major joke! How about Enron, WorldCom, Merrill Lynch, just to name a few! (female student at a state university).

Inside colleges and universities, students receive repeated signals that suggest cheating is acceptable. Peer behavior, as noted above, represents one source. Cheating behavior among peers sends a message that cheating is not just acceptable but perhaps even necessary. This is exacerbated by the fact that students are generally reluctant to turn in their classmates when they observe them cheating, even when anonymity is ensured. This leads to a sense of ambiguity about the appropriateness and inappropriateness of cheating.

Faculty and administrators often contribute to this problem by failing to monitor cheating behavior, turning a blind eye when cheating is reported, neglecting to clearly communicate expectations regarding appropriate and inappropriate behavior on assignments and tests, disregarding academic integrity guidelines and policies, failing to demonstrate that academic integrity is a priority, and giving students mixed signals about appropriate and inappropriate behavior. For example, we know of professors who teach students about the virtues of collaboration and then admonish students for collaborating. Some students perceive what they believe to be cheating on the part of certain faculty and administrators and condemn what they view as hypocrisy. They reason that if it is acceptable for faculty and administrators to cheat, why not students.

All of this creates an environment of ethical ambiguity that conveys mixed messages about the appropriateness of cheating. Our research suggests that this contributes to some students' belief that what many professors consider cheating (e.g., unauthorized collaboration) more accurately falls into an ethical "gray area" (McCabe, Treviño, and Butterfield 1999). By appealing to gray areas, and otherwise stretching the definition of "not cheating" beyond normal standards, students can often justify or deny any wrongdoing.

Of course, cheating is not limited to college campuses. A series of recent high-profile scandals in corporations, government, and athletics has focused attention on ethics and cheating in the larger culture. Today's students have grown up in a society where ethical transgressions among business leaders, government officials, and sports figures are common, often leading to no real punishment. A good overview of these trends and their impact is found in *The Cheating Culture* (Callahan 2004).

For example, as we were writing this chapter, the Securities and Exchange Commission charged Texas financier R. Allen Stanford with fraud for allegedly bilking investors out of $8 billion by misrepresenting rates of return for certificates of deposit and losing much of the proceeds through a "black box" of risky investments (Scannell, Bustillo, and Perez 2009). This scheme would have been more prominent news if not for Bernard Madoff, the former chairman of the NASDAQ stock exchange, who was charged with committing what is believed to be the largest securities fraud in history. Madoff defrauded investors out of $50 billion through a classic Ponzi scheme, paying off early investors with funds from subsequent clients to maintain an illusion of profitability (Zambito and Smith 2008). In sports news, baseball star Roger Clemens was charged with obstruction of justice and perjury with regard to long-standing allegations on the use of performance-enhancing drugs (Sheinin and Hsu 2010). In politics, we saw the far-reaching political corruption investigation of former lobbyist Jack Abramoff. Abramoff was convicted of crimes that include grossly overbilling clients from Indian casinos and using the proceeds for political gifts and illegal campaign donations. The Abramoff scandal led to the conviction of at least two White House officials and ten other lobbyists and congressional aides, as well as the resignation and imprisonment of U.S. representative Bob Ney (Frieden 2009). These headlines are routinely accompanied by less sensational stories such as employers who fail to terminate employees who falsified their credentials, managers who seem not to care that a job applicant cheated throughout college, and employees who cheat on personality tests during the application process (O'Connell 2009).

Many students perceive that such violations are punished minimally, if at all. Not surprisingly, this sends a strong message to the current generation of students that cheating is acceptable and perhaps even necessary. Some adopt cynical attitudes and find themselves asking questions such as "Doesn't everyone do it?" and "Who cares if students cheat?" They reason that in a "win at all costs" atmosphere, one must use any and all means necessary to get ahead, including cheating. If we do not do something to alter this trend, students will continue to rationalize that it is okay to cheat.

Today's College Students Represent Tomorrow's Leaders

Values and beliefs—circumstances may change from time to time, but having values might make a person less prone to changing his or her mind in tough situations. The university should be a place with people who have strong values and convictions even in stressful situations, especially if these are future leaders of the country/world (male student majoring in the social sciences).

Perhaps the most important reason that we should care about academic integrity is that college students are likely to become tomorrow's leaders in virtually all areas of society, including education, medicine, law, politics, and business. The decision to cheat or not to cheat on academic work is one of the most basic ethical decisions faced by college students. If they cannot pass this test, this does not reflect well on our shared future.

Thus, we view this as a fight for the future. Unfortunately, many colleges and universities have not been doing a very good job, particularly in terms of creating and maintaining the kind of culture that promotes academic integrity. Unless we do a better job of teaching the next generation of college students about honesty and integrity, we may well be contributing to their cynicism about ethics, leading to further ethical erosion in our academic institutions and in the broader society.

Our goal is to bring together in one volume what we have learned in our two decades of study, from our own research and that of others. Some may argue that cheating has been around as long as humans have—there's nothing new and not much can be done. We disagree. We have seen change over the past twenty years and sense a growing attitude among many of our students that it's time for students and institutions to take action. Part of the current problem may be that students and faculty have different definitions of what is acceptable behavior and what constitutes cheating. To see this, one only needs to talk to a few faculty members and a few students about the appropriate use of the Internet in preparing written assignments. But we get a strong sense that many students are willing, in some cases eager, to attack the biggest problems—such as the preparation of term papers by ghost writers or explicit cheating on a test or exam. A critical question in our minds is whether faculty and administrators are willing to work with students to achieve this goal, especially when it might mean faculty ceding some "control" to students to assure their buy-in.

Our hope is that, in some small way, the research summarized in this book will help faculty and administrators understand that taking action to support academic integrity makes sense and that it is time to do so. Many forces undermine academic integrity, and sometimes they may appear insurmountable—cynicism, relativism, and apathy among students, and skepticism, indifference, and resistance to change among faculty and administrators. Less apparent sources include faculty who give students mixed signals about the inappropriateness of cheating and faculty curmudgeons who focus on maintaining law and order through fear and retribution.

Fortunately, there are also forces working to promote academic integrity. We have been privileged to work with many faculty members and administrators who are genuinely concerned about the issue and have rebuilt courses, revamped their curricula, and strengthened their institutional cultures. We have also been encouraged by the growing number of students who take a stand against cheating and for academic integrity in their institutions. Many students devote considerable time and effort to tackle ethics-related tasks that are often avoided by faculty, such as designing and enforcing honor codes and serving on judicial boards. These people inspire us to be positive and aspirational, in both the focus and the tone of our writing.

What Can We Do?

We believe that faculty and administrators can make a difference, if they are genuinely concerned about academic integrity and are willing to devote time and effort to promoting it. An increasing number of colleges and universities are refocusing their efforts to promote academic integrity among students, as part of their strategy to enhance students' ethical development and reduce the level of cheating on campus. These efforts include orientation and training sessions, website pages and chapters in student handbooks devoted to academic integrity and codes of conduct, and development of course syllabi to include definitions, consequences, and other content related to academic integrity. Many institutions are also expanding their efforts to teach ethics to students, and some have even tried to include some judgment about an applicant's ethical inclinations in their admissions process. In addition, the number of colleges and universities that have joined the Center for Academic Integrity, a consortium of institutions with a common interest in promoting academic integrity, grew from less than fifty to more than three hundred in less than two decades. (The current membership of the center has since dipped below three hundred as schools cut budgets in this time of austerity.) The number of schools adopting some form of academic honor code, or at least the principles generally embodied in such codes, has risen as well. We believe these trends are an indication that, today, more academic institutions are taking academic integrity seriously.

Those familiar with our work know that we started out as unabashed fans of honor code strategies to promote academic integrity and reduce student cheating. But, as this book clearly reflects, a funny thing happened on the way to our celebration of honor codes. First, we "discovered" that it is not the presence or absence of a formal code itself that is the key to addressing academic dishonesty. Second, it seems that the influence of honor codes, at least as they have been implemented at many schools, has eroded over the past two decades. For reasons we discuss in the final chapter, we are still committed to strategies that involve the principles embodied in honor codes.

Although Bowers's perspective on the general problem of cheating was broad, he also looked at the impact of academic honor codes on the self-reported cheating of students at the 99 schools he surveyed. This focus is more explicit in our work, but Bowers's early work allows us to make some longitudinal comparisons on the effectiveness of honor codes, as well as other approaches to promoting academic integrity. Indeed, an underlying objective in the initiation of our original project was to determine whether honor codes still held a significant influence over students, as Bowers reported. Two of us fondly remembered the honor code experiences we had as undergraduates at two different schools and wondered whether codes still had a similar impact. This was the central design criterion in our sample selection. Fourteen of the 31 schools in our original sample had traditional academic honor codes, and 17 did not. The 14 code schools "trusted" students to do honest work, and most did not proctor exams. Instead, they relied on a campus culture created and nurtured by their honor codes to help students understand the positive values associated with living in a community of trust and the negative outcomes associated with the alternative. In essence, our original research question was whether honor codes still "worked" in nurturing high levels of academic integrity on campus. Although this is still a question that interests us greatly, our objective has morphed somewhat over time. First, we learned that academic honor codes are not the only successful approach to improving levels of student academic integrity. Second, the literature on student cheating blossomed simultaneously with our growing interest in the topic. A wave of new research seemed to be developing, at least some of which, we hope, was catalyzed by some of our own work. While this growing interest is certainly a positive development, it compounds the task we hope to accomplish in this book. Our underlying goal is to further the dialogue that our work and the work of others has precipitated over the past twenty years and provide a meaningful summary of the state of the art in academic integrity—what students believe academic integrity is, what might motivate students to behave with increased integrity (including to cheat less), what contextual settings seem to be associated with higher levels of academic integrity (e.g., honor codes), and so forth.

So, while our own work over the past two decades will serve as an organizing principle for this book, we also hope to provide a comprehensive review of the literature on academic integrity. We aim to create a compendium that will serve as a resource both for future researchers who will work on the many unanswered questions that remain and, perhaps even more important, for schools interested in reviewing and perhaps upgrading their existing integrity policies.

How the Book Is Structured

We hope that our readers will come to better understand

- why academic integrity is important;
- what is known about cheating in college, including why students cheat; and
- what works to promote academic integrity and reduce cheating.

We have tried to make the case as to why this topic and this book are important. In the next chapter, we discuss what college students bring with them from their high school experience. Then we review research on cheating and academic integrity, including prevalence, types, and methods of cheating, and trends over time, such as Internet-based cheating (chapter 3). We move from there to consider personal and contextual reasons why students cheat (chapters 4–7). It is helpful to understand both personal and contextual influences because interventions can be targeted toward groups that cheat more (e.g., business majors) and contexts that support cheating (e.g., fraternities and sororities). Although most research on academic integrity focuses on undergraduates, we also look at professional schools (chapter 8). We conclude by looking ahead and offering practical advice for faculty and administrators interested in promoting academic integrity in their institutions (chapter 9). We focus in particular on the role of the institution's ethical culture. We offer an ethical community-building approach that colleges and universities can use to send clear and unambiguous messages to students and help them form a solid foundation for ethical decision making.

Although our focus is on the positive, aspirational side of these issues, we are not naive—cheating has always been and will always be with us. We have researched this topic for two decades and have published many scholarly papers in this area. We have talked with students, faculty, and administrators. We know a lot about what matters and what seems to work. Our goal here is to take what we know and present it in a practical and interesting way, but also in a way that is grounded in solid research findings—both our own and those of others. We offer no magic elixirs or shortcuts to achieving success. Improving the climate of integrity on our campuses is hard work, but work that is essential and important.

CHAPTER TWO

Where to Begin

Academic Dishonesty among High School Students

As noted in chapter 1, our work has primarily focused on the college level. However, about a decade ago, we made the decision that to better understand what we were observing among college students, we needed to develop some understanding of the experience they brought with them from high school. Because the available research on the level of cheating among high school students was limited (e.g., Brandes 1986; Schab 1991), we decided to generate some of our own data. In this chapter we discuss what we have learned about the attitudes and beliefs concerning academic integrity and dishonesty that college students carry with them from high school to their higher education experience.

Work Begun by Others

We begin by summarizing what we know about high school students' attitudes and cheating behavior from notable work in this area. For example, Davis and his colleagues (1992) did some important empirical work, but their research focused more on the relationship between cheating and individual attributes than on the institutional perspective that is of more interest to us. In addition, although they did discuss high school cheating, their primary focus was on college cheating. Indeed, their data on high school cheating were obtained from a sample of college students at 35 schools (including 13 private schools and 8 two-year colleges) whom they surveyed concerning their cheating experiences in both high school and college. These researchers reported, as we corroborate later, that students admit to cheating at even higher rates in high school than in college. For example, using the college attended by

The authors acknowledge Joseph Gaspar, a doctoral student at Rutgers, for his assistance in preparing the literature review for this chapter.

students as their unit of analysis, Davis et al. found self-reported levels of high school cheating ranging from a low of 51% to a high of 83%, compared with self-reported levels of cheating in college ranging from 9%, reported by a sample of women at a small liberal arts college, to 64%, reported by a sample of men at a regional university.

Much of the other literature available in 1999, when we started surveying high school students, focused primarily on such variables as willingness to cheat (e.g., Coles, Hunter, and See 1989), the seriousness of cheating as perceived by both faculty and students (e.g., Evans and Craig 1990), and the role of moral reasoning (e.g., Bruggeman and Hart 1996). Bruggeman and Hart found self-reported levels of cheating among high school students that fell well within the range reported earlier by Davis and coauthors: in the Bruggeman and Hart survey, 70% among 90 students attending a religiously affiliated high school versus 78% reported by 131 students attending a private but secular high school in the same region.

Evans and Craig (1990) did not attempt to quantify the level of cheating, but their survey is important. They administered a 109-item Likert-type survey to 1,763 students and 107 teachers in four middle schools (grades 7 and 8) that fed two senior high schools (grades 9 through 12) in a single school district in Washington State. As defined by the authors, the survey covered four domains: problem awareness and seriousness, knowledge of cheating, causal attributions for cheating, and "a subject's beliefs about the efficacy of various strategies designed to prevent or reduce cheating" (Evans and Craig 1990, 45). Much of what the authors described as the major findings of their survey is not surprising. For example, they reported that both students and faculty were sensitive to (aware of) the incidence of cheating—a result that has received widespread support in other work, including our own. Another of their findings that we have also observed in our own work was that students were more likely than teachers to attribute the presence of cheating to such factors as their classrooms and teachers, as well as themselves— for example, students saw part-time work as a more significant correlate of cheating than did teachers. But both groups were skeptical about the ability of various strategies to reduce cheating, including the use of honor codes. We were not surprised to learn that students and teachers who had never "lived" under such a code would be skeptical about its effectiveness. But we have also seen students and teachers who, when introduced to an honor code environment, grow to understand its benefits and become comfortable with its "restrictions," ultimately reducing the level of cheating. We cover this topic in greater detail in later chapters, when we discuss our own research, but we should note here that we do believe that honor codes are more difficult to introduce in a high school than in a college setting.

The efforts of Brandes (1986) and Schab (1991) stand out as good examples of empirical work at the high school level. Both authors used self-reports by students, despite the shortcomings of such reports, to quantify the level of high school cheating. Some subsequent efforts to do this, including our own and that of the Josephson Institute of Ethics, are discussed below. Brandes (1986) conducted a large-scale study of middle school students (1,037 sixth graders) and high school students (2,265, mostly eleventh graders) enrolled in public schools, as well as 109 school staff members, in California in the spring of 1985. Among the highlighted findings reported by Brandes (1986, 5–6) were the following: (1) The incidence of all types of cheating was higher among the high school students. (2) Major forms of cheating among the sixth graders included copying from another student on a test (39%) and plagiarism (41%). (3) Major forms of cheating among the high school students included their use of crib (or cheat) notes during a test (74% acknowledging they had done this one or more times) and copying from another student during a test (for which fully 75% acknowledged one or more transgressions). And (4), 97% of the high school students indicated they had seen another student copy on a test at least once, and almost 93% had seen this occur at least a few times or more. While other researchers, ourselves included, have used slightly different approaches to estimate the amount of cheating in either high school or college, there are no "big surprises" in the Brandes data. Of further interest from the Brandes study is a priority ordering of high school students' opinions on what they believe contributes to cheating. Number one is a failure to study and prepare, followed by fear of failing and the pressure parents put on their children to do well. Ranked seventh of the eight items presented as possible choices is "They are not afraid of punishment." One must ask whether this suggests that schools are contributing to the problem through leniency around cheating.

Schab (1991) conducted one of the few longitudinal studies of high school cheating that was available before the Josephson Institute began its work in the 1990s. The Schab study is a major contribution to the literature, but it has two obvious shortcomings: first, it includes only students from central Georgia (reflecting Professor Schab's location at the University of Georgia), and second, subsequent to his 1989 study, Schab retired. McCabe contacted Schab in 1999 in an attempt to offer his assistance to continue this study, but without success. So we have a longitudinal study that includes surveys conducted in 1969, 1979, and 1989, with more than a thousand students participating in each of those three years, although the generalizability of the data may be limited by the unique focus on students from central Georgia. Over the years, we have noticed in our data that schools in the South and Midwest tend to report somewhat lower levels of cheating than schools on the east and west coasts. Although most of Schab's survey questions are somewhat different from those used by Brandes, there is at least one identical question—concerning the use of crib notes. While Brandes (1986) reported that 74% of the primarily high school juniors in his survey had used crib notes at least once, Schab's (1989) number is a somewhat lower 68%. Certainly, both numbers indicate that a significant problem exists and, indeed, they seem quite comparable, especially given that the Schab sample includes more than just juniors (which is implied but not explicitly stated). There is also evidence from a number of surveys, including our own, that the level of cheating in high school correlates positively with grade level, as well as showing the regional effect. Other interesting highlights in the Schab survey include the following: (1) Over time, students reported being more aware of cheating among their peers. (2) Over time, respondents became more certain that higher levels of cheating occurred in high school than in elementary school and college. (3) The Schab and Brandes respondents listed the same three items—failure to study ("too lazy to study" in Schab's listing), fear of failure, and parental pressure—as the major explanations of why students cheat. And (4), most important from our perspective, Schab clearly demonstrated that self-reported levels of cheating among high school students between 1969 and 1989, at least in central Georgia, were increasing. For example, letting others copy your work increased from 58% to 98%; using a cheat sheet, from 34% to 68%; and self-reports of copying something word-for-word from a book, from 67% to 76% (Schab 1991, 843). Indeed, it was this knowledge of how significantly cheating seemed to be increasing at the high school level that made us realize we might be on the cusp of a major increase in cheating at the college level, and thus we needed to do more to understand how this might affect colleges and their students.

Our Research Begins

Our first attempt to gather our own high school data centered on a survey of four public school districts and one private school in New Jersey in the spring of 1999 (McCabe 1999). Our goals were strictly exploratory at this point. We administered a brief written survey to a sample of 455 students (mostly eleventh graders) at the five senior high schools, and we were able to administer a comparable survey to 593 junior high school students (primarily seventh and eighth graders, but also some sixth graders), although only at four schools, as one of the public school districts opted out of this part of the survey. Highlights of the results included: (1) cheating on tests was self-reported by 74% of the junior high students and 78% of the eleventh graders; (2) 87% of the junior high students reported that they had observed someone else cheating on a test, versus 90% of the senior high students; (3) self-reported plagiarism was slightly higher among the junior high students—41% versus 39%; and (4) the open-ended comments provided by the senior high students, in particular, suggested views of cheating that were already fairly hardened. For example, here is a small sampling of the comments offered by senior high students in this survey:

Cheating is an inevitable part of life. Society teaches that the cheater usually succeeds more than the honest man, so based on what we observe, cheating makes sense.

If you don't get caught, you did the job right.

I don't think many people care about cheating.

Although similar in many ways, the comments from junior high students in this survey were a little less negative. Junior high students generally acknowledged that a high level of cheating was occurring among their peers, but many seemed to feel that more serious cheating (e.g., copying from someone on a test) was less frequent than activities such as copying homework. Indeed, many expressed views that questioned whether copying of another student's homework was cheating at all or wondered how they could possibly refuse a classmate who had asked for such help. They also seemed to place a significant share of the blame for the cheating they observed on their teachers. For example:

Lots of people have cheated off me and the teachers just sit at their desks not even bothering to look for cheaters.

Some students get away with cheating and the teachers act like nothing has happened.

Teachers are stupid, or they just don't care. When I [cheated] my teacher saw, she didn't do anything. They don't give a damn.

These findings are consistent with research by Murdock and colleagues (Murdock, Beauchamp, and Hinton 2008; Murdock, Miller, and Kohlhardt 2004), who examined the role of classroom characteristics and teacher behaviors on cheating-related outcomes. These studies showed that poor pedagogy, ineffective goal structures, and low teacher caring influence the degree to which students blame their teachers for cheating behavior, how students reason about the acceptability of cheating, and students' actual cheating behavior.

One other distinguishing feature of our junior high survey, however, was the observation by more than a few students that some, perhaps many, students completing the survey were not taking it seriously and were making a "joke" of it. Student comments suggested that the self-reports of cheating we were seeing might be intentionally inflated. While this indicates that we must interpret our junior high school results with caution, even the fact that students would elect to treat the topic in this fashion might be revealing of their true feelings about cheating. The comments offered by both the junior and senior high school students we surveyed at this time definitely suggest that many students, maybe even most, simply did not see day-to-day cheating (on quizzes, homework, and written assignments other than term papers) as a big deal. It seems they had become quite comfortable with such cheating and, in at least some cases, viewed cheating as essential to remaining competitive in what they perceived as the "great GPA race." This seemed especially true among senior high school students, most of whom were aspiring to go to college. They felt pressure from their parents and from themselves to maintain as high a GPA as possible. So when they saw others cheating, even on minor assignments, they felt the need to do the same so that they would not be at a disadvantage.

To try to gain some additional insight into these issues, in the spring of 1999, with funding from Educational Testing Services, we conducted two focus groups involving a total of 18 college-bound high school seniors and one junior from eight high schools in New Jersey that represented a mix of urban and suburban, public and private, and single sex and coed (McCabe 1999, 682). In addition to confirming the role that teachers might play in failing to prevent cheating, as well as their comments on the then increasing role of technology in cheating, these students provided some additional insight into changing student attitudes on cheating. For example, some comments we reported earlier (McCabe 1999, 682):

I think times have changed. Cheating is considered, I don't know, just a kind of daily thing that's out there, almost kind of acceptable. Teachers know it and students know it.

Maybe when our parents were growing up or their parents were growing up, it was a lot tighter and stricter on people cheating. Today it's just not happening. I think grown-ups have gotten a little bit more with-it in terms of knowing that you're just going to kind of cheat.

It's almost a big deal if you don't cheat.

We came away from our first survey and these focus groups with the sense that, first, cheating habits develop early and, second. there was something to be learned from high school students. It was on this basis that we decided to pursue further work with these students, and we put together a sample of 26 schools—14 public and 12 private, geographically dispersed in 18 states, ranging from Massachusetts to California, South Dakota, and Texas—for a second study. Although we were successful in recruiting these 14 public schools, we quickly learned how difficult it would be to get public schools, in general, to participate in our survey process. It seemed that individual teachers were afraid of what the principal might say if they helped us, while principals generally felt they needed to get their superintendent's permission to do our survey. The typical response from the superintendents was that they would not proceed without approval from the Board of Education, and they already had too many priorities in front of the board to add this to the list. We also got the feeling that fear of adverse publicity and potential problems with parents were probably the bigger issues for most schools. Also evident was the worry that if the schools did the survey and discovered there was a problem, they would have to do something about it. The resulting underrepresentation of public schools in our high school samples has become a constant. The headmasters, headmistresses, or principals at private (secular) and parochial schools generally have not expressed similar concerns and have more typically approved our survey process. While they recognize the potential downside, most seem more interested in gaining a better picture of what is going on in their schools with regard to academic integrity, so they can address it. Of course, some of these private (both secular and parochial) schools have an honor code tradition that goes back decades or more, and they would expect to see less cheating at their schools. Although our survey data bear this out, as we discuss shortly, private secondary schools with honor codes are hardly issue-free in the area of students' academic integrity.

In this second survey, conducted in 2000, we again focused primarily on high school juniors. The survey included 2,342 juniors, with 1,459 enrolled in one of the 14 public schools participating and 883 in one of the 12 parochial schools (423 students in 4 schools) or private schools (460 students in 8 schools). As in our first high school survey, we found high levels of self-reported cheating in general, with 81% of the public school students acknowledging one or more instances of plagiarism or one of four forms of test and exam cheating (copying from another on an exam, with or without the other's knowledge; unpermitted use of crib notes or cheat notes; and helping someone else to cheat on a test or exam). Somewhat surprisingly, 82% of the students at the four parochial schools admitted cheating, versus 67% at the eight private schools. While the private school number is notably lower, we trust most readers would agree that it is still unreasonably high. It seems particularly high to us when we factor in that two of the eight private schools had strong honor code traditions, and "only" 54% of the students at these schools self-reported any cheating.

It was this finding on honor codes in our second survey that led us to contact an association of private schools on the East Coast and suggest a survey to study the honor code issue more deeply. This survey was conducted in the spring of 2004 and included a total of 27 schools—21 private (secular, but some with historical religious roots) and 6 parochial. (Since we were working with a private and parochial school association in this case, there was no public school comparison group.) Central to the objective of exploring the impact of honor codes on secondary school students, of the 27 schools in this sample, 9 had academic honor codes of relatively long standing. We also hoped to develop some further insight into the higher level of self-reported cheating observed at parochial schools by looking at a comparison of private schools with no honor code and the parochial schools, none of which had an honor code, so we might be able to hypothesize whether this higher level of cheating at parochial schools was due to the absence of a code or something else. Of course, the modest sample size in each group would prevent us from reaching any definitive conclusion.

Analysis of data from this survey led to two important observations on the level of cheating: first, honor codes are associated with reduced cheating levels at the secondary school level, and, second, the absence of an honor code tradition does not seem to explain the difference in cheating between parochial and private schools—that is, higher levels of self-reported cheating in parochial schools seem to persist even when we control for the potential influence of honor codes. Regarding honor codes, whether we look at juniors only or all students, we see a notably lower level of cheating in schools with honor codes. For example, looking at the same summary statistic used in our first study, which captures both plagiarism and four forms of serious test cheating, we see that 65% of the 1,959 students in no-code private schools self-reported one or more incidents of cheating, compared with 57% of the 1,993 students in private schools with honor codes. The difference is slightly greater among juniors only (64% in no-code vs. 54% in code schools). We should note that our definition of a traditional honor code in our research at the college level has been stricter than that used by many secondary schools when referring to an honor code. Both types require or encourage the reporting of any incidents of cheating that a student might observe, often utilize students at some point in the adjudication process for alleged violations, and often require the signing of some form of honor pledge, but the use of unproctored exams seems to be much less frequent, indeed almost nonexistent, at the high school level.

Among high schools, whether public or private, being able to say your school had an honor code seemed to be a particular point of pride in the mid-2000s. But often, what a school described as its code was little more than a statement of aspirations and a listing of penalties for typical cheating violations. There was and still is little difference between what many nonprivate schools already had in place (e.g., a listing of potential offenses and punishments) and what was referred to as an honor code. For example, entering the phrase *high school honor code* into Google generates a site "Your Code of Ethics: Schools—High School Honor Codes," sponsored by the Writers Center (2007). The site lists 12 secondary schools purported to have honor codes, 7 of which are public schools—although 3 of these are statewide math and science academies (Illinois, North Carolina, and Virginia), which have some characteristics of private schools (e.g., students living in residence, competitive admissions processes). Even including these three schools, at least five of the seven public schools seem to have a simple listing of offenses and penalties and some aspirational statement labeled as an honor code. Of the other two public school codes, neither really qualifies as an honor code, but one school (one of the math and science academies) does require students to sign a statement acknowledging the goals of the "honor" code, and the other allows but does not mandate some student input in the judicial process. We also note the date of the Writers Center site's most recent update—late 2007—and the dates on the many high school sites produced by the same Google search: in the period 2005–2008, with most in the 2005–2006 range. This seems to be the time frame when it was still fashionable to be introducing a code at the high school level—often leading to much desired publicity portraying the school as one that cares about integrity and is doing something about it. Unfortunately, for at least some schools, the publicity may have been longer lasting than the school's dedication to a meaningful, proactive program of academic integrity.

The second finding of import in this second high school survey was confirmation of significantly higher levels of self-reported cheating among the parochial school students than among their private school peers, even at those private schools without honor codes. This continues to puzzle us, as does a finding of many years ago in one of our college studies in which we inquired about religious background. Although the difference was not great, it was large enough to be statistically significant, in the light of our large sample size, and suggested that Roman Catholic students self-reported more academic dishonesty than any other group—including those with no religious preference. In the case of high school students, especially given what we know about the schools in our sample, we do not think it unreasonable to expect equal or lower levels of cheating in these parochial schools, as many parents seem to be making a financial sacrifice to send their children to these schools—ostensibly so that they might receive religious (and moral) instruction. Yet, self-reported cheating is higher in these schools. Parochial schools are often known for their strict levels of discipline, and several parochial school faculty members whom we surveyed suggested they would not consider reporting a student for cheating, because they believed the consequences at their school were overly punitive. We have suggested in training sessions conducted at several Catholic schools over the past ten years that perhaps the higher level of self-reported cheating by Catholic students relates to the power of the confessional, and Catholic students simply have a greater felt obligation to report their own cheating when asked.

TABLE 2.1. Results of the Josephson Institute of Ethics surveys "The Ethics of American Youth," 2000–2010 (% of respondents reporting)

Year	Self-reported test cheating	Self-reported Internet plagiarism
2000	71	—
2002	74	—
2004	62	—
2006	60	33
2008	64	36
2010	59	34

Our need to continue studies of high school students was relieved somewhat by the efforts of the Josephson Institute of Ethics (2010), which now conducts a large biennial survey, "The Ethics of American Youth." Its website (www.josephsoninstitute.org) provides summaries of reports for 1998 forward and detailed information on its most recent surveys. Although the Josephson survey is more expansive than simply classroom issues, it does include some key questions that are germane to academic integrity. In particular, the survey includes a question about engaging in test cheating and, more recently (2006–2010), a question about the use of the Internet to engage in plagiarism on an assignment. The trend since 2000 is summarized in table 2.1.

Examination of the data on test cheating suggests a generally declining trend over the period, while the three years of data on the Internet as a mechanism for cheating suggest a small increase from 2006 to 2008 and then a small decline for 2010. As we discuss in subsequent chapters, we have observed similar trends in self-reported cheating among college undergraduates—some decline in test cheating and some increase in Internet-based plagiarism. These trends may reflect real changes in cheating or, as we suggest later, may reflect changing student attitudes about what constitutes cheating. The thousands of open-ended comments we have collected from both high school and college students seem to suggest a sea change in what many students consider to be cheating. On many of our surveys, students say they have never engaged in a particular activity (whether test copying or Internet plagiarism), but in open-ended comments, they might say they actually have engaged in these behaviors, but then explain why, when they did so, it wasn't really cheating (e.g., the test was unfair; I had too much work to do and could not get it all done so I had to copy part of it, something I don't do often), so in the survey itself they selected the response no, they've never done it.

Returning briefly to the work of the Josephson Institute, we see further evidence that today's students may have unique views of what's right and wrong in the classroom, or at least views that seem to differ from those of older generations. In particular, the Josephson survey in 2008 asked students whether they were satisfied with their own ethics and character. While it's encouraging that 92% answered affirmatively, this seems at odds with the results for the three questions in the Josephson survey that focused on academic integrity behaviors in the classroom. For example, 36% of respondents acknowledged copying from an Internet document for a classroom assignment; 64% acknowledged cheating on a test at school, with more than half of the group acknowledging they had done this more than once; and 82% indicated they had copied homework from someone else, with slightly more than three-quarters of this group acknowledging they had done so on multiple occasions.

To us, this suggests that students may be more interested in simply getting their work done than in what they are actually learning. To some extent at least, this seems to be confirmed by a quick tour of the website of the Higher Education Research Institute (HERI) at the University of California, Los Angeles, which has conducted the American Freshman Survey over the past forty years (http://heri.ucla.edu). This site highlights a significant trend uncovered by HERI that may provide at least some insight into students' motivations for cheating. In 1987, almost half of the students completing the HERI survey indicated that they spent more than six hours a week on homework in their senior year of high school. While this amount of homework time may seem low to at least some adults who went to high school in an earlier time, the bad news is that the proportion doing six hours a week has been steadily declining since this question was added to the HERI survey in 1987. In 2005, only about one-third of participating students indicated they were studying at this level—which amounts to about an hour per day. And we remind the reader that *all* of these participants were college bound. Making this even more troubling is that we have read numerous student comments in our own surveys that attribute cheating to the unreasonable workloads imposed by the school and teachers and discuss how such workloads interfere with students' social lives, jobs, athletics, and so forth. We are also aware of the national debate on grade inflation—students studying less yet getting better grades (e.g., Arum and Roksa 2011). While all of this may not make sense to an older generation, students have less trouble reconciling it. As suggested almost daily in the media, the younger generation's fascination with and dependence on electronics may be a key. Anything and everything they need or want seems to be accessible on their electronic devices. When any answer they need is so readily accessible, it becomes harder to convince students not to use such assistance in their academic work.

Students also may feel free to do whatever it takes to get the job done and get the grade desired in the time allotted, and *they* will determine how much time they have to allot to their academic obligations, after their other activities are complete—social, athletic, relaxation, and so on. And, of course, getting the grades they feel they need in order to get into their first-choice college and satisfy their parents' expectations appears to be a major motivator. Unfortunately, in our view, many students have transferred this pressure to their teachers, in high school and in college, putting upward pressure on individual grades and overall grade distributions. As more faculty members have given in to such pressure, often to avoid the hassle of dealing with parents who feel their high school children deserve better grades, the collective result seems to have been grade inflation. Not surprisingly, if one student succumbs to this grade pressure and gets away with cheating, it motivates others to do the same so that they are not left behind in the great GPA race for college admission. In many cases, students feel little, if any, guilt engaging in this behavior, due to neutralization techniques such as rationalizing or blaming the instructor (McCabe 1992; Sykes and Matza 1957).

This seems to be further confirmed by the aggregated data we collected at the high school level between 2000 and 2010, which include the private school data discussed above (for comparative purposes). However, in our other studies we surveyed some schools in the fall, so we are excluding first-year (freshman) high school students from our analysis here to make sure students are responding only with their high school experience in mind and are not including any incidents of cheating that may have occurred in eighth grade. Eliminating these students and using the same indices used earlier to measure cheating behavior, with one exception, results in the data shown in table 2.2. (The exception relates to plagiarism. It has become clear over the years that students

TABLE 2.2. Rates of self-reported high school cheating, 2000–2010 (% of students, excluding first-year students, reporting behavior)

Group	N	Reporting test cheating (%)	Reporting written cheating (%)	Reporting any cheating (%)
Private schools with honor code	2,254	41	41	57
Private schools, no honor code	3,751	47	41	62
Public schools	7,341	73	58	82
Parochial schools	7,319	67	61	80
Total	20,665	63	54	75

seem to be including instances of "cut-and-paste" plagiarism from written sources in our measure intended to capture larger instances of written plagiarism. As a result, our plagiarism measure includes only three of the four factors used earlier: cut-and-paste plagiarism from the Internet or from written sources and downloading of larger sections of text from the Internet.)

The data in table 2.2 are largely consistent with those we reported and discussed above, with one exception: the identical self-reports of cheating on written work at code and no-code private schools. This may have something to do with our measure of self-reported plagiarism. Inspection of the data in the table suggests that students in code and no-code schools are self-reporting almost identical levels of cut-and-paste plagiarism, which, as we will see shortly, the majority of students view as trivial cheating or not cheating at all. When looking at more serious instances of plagiarism such as downloading most or all of a paper from the Internet, we find the numbers are small in both cases: only 4% of the students in an honor code environment report such activity, while 6% self-report this behavior in a no-code environment. Nevertheless, the data in table 2.2 do seem to confirm some of our earlier findings: cheating in high school is widespread, cheating in both public and (surprisingly, to at least some degree) parochial schools is notably higher than in private (secular) schools, and honor codes, even in high school, seem to reduce the level of some self-reported cheating—test, if not written, cheating.

As we suggested earlier, honor codes are one tool available to high school administrators and faculty to help combat academic dishonesty.

Although they are difficult to implement at the high school level, honor codes can still make a difference. A big issue is how much of a commitment a school is willing to invest in developing and implementing a code. Honor codes require a great deal of patience and attention, and they take time to truly become part of an institution's tradition. One possible exception we are aware of is a school in the Midwest, which McCabe has worked with, that introduced a modified honor code, primarily aspirational in nature, several years ago. We first surveyed the school immediately before the code was enacted. After it had been in effect for only two years, before it really had time to take hold as part of the school's institutional fabric, we were asked to conduct a follow-up survey. There were still skeptics when we surveyed the school this second time. But a typical comment from students was "I think we've gotten better with academic honesty. At least I have." While two years does not seem to be enough time to truly change a school culture, this school seemed to be off to a good start. The most important thing about this progress may be that it occurred at a school with an enrollment in excess of twelve hundred students, suggesting that, although smaller private schools may have an advantage in implementing honor code strategies, they may not have a monopoly. The code at this Midwest school has now been in effect for almost five years, and we look forward to resurveying the students.

Whether honor codes are effective or not, we doubt there will be any rush among high schools to adopt them. First, at public schools, it would almost demand parental approval before a full-fledged code (with a student hearing board, reporting requirements, etc.) could be adopted. We aren't aware of many principals who would be willing to take the risks associated with such a strategy, unless they have had a major and public problem with a cheating incident. However, an aspirational code such as those already adopted by a number of public high schools throughout the country may be a worthwhile response to such concerns. The code may take a variety of forms. Anyone interested in this may find the manual *Honor above All*, compiled by the Josephson Institute (Josephson and Mertz 2004), to provide useful guidance.

For any private school interested in introducing a code, we suggest the manual *A Handbook for Developing and Sustaining Honor Systems* (Gould and Roberts 2007) as a useful guide. Among the high school honor code websites worth viewing, we suggest those of Norfolk Academy, a coed private school (www.norfolkacademy.org); the Hutchison

School, an all-girls private school in Memphis (www. hutchisonschool .org); and the Haverford School, an all-boys private school in Pennsylvania, founded in the Quaker tradition (www.haverford.org). We believe the Haverford School code is particularly interesting because of the significant involvement of students in the resolution of allegations of cheating. Acting as a jury, students make recommendations to the head of school on all cases and also take the initiative, in appropriate cases, of informing parents of penalties or sanctions meted out by the committee to their child. Part of this communication explains why the penalty selected is considered appropriate and that parental support of the proposed sanction is expected. We assume this support is typically forthcoming, since the system's goal "is to promote personal growth and to support community standards [and to] consider mitigating and extenuating circumstances when making its recommendation." Having had the opportunity to observe some sample letters to parents, we find that students on the honor council take the rehabilitation goal of the system seriously and design imaginative sanctions clearly aimed at this goal.

Reminding ourselves that we are *educators*, we believe such rehabilitation should have a prominent place in our arsenal of strategies to address issues of academic dishonesty. For example, what is the appropriate reaction to a first-year student, whether high school or college, who is involved in a minor incident of Internet plagiarism? As educators, perhaps the best response is to use this first-time incident as a "teachable moment" to ensure that the student becomes fully informed about plagiarism and the school's academic integrity policy in general. Not only is this a constructive, educational approach, but it also creates a written record that this particular student has clearly been informed of the policy, and thus any subsequent offense can be treated more seriously. Sometimes a student's first offense may be so serious that such a rehabilitative approach is not appropriate (e.g., a student who breaks into a faculty member's computer to get an advance copy of an exam), but we believe that relatively minor first offenses are better handled through rehabilitative rather than punitive approaches. If done correctly, these approaches not only address the problem but also potentially "save" and educate a good student. Other students and faculty may also be more willing to report an offense if they understand the system to be rehabilitative in orientation.

One issue in implementing such an approach is finding ways to convince students that certain behaviors are truly inappropriate. Among

TABLE 2.3. Ratings of seriousness of selected behaviors by faculty and students at an East Coast public high school, 2010 (% of respondents giving rating)

Behavior	Faculty ratings		Student ratings	
	Not cheating	Serious cheating	Not cheating	Serious cheating
Copying on test/exam	3	90	7	35
Use of crib notes	0	95	14	46
Receiving information on test that a friend took earlier	0	58	16	17
Parents doing more than half of the work on graded assignment	0	78	23	26
Unpermitted collaboration	0	39	34	9
Letting other student copy homework	0	54	20	11

high school students today, views of what constitutes cheating probably differ from those held by most adults. For example, one of the high schools we surveyed in the spring of 2010—a suburban public school in an upscale community on the East Coast—allowed us to survey both students and faculty. Looking at the data provided by each group in their ratings of the seriousness of various forms of cheating, we see a very obvious difference in attitudes. The variable we used in both cases was simply a four-point Likert scale that allowed respondents to rate various behaviors as not cheating, trivial cheating, moderate cheating, or serious cheating. Only 35% of the 396 students completing the survey rated copying on a test or exam as serious cheating, and 7% suggested it was not cheating at all. In comparison, an overwhelming 90% of the 48 faculty completing the survey rated such copying as serious cheating, and only 3% saw it as not cheating at all. As table 2.3 shows, this pattern repeated itself over a variety of behaviors.

For every behavior (including others not listed in the table but for which we have data), and for each of the four schools for which we have faculty data that allow such comparisons, we see the same pattern. Clearly, students have a very different perspective on what constitutes serious cheating. Whatever process students have used to arrive at these judgments, these data help us understand why academic integrity is a difficult concept to get them to accept. There seem to be so many underlying factors that help students conclude that many of these behaviors are often, if not always, acceptable and do not represent serious cheating.

Unfortunately, as the following comments from students suggest, some place success before integrity, whether it be to please their parents, to achieve a personal goal, or to avoid a hassle with teachers or parents. Even when they feel they are doing something wrong, for many students, personal gain overrides personal integrity.

Because it is so easy to do and is not often found, cheating provides students with an easy way to get ahead in school. In an extremely competitive district like [district X], students often search for any advantage they can gain, however immoral.

Especially in this school, there is a great deal of pressure to attend a top 20 college. Many students become so engrossed in this idea that they disregard their morals and ethics. They will do ANYTHING *to get the grade.*

The atmosphere of the school leads to a pressure to do well, especially in order to get into a desired college. Also, harder assignments that may be "unfair" lead to cheating, as do long assignments without much purpose. Furthermore, some students, often rightfully, do not consider sharing as cheating.

In such an environment, cheating becomes the norm. Even students who would prefer not to participate are probably being asked to produce their homework for copying on occasion, and they become suspect as a potential "snitch" if they do not go along. This is why we believe the "adults" in the system (faculty, parents, and administrators) have to do most of the heavy lifting here and, at a minimum, find ways to encourage greater personal responsibility on the part of our high school students. While students must be engaged in the effort, they need the help of the adults in the system to develop the critical mass that is probably required to make any meaningful progress. To sit back and engage in "ain't it awful" thinking adds nothing worthwhile. As we have visited schools and talked to many students over the past decade or two, as part of our project, we have heard from a large number of students who care about these issues and worry about them at least as much as we do. They need our help to move forward in a positive and substantive way, but we (the adults) need to figure out what our appropriate role is in the process. Unfortunately, many students seem to have little confidence in the ability of the older generation—the generation that brought them Enron, the collapse of Wall Street, two unpaid-for wars, and a myriad of other issues—to serve as moral exemplars. Students seem to be cynical when members of the older generation express any degree of moral superiority, either practical or intellectual. Many seem to feel the older generation has had its chance and failed. So, finding the right balance between student leadership and initiative and adult support remains a challenge.

Conclusion

A few key conclusions can be drawn from the research that we and others have conducted on academic integrity among high school students.

1. Cheating habits develop long before college. Cheating is widespread across all types of high schools—public, private, and parochial—and most college-bound students are exposed to significant cheating cultures during their secondary education.
2. High school students cheat for many reasons, including parental expectations, pressure to get good grades, and attribution of blame to others (e.g., teachers).
3. Rates of self-reported cheating that is enabled by the Internet (e.g., cut-and-paste plagiarism) are on the rise, while rates of self-reported test and exam cheating are declining.
4. A major shift has occurred in cheating-related attitudes and definitions among students. This shift has contributed to significant gaps between students and faculty regarding what constitutes cheating and may be a key reason for the decreasing rates in self-reported test and exam cheating.

The picture that emerges helps us understand the cheating environment that students experience in high school and the attitudes and beliefs about academic integrity and dishonesty that they bring with them to college. Many students view the primary goal of high school as gaining admission to the college of their choice. They seem to find their academic work in high school somewhat irrelevant—more of an obstacle to college admission than a true learning experience. When they arrive at college, they expect it will be different from high school—that this will be where true learning begins. When they hear college administrators and faculty talk about the importance of academic integrity, such as during orientation, this fits with their expectations; after all, this is not high school any more. We believe that most new college students, despite their experience with cheating in high school, are prepared to internalize this message and begin their college experience with a positive attitude about the need for academic integrity. However, their idealistic view often degenerates all too quickly, as we discuss in later chapters. In most colleges, the reality sets in that college is not that different from high school after all.

CHAPTER THREE

Prevalence, Types, and Methods of Cheating in College

Although we probably do not need to convince anyone that student cheating is a significant problem at colleges and universities today, we begin our discussion of college-level cheating with a very brief summary of some recent popular press articles that illustrate the scope of the problem and its global nature. Then, to establish a foundation for the rest of the chapter, we discuss some major research findings by other scholars on the prevalence of cheating, including the major types and methods of cheating. With a greater emphasis on our own work, we then address two frequently asked questions: "How widespread is cheating on college campuses?" and "Is cheating on the rise?" We organize these discussions historically, beginning with the early 1990s and continuing through 2010; we are also able to compare these findings with the work of Bill Bowers from the early 1960s. We then review what we have learned about a variety of topics such as the prevalence of cheating in cross-cultural contexts and among graduate students, changing perceptions of the seriousness of cheating, differences in the prevalence of cheating between two- and four-year colleges, and the impact of the Internet.

Much of this discussion includes analyses of data not previously reported. In undertaking the task of attempting to understand prevalence, we are reminded of the unattributed logic that the more you learn about something, the more you realize how little you really know about it. Certainly, our two-decade effort to understand the issues associated with student cheating raises as many questions as it answers, and prevalence data remain particularly problematic.

The Popular Press Perspective

If any reader feels e-mail deprived, signing up for Google alerts with the keywords *plagiarism* and *cheating* will certainly help (although *cheating* will also generate links describing instances of marital infidelity). Rather than attempt to provide any comprehensive summary here, we simply review a few recent headlines and capsule summaries that appeared in Google news alerts during the last two weeks of November 2009.

- "49 Disciplined for Plagiarism"—The *Otago Daily Times* in New Zealand reported that, in the previous two years, 49 students had been found responsible for plagiarism at the University of Otago (Rudd 2009).
- "Poll: 17 Percent of Students Say They Have Cheated"—The *Brown Daily Herald*, the student newspaper at this Ivy League stalwart, reported the results of a study of 687 students that it had conducted, which revealed that close to 20% of Brown students self-reported cheating in the previous semester (Simons 2009).
- "Checks Catch Thousands of Uni Students Cheating"—The *Courier-Mail* in Australia reported that "about 2000 students studying at universities in Queensland have been found guilty of cheating during the past three years. Figures made public for the first time following an investigation by the *Courier-Mail* show the number of students caught cheating is rising at most universities, despite the introduction of sophisticated text-matching software" (Wenham 2009).
- "Case of the Purloined Term Paper; When Work Is Resold"— Although it doesn't contain any estimates of the size of the problem, this *USA Today* article discusses the practice of students simply buying term papers online for submission as their own work (Marklein 2009).
- "Academic Dishonesty—Day 2: 100-Level Courses Rife with Cheating"—The *Exponent*, the student newspaper at Purdue University, notes that 47% of the cases of academic dishonesty reported in the 2008/2009 academic year occurred in 100-level courses. Of course, this implies that students leaving high school and entering college are already predisposed to cheating. It seems that at least some campuses use such data to justify throwing up

their hands and claiming there is nothing they can do (Hammer 2009).

Clearly, the perception is that academic cheating is a problem, and it is not limited to the United States. So, let's see what we know about how serious a problem it is.

What Others Have Taught Us

A significant amount of empirical research supports the conclusion that cheating in colleges and universities is widespread. For example, Genereux and McLeod (1995) reported that 83% of survey respondents self-reported cheating in college. Roig and Caso (2005) found that 72% of undergraduate students participating in their study claimed to have used a fraudulent excuse in college at least once. In a study of graduate students, Wajda-Johnston et al. (2001) found that between 3% and 55%, depending on the behavior, self-reported engaging in academically dishonest behaviors.

We have learned, however, that such numbers must be interpreted cautiously (Crown and Spiller 1998), as significant disparities exist in research estimates of the percentage of college students who engage in academic dishonesty, ranging from 3% (Karlins, Michaels, and Podlogar 1988) to 98% (Gardner et al. 1988). These discrepancies largely stem from differences in research methodology, including research design (e.g., survey vs. experiment), how cheating is defined and operationalized (e.g., self-reports vs. observed or actual cheating), and the time frame examined. For example, Karlins and colleagues (1988) measured cheating as the number of students who plagiarized a single assignment, while Gardner and colleagues (1988) examined cheating on homework assignments across an entire semester. In addition, social desirability bias is always a problem when surveys ask students to self-report on sensitive questions such as academic dishonesty.

Some recent studies have found innovative ways of addressing these methodological issues. Yardley et al. (2009) examined the prevalence of cheating by surveying college alumni, who arguably have less of a vested interest in hiding their dishonest behavior as undergraduates. A whopping 81.7% reported having engaged in some form of cheating during their undergraduate careers. Martin, Rao, and Sloan (2009) examined prevalence by studying actual plagiarism, as opposed to self-reported or witnessed plagiarism behavior, and found that 61% of the students in their sample engaged in plagiarism.

The majority of this research claims that cheating in college has increased over the past several decades (Baird 1980; Davis et al. 1992; Diekhoff et al. 1996; Singhal 1982). However, as already noted, these findings must be interpreted cautiously due to differences in methodologies across studies. Notably, when controlling for different research methods, Spiller and Crown (1995) found no evidence to support an increase in cheating behavior.

One of the most important confounding factors in this research may be the changing student definitions of what constitutes cheating, particularly in areas such as plagiarism and unauthorized collaboration. Research has supported the idea that students and faculty often disagree on definitions of cheating. For example, Burrus, McGoldrick, and Schuhmann (2007) argued that students do not always understand what constitutes cheating. Their study showed that students are much more likely to self-report cheating after being given an explicit definition. Students also do not always understand what constitutes plagiarism. Roig (1997) found that plagiarized versions of a paragraph were misidentified by as many as 50% of the student subjects as having been properly paraphrased. In a subsequent study, Roig (2001) showed that college professors disagree among themselves about whether written text has been plagiarized. When asked to paraphrase a paragraph, as many as 30% of the faculty in the study copied at least some text directly from the original paragraph. One result of this confusion may be that what students classified as plagiarism years ago may not be considered plagiarism by students today. Although most students seem to understand that word-for-word quotation requires an appropriate citation, they seem less clear on the need to provide a citation when presenting someone else's ideas in their own words. And with the Internet, this confusion has only grown.

Our research has shown an increase in collaborative cheating. In many college courses, students are assigned to teams and are encouraged to collaborate on team projects. However, students often receive mixed messages about the acceptability of collaboration. In some cases, instructors do not explicitly and unambiguously communicate standards of acceptable and unacceptable behavior. Another problem occurs when instructors teach students about the importance of collaboration and teamwork (in an organizational behavior course, for example) but then forbid students to collaborate on course work. Given these mixed messages, it is not surprising that some students conclude that collaboration is acceptable, even when the instructor asks for individual work. Evidence of this phenomenon was offered by Rabi et al. (2006), who found that 16.3% of students admitted to cheating during pharmacy school, but 74% admitted that either they or their classmates had worked on an individual assignment with a friend. Clearly, not all of these students perceived unauthorized collaboration to be cheating. If students' definitions of cheating are becoming less stringent, this may help to explain why students' self-reports of cheating are lower today than ten to twenty years ago. More than once, recently, students have submitted surveys to us in which they claim they have not engaged in certain behaviors, but in the open-ended responses that we encourage students to complete at the end of our surveys, they explain that, yes, they actually did engage in that type of behavior, but they checked "no" on the survey because, when they did it, it was not cheating, because . . . We have seen several typical explanations or justifications here that students may use to convince themselves that, at least in the unique circumstance in which they engaged in the behavior, it was not cheating. Most of these explanations—the assignment was hard, I didn't have enough time, the assignment had no learning value, the assignment counted for only a very small portion of my overall grade, and the like—seem unconvincing, except perhaps to the student engaging in the behavior. In any event, such "justifications" seem to have become more common since our research began in 1990.

The Early Work of Bill Bowers

We consider the real start of research on student cheating to be the work of William J. Bowers, who conducted the first large-scale, multi-campus study of student academic dishonesty in the early 1960s, culminating in his work *Student Dishonesty and Its Control in College*, published by the Bureau of Applied Social Research at Columbia University in December 1964. Bowers's work on student cheating provided an important starting point and remains a standard. References are made to his work in almost every chapter of this book, but here we limit our coverage to the Bowers data on the prevalence of different forms of academic dishonesty found on college campuses almost fifty years ago.

TABLE 3.1. Types of cheating as compiled by Bowers

1. Copying a few sentences of material without footnoting in a paper
2. Getting questions or answers from someone who has already taken the same exam
3. Copying answers from a text or other source instead of doing the work independently
4. "Padding" a few items on a bibliography
5. Giving answers to other students during an exam
6. Copying from someone's test or exam paper without his knowing about it
7. Working on the same homework with several other students when the teacher does not allow it
8. Copying from someone's test or exam paper with that person's knowledge
9. Writing a paper for another student
10. Arranging to sit next to someone who will let you copy from him during a test or exam
11. Arranging with other students to give or receive answers by use of signals
12. Taking an exam for another student
13. Having another student take an exam for you

SOURCE: Reprinted with permission from W. J. Bowers, *Student Dishonesty and Its Control in College* (New York: Bureau of Applied Social Research, Columbia University, 1964).

One of Bowers's many contributions was his decision to distinguish among the many types of cheating, including plagiarism, cheating on tests and exams, and "collaborative cheating." He identified more than a dozen different forms of cheating in his survey, many of which are part of larger categories such as plagiarism and exam cheating. For example, he distinguished between copying from another student's exam and allowing others to copy from one's own exam. He also differentiated behaviors such as working with several other students on course assignments "when the teacher does not allow it" (which we termed "unpermitted collaboration" in our later studies) and "copying answers from a text or other source instead of doing the work independently." Table 3.1 shows 13 behaviors highlighted by Bowers. Of course, computers and other electronic technologies that are used to cheat today were not available at the time.

Bowers reported that 75% of his respondents admitted engaging in one or more of these acts. He also found that just over half (51%) reported engaging in two or more of these behaviors. In table 3.2 we reproduce the Bowers data on the percentage of students admitting engagement in one or more of the behaviors (Bowers 1964, 48, table 4.7).

TABLE 3.2. Percentage of students admitting various numbers of acts of academic cheating, 1962/1963

No. of acts	Committing each number (%)
None	25
One	24
Two	19
Three	13
Four	7
Five	5
Six	3
Seven	2
Eight or more	2
Total	100 (5,422)

SOURCE: Reprinted with permission from W. J. Bowers, *Student Dishonesty and Its Control in College* (New York: Bureau of Applied Social Research, Columbia University, 1964).

We can draw two quick conclusions from this table: first, a lot of students admitted to engaging in some form of academic dishonesty, and second, a minority (19%) are what one might label "active" cheaters—having engaged in more than three of the acts that Bowers studied. The bottom line is that student dishonesty has long been an issue—our data confirm this over a nearly fifty-year period.

Bowers used a lengthy questionnaire in his work and was able to evaluate the question of the prevalence of cheating in several ways. In addition to the behaviors we have just discussed, he also asked students a brief series of questions to solicit information on how often they had engaged in what Bowers labeled four different "forms" of academic dishonesty: cheating on tests, plagiarism, submitting work done by another as one's own, and using unpermitted materials during a test or exam. The actual items Bowers used, and the data supplied by his respondents, are reproduced in table 3.3 (Bowers 1964, 43, table 4.4).

Combining these data into the same format used to report Bowers's more detailed behaviors (as in table 3.2), we find that only 50% of the students admitted to engaging in academic dishonesty, versus the 75% reported by Bowers based on his more detailed questions. Given our work in the past two decades, this finding does not surprise us, and it

TABLE 3.3. Students admitting having engaged in various forms of cheating since coming to college, 1962/1963 (% of students reporting behavior)

Type of cheating	Never	Once	A few times	Several or many times
Copied from another student during an exam	71	13	15	1
Plagiarized from published material on papers	72	9	16	3
Turned in papers done entirely or in part by other students	86	7	6	1
Used crib notes during an exam	87	6	6	1

SOURCE: Adapted with permission from W. J. Bowers, *Student Dishonesty and Its Control in College* (New York: Bureau of Applied Social Research, Columbia University, 1964).

may shed some light on the often large variation we see in prevalence reports. First, the results are clearly sensitive to what is included in one's definition of cheating, and second, our work suggests that a number of students, sometimes a large number, who are classified as cheaters by the researcher's definition of cheating would not classify themselves as cheaters. For example, in the Bowers scheme above (table 3.3), how inclusive is the form "plagiarized from published material on papers," to which 28% of his total respondents (those at both code and no-code institutions) replied in the affirmative? In the data reported by Bowers (1964) in his table 4.6, he notes that 43% of these same respondents replied in the affirmative to his question about "copying a few sentences of material without footnoting in a paper." We believe this is an example of the phenomenon of students interpreting the researcher's specific terms in the manner most favorable to them. In our view, at least some of the difference of 15 percentage points in the Bowers case, for example, represents students who have convinced themselves that "copying [just] a few sentences of material" is not plagiarism. The bottom line is that it is often difficult to understand what prevalence numbers actually mean and to compare numbers obtained by different researchers. But it appears that the more items that are used to capture different types of academic dishonesty, the more likely it is that a higher percentage will report cheating. With specific questions, we are encouraging, if not forcing, respondents to broaden their definition of cheating—our dependent variable.

1990/1991 McCabe and Treviño Study

Our first study of student academic dishonesty had as its primary aim to establish whether cheating was lower in institutions with honor codes (McCabe and Treviño 1993). Bowers's work suggested this in the early 1960s, but no large-scale, multi-campus studies of student dishonesty had been conducted since Bowers. In addition, this subject was of particular interest to McCabe and Treviño, both of whom had experienced honor codes as undergraduates. The honor code aspect of our work is discussed in detail in chapter 5, where we show that the prevalence of self-reported cheating is lower in honor code institutions. In this chapter, we highlight the prevalence results from the 17 schools participating in this initial project that did not have honor codes. Because most colleges and universities do not have formal honor codes, we believe that prevalence data from these schools are probably more representative of the general level of prevalence of student cheating in the United States.

To begin this work, McCabe contacted several academically selective schools. He benefited greatly in this effort from the assistance of colleagues at Princeton, his alma mater, and from the summary of a conference on honor systems that Princeton had organized in the spring of 1988. This summary, *The Princeton Conference on Honor Systems*, was published by the Princeton Honor Committee of 1987/1988, and the McDonnell Douglas Foundation was the conference sponsor. Thirty-seven schools participated in that conference, more than half of which have now participated in our ongoing project.

The other tool used to identify potential study participants was a report written by Brian Melendez in September 1985 at the request of the dean of the Faculty of Arts and Sciences at Harvard, to help the Harvard community begin to think about the possibility of an undergraduate honor code. Twenty-five of the 70 schools responding to Harvard's survey were among the 31 schools in our study. Using the slightly more stringent version of the typology suggested by Melendez (vs. that of the Princeton conference), 14 of the 31 schools in our final sample were classified as having a traditional academic honor code, and 17 were considered not to have such a code.

TABLE 3.4. Students' engagement in nine types of cheating at no-code schools, Bowers 1962/1963 and McCabe and Treviño 1990/1991 survey results (% of students reporting behavior)

Type of cheating	Bowers 1962/1963	McCabe and Treviño 1990/1991
Copying a few sentences of material without footnoting in a paper	53	41
"Padding" a few items on a bibliography	35	25
Plagiarized from public material on papers	36	19
Getting questions or answers from someone who has already taken the same exam	43	19
Copying from another student on a test or exam	31	31
Working on the same homework with several students when the teacher does not allow it	14	40
Turned in papers done entirely or in part by other students	20	13
Giving answers to other students during an exam	27	27
Used crib notes during an exam	21	21
Any of the nine behaviors	83	74
N	2,313	2,854

Focusing for the moment on these 17 no-code schools in our 1990/1991 study, the findings were similar to those of Bowers in a number of ways. In comparing our work with that of Bowers, we focus on 10 items that simply asked students whether they had participated in any of a list of particular behaviors at their current college. In our 1990/1991 and subsequent surveys, we were able to closely duplicate these 10 Bowers items, which allows us to look at prevalence trends in cheating over time. In the case of two questions related to copying from other students on a test or exam, we combined these into a single item, logically labeled "copying from another student on a test or exam." Thus we compared nine cheating behaviors between our surveys and the Bowers survey. The student self-reports detailing the level of engagement in these different behaviors are shown in table 3.4, for both the Bowers survey (conducted in 1962/1963) and our 1990/1991 survey. In this table, we include Bowers's original wording as it appeared on questions 58b and 59 of his survey (Bowers 1964, 267–268). As noted, however, this comparison includes only 10 of the items that Bowers used in questions 58b and 59 of his survey, and we have combined the two test/exam copying behaviors into a single item so that 9 individual items are presented in the table, along with a composite index representing the 9 behaviors combined.

For these comparisons, we eliminated first-year students from the calculations, which accounts for the small differences in N between table 3.3 (adapted from Bowers 1964) and the Bowers and 1990/1991 McCabe and Treviño samples in table 3.4. Both we and Bowers did some of our surveying in the fall semester, and we concluded that it was not appropriate to include first-year students who had very limited experience in college at the time. (Note: Many of these data have been discussed elsewhere, and freshmen were included in these discussions [e.g., McCabe, Treviño, and Butterfield 2001]. While the relative comparisons are essentially the same, the levels of self-reported cheating discussed here are typically 1 to 3 percentage points higher, reflecting the fact that self-reported cheating among freshmen, especially first-term freshmen, was generally lower than that of upperclassmen.)

In table 3.4 we report rates of engagement in cheating behaviors for the no-code schools in both the Bowers and the 1990/1991 McCabe and Treviño samples. One of the many interesting findings that Bowers simply did not have room to discuss in great detail in his 1964 report involved a question on his survey that asked respondents whether their school had an honor code. We were able to use this question to appropriately sort the Bowers sample of 99 schools into 32 code schools, 64 no-code schools, and 3 schools that we eliminated from this analysis due to some apparent student confusion about whether or not their campus had a formal academic honor code. In this chapter, we are using the sample of 2,313 students attending one of the 64 no-code schools in the Bowers sample.

One of the more obvious findings evident in table 3.4 is how modest the changes are between 1962/1963 and 1990/1991 for cheating associated with tests and exams, with the exception of the substantial decrease reflected in the behavior "getting questions or answers from someone who has already taken the same exam." The marked decrease in this collaborative cheating behavior at no-code schools seems at odds with the significant increase in "working on the same homework with several students when the teacher does not allow it," the one behavior that increased dramatically in the same period. Yet students' anecdotal comments in our 1990/1991 survey suggest there may be a fair amount of "rationalizing" among students concerning discussion of test content. While some argue that this behavior is not at all problematic, many others go to some length to point out that they were given only questions, not answers, or they just received a general indication of what was on a test, not specifics. These students do not see these behaviors as cheating, or certainly not as serious cheating, and do not seem likely to report this activity as cheating. Students seem readily able to justify collaborative behaviors for a variety of reasons—too much work to do, not understanding an assignment, lack of availability of their teacher for clarification, and so forth.

Several important conclusions are evident from these data. First, as we have noted already, self-reported dishonesty on written assignments decreased in most cases between 1962/1963 and 1990/1991, whereas changes in cheating associated with tests and exams were essentially nonexistent. Although our earlier explanation of how easily students can justify such behavior may well account for much of the difference, it's not clear that the comparison we have made here is truly appropriate. The 1990/1991 sample included only schools whose level of academic selectivity in the admissions process was very high—certainly much higher than the average school in the Bowers sample. And although we do not have any conclusive data on this point, we do have some data that suggest cheating is lower on smaller, more selective campuses. Thus it's not clear that we are comparing apples and apples here. We also note (see table 3.4) that students reported higher rates of engagement in cheating on written work versus tests and exams. For example, if we compare summary rates of engagement in the four behaviors related to test cheating with the five behaviors involving written work, we find self-reported rates of test cheating and cheating on written work of 59% and 70%, respectively, in the Bowers sample and of 47% and 65% in our 1990/1991 sample of no-code schools. In our more recent surveys, we see some evidence of different and changing perspectives on the seriousness of test cheating versus written cheating that may help us understand these differences.

For now, we'll move on to a brief review of our 1993/1994 project involving nine medium to large state universities that had also participated in the Bowers study in the 1960s. The underlying objective of this next study was twofold: first, to allow a more direct comparison of the Bowers data with data gathered more recently from schools that had participated in his original study, and second, to see whether the trends we had observed in smaller, more selective schools would also hold at larger, somewhat less academically selective schools.

1993/1994 Study of Nine Medium to Large Public Universities

Seventeen medium to large public institutions (schools with a minimum enrollment of four thousand undergraduates) from the Bowers sample were contacted as potential participants in the new study, and 10 agreed to participate in this replication, thirty years later, of Bowers's original work (McCabe and Treviño 1997). One school was eventually eliminated from the analysis, since it was the only school that had a long-standing honor code in place to address student academic dishonesty. Based on our earlier results, we thought that honor codes could create a distinctly different context on a campus around the question of student honesty and that this school's data should not be analyzed in the same sample as the other nine schools. As detailed in our report (McCabe and Bowers 1994), 200 seniors, 150 juniors, and 150 sophomores at each school were mailed a revised version of the McCabe and Treviño 1990/1991 survey, which they were asked to complete. At one school, the sample was mistakenly expanded to include 220 seniors, 200 juniors, and 200 sophomores, and another school elected to include a small sample of first-year students, so the final distribution at this school included 200 seniors, 200 juniors, 100 sophomores, and 100 first-year students. However, these first-year students were not included in our final sample. A total of 1,793 surveys were returned, a 39% response rate, which was comparable to the overall response rate of 38% obtained in our 1990/1991 study—although the response rate at schools with no honor code was slightly lower (36%) in that survey. In Bowers's original survey, the response rate was 60%, and this decline of more than 20 percentage points signals the need for some caution in comparing results. This problem became even more of a concern when we switched our methodology to web-based surveys in 2002. Response rates for those surveys have dropped to around 20%. The reader should keep these "low" return rates in mind, along with the self-report nature of our data and those of Bowers.

The rates of self-reported cheating observed in this 1993/1994 (mostly 1993) survey of medium to large universities are shown in table

TABLE 3.5. Students' engagement in nine types of cheating at no-code schools, 1993/1994 survey results compared with Bowers 1962/1963 and McCabe and Treviño 1990/1991 results (% of students reporting behavior)

Type of cheating	Bowers 1962/1963	McCabe and Treviño	
		1990/1991	1993/1994
Copying a few sentences of material without foot-noting in a paper	53 (53)*	41	54
"Padding" a few items on a bibliography	35 (35)	25	29
Plagiarized from public material on papers	36 (35)	19	26
Getting questions or answers from someone who has already taken the same exam	43 (46)	19	29
Copying from another student on a test or exam	31 (27)	31	52
Working on the same homework with several students when the teacher does not allow it	14 (12)	40	49
Turned in papers done entirely or in part by other students	20 (21)	13	14
Giving answers to other students during an exam	27 (25)	27	37
Used crib notes during an exam	21 (17)	21	27
Any of the nine behaviors	83 (83)	74	87
N	2,313 (306)	2,854	1,744

*Numbers in parentheses are the Bowers data for only the same nine schools that we surveyed in 1993.

3.5, where we have simply added this information to the data for no-code schools given in table 3.4. In addition, in the Bowers column, in parentheses, we show the data that Bowers obtained at just the same nine schools that we surveyed in 1993. Unfortunately, this reduces the Bowers sample to 306.

Perhaps one of the more obvious findings in table 3.5 is the results for cheating on written work. In three of the five comparisons, we see a similar change between 1962/1963 and 1990/1991 and between 1962/1963 and 1993—a notable decline in the level of self-reported cheating. We see a similar decline in 1990/1991 for "copying a few sentences of material without footnoting in a paper," but the 1993 number is roughly equal to 1962/1963 in this case. The item "working on the same homework with several students when the teacher does not allow it" shows a dramatic increase from 1962/1963 forward to the 1990s, in both cases. Some might attribute this to the slightly different wording used for this item in our 1990s surveys ("worked on an assignment with others when the instructor asked for individual work"), as one might argue that it includes more than just homework. But we think a more appropriate explanation involves the changing student attitudes about such collaboration, as 61% of our respondents in 1993 rated this behavior as trivial cheating, and another 23% felt it was not cheating at all. The only other written cheating behavior for which at least 70% of the students classified the behavior as not cheating or trivial cheating was "copying a few sentences of material without footnoting in a paper"— the one other behavior for which self-reported engagement did not drop significantly between 1962/1963 and 1993. As also suggested by later studies, it seems that students may be developing a logic that says some behaviors, those that save them a lot of time and do not seem too serious to them, are acceptable—what one might call a time-management perspective. Today's students are extremely busy with social commitments, extracurricular activities, paid work, and texting and e-mailing friends. Anything that saves them time in getting their school work done and is not considered serious cheating seems to be okay. Students now seem to feel much freer to define for themselves the value of assignments they receive. For anything that, in their view, does not help them learn the course material, taking shortcuts (which the instructor might consider cheating) often not only is acceptable but makes sense to them.

This view appears to be especially strong when students are discussing mandatory distribution requirements that are not—again, in their opinion—relevant to their chosen major. The most striking remarks that we have heard from students in this regard come from science and engineering majors, who bemoan distribution requirements in a course such as English literature. A typical "rationale" for cheating in such courses focuses on the argument that the student has never been good in the subject (that's one of the reasons he or she is majoring in science or engineering), and why waste time on such subjects? Cheating is often further rationalized in these cases by a logic that suggests poor performance in the course will adversely affect their graduate school admission choices, so they have no choice but to cheat to make things "fair" again—it's the school and its distribution requirements that are respon-sible for their cheating, not them. This does not necessarily mean we should do away with distribution requirements, if we believe they have value, but maybe we need to find ways to convince students of their value, too. Whatever we decide to do with distribution requirements, the important message about written work (as evident in table 3.5) is that most forms of cheating may, surprisingly, be on the decline. Of course, we have to qualify this statement with the word *may*, because we cannot be certain that this result doesn't simply reflect the lower survey response rates, with perhaps those cheating the most being the least likely to respond. But the importance of understanding these de-clines may lie in understanding why, between 1962/1963 and 1993, we have seen such a strong increase in cheating on collaborative work and virtually no change in "copying a few sentences of material without footnoting," or cut-and-paste plagiarism.

Once again, we see a different picture when looking at changes in self-reported test and exam cheating between 1962/1963 and 1993. Un-like in the 1990/1991 study, in 1993 we see increases in most forms of self-reported test cheating (the one exception being "getting questions or answers from someone who has already taken the same exam"), with the composite level of cheating (engaging in any of the four test cheating behaviors shown in table 3.5) increasing from 60% for the four such behaviors in the Bowers no-code sample in 1962/1963 to 70% in our 1993 state school sample. The difference is even more dramatic if we exclude the question about getting advanced information on the con-tents of a test: at no-code schools, 44% acknowledged engagement in at least one of the other three test-related behaviors in 1962/1963, versus 64% in 1993. If we focus on just the nine schools in both the Bowers sample (data in parentheses in table 3.5) and our 1993 sample, the con-trast is even larger: 41% versus 64%. In either case, however, it is clear that self-reported test-related cheating increased between 1962/1963 and 1993, using the Bowers measures. In fact, the increase in test cheat-ing in 1993 is large enough to offset the decrease in cheating on written work. And rather than the modest increase in overall cheating that we see when comparing no-code schools in 1962/1963 and 1990/1991, when comparing 1962/1963 and 1993 we see a small increase in overall cheating. We believe these mixed results support a view that cheating changed very little between the early 1960s and the 1990s.

1999/2000 Center for Academic Integrity Assessment Project

Our 1999 study was the first research project we conducted in direct collaboration with the Center for Academic Integrity (CAI). A consortium, by 1999, of more than three hundred colleges and universities and other interested parties, including some secondary schools, the CAI represents a tangible outcome of the research project we have been describing. On completion of our 1990/1991 study on honor codes, and at the suggestion of John Margolis at Northwestern University, McCabe was able to raise enough money from corporate contacts to sponsor what turned out to be the formative meeting of the center. At this meeting, held in Newark, New Jersey, in 1991 and supported largely by Verizon (then Bell Atlantic), McCabe gathered representatives of 26 schools (all but 5 of which had participated in the 1990/1991 survey), with a total of more than fifty people, including primarily administrators but also a small number of faculty and a moderate number of students. After reading the *many* thoughtful student comments he had received in the first survey (1990/1991), McCabe was convinced that students deserved a voice in the discussion if we really hoped to better understand the issue of student integrity and develop strategies that work. Indeed, students who attended this first meeting made important and relevant contributions. When the CAI was formally chartered about a year later, students were given a key role in its management, and students continue to participate fully in the center, now part of the Rutland Center for Ethics at Clemson University. A detailed history of the CAI and some additional information on the center's Assessment Project can be found on the center's website (www.academicintegrity.org). Note, however, that if you make the mistake of going to www.academicintegrity.com, you will be greeted by the headline "College Term Papers Made Easy" and offered the "opportunity" to purchase a variety of papers. In the Environmental Ethics section, for example, you can purchase a seven-page paper entitled "The Impact of Deer on Forests and Forest Regrowth." It's only $9.95 per page (as of February 2011) and includes a free bibliography! Of course, same-day delivery is possible, just in case you've waited until the eleventh hour to complete your assignment. This is only one of probably dozens, maybe hundreds, of sites that offer similar services.

In 1998/1999, the CAI developed a strategy for an academic integrity assessment project, obtained needed funding from the John Templeton Foundation, and enrolled 12 competitively selected schools as official participants in the project—which was designed to help schools assess their existing academic integrity policies. In addition, another 10 schools participated in the integrity survey, which was part of the assessment process, and both students and faculty were surveyed at these schools. The 12 fully participating schools provided extensive feedback on the guide and the survey and met at Vanderbilt University in 2000 to review the overall process. Based on this input, the CAI assessment guide was revised and then released in 2001. Although several modest changes have been made to the guide and survey since then, the basic format has remained relatively constant. The most significant change is putting the surveys (student and faculty) online, resulting in some data comparison problems, as we discuss in the next section. But first let's review the results of the 1999/2000 (early 2000) survey process that initiated the CAI Assessment Project and represents our last major written survey at the college and university level. As noted above, 22 schools participated in this survey in the 1999/2000 academic year, but one of these schools was a two-year college and is excluded from our analysis. Thus, the sample for this phase of our project includes 21 schools and, after elimination of 129 first-year students and 8 students who did not specify their class standing, 2,468 students: 640 sophomores, 724 juniors, and 1,104 seniors.

The project also provided one of the first opportunities to study what have become known as modified honor codes—an attempt by campuses, usually larger campuses, to capture some of the benefits of an honor code tradition without introducing unproctored exams or a student reporting system. We reserve our detailed discussion of modified honor codes for chapter 5. Here we focus on the 693 students who attended institutions without any form of honor code. However, there is no rigid definition of what a campus might consider a modified honor code, and some researcher bias is possible in making such distinctions in classifying schools. In the present case, though, we are confident that the no-code sample of 693 students, representing eight schools, does not include any school that had an honor code at the time of the survey.

In table 3.6 we summarize our general findings on the prevalence of cheating, by adding the 1999/2000 data to the table 3.5 data. We can

TABLE 3.6. Students' engagement in nine types of cheating at no-code schools, 1999/2000 survey results compared with Bowers 1962/1963 and McCabe et al. 1990/1991 and 1993/1994 results (% of students reporting behavior)

Type of cheating	Bowers 1962/1963	McCabe et al. 1990/1991	1993/1994	1999/2000
Copying a few sentences of material without footnoting in a paper	53 (53)*	41	54	45
"Padding" a few items on a bibliography	35 (35)	25	29	26
Plagiarized from public material on papers	36 (35)	19	26	19
Getting questions or answers from someone who has already taken the same exam	43 (46)	19	29	56
Copying from another student on a test or exam	31 (27)	31	52	34
Working on the same homework with several students when the teacher does not allow it	14 (12)	40	49	51
Turned in papers done entirely or in part by other students	20 (21)	13	14	8
Giving answers to other students during an exam	27 (25)	27	37	27
Used crib notes during an exam	21 (17)	21	27	19
Any of the nine behaviors	83 (83)	74	87	83
N	2,313 (306)	2,854	1,744	693

*Numbers in parentheses are the Bowers data for only the same nine schools that we surveyed in 1993.

glean several observations from table 3.6 that may add to our understanding of how student cheating might be changing over time.

- Generally, most of the rates of self-reported cheating at no-code schools in the 1990s are roughly the same as or lower than the rates reported by Bowers at his no-code schools in the early 1960s.
- The most notable exception to this trend is the "offense" of collaboration or, in Bowers's original wording, "working on the same homework with several students when the teacher does not allow it." The level of this behavior as self-reported by students was up dramatically in 1990/2000. While one could argue, as we noted earlier, that the alternative wording that we used, "worked on an assignment with other students when the teacher asked for individual work," is responsible, we think the wording difference is small enough that other factors probably account for this change. Collaboration is simply a behavior that today's students don't view as cheating, regardless of a faculty member's instructions for a given assignment. This attitude is suggested by the finding that 87% of respondents at the no-code schools in the 1999/2000 sample classified such collaboration as either not cheating (30%) or trivial cheating (57%), and only 13% classified it as serious cheating. There is also a notably higher level of cheating by copying from someone on a test or exam in the 1993 sample and a moderately higher level in the 1999 sample, compared with the Bowers sample. The particularly high level of copying on tests in 1993 may reflect a relationship between campus size and level of overt test cheating—that is, behaviors that may well be observed by others in the exam room. While this apparently did not affect the level of self-reported cheating in Bowers's original work (with the sample of nine large campuses, in parentheses in tables 3.5 and 3.6, showing a somewhat lower level of such explicit test/exam cheating), we speculate that, today, such test/exam cheating is greater at larger schools than at smaller schools, all else being equal. Our logic rests on two points: first, it may be easier to create a campus ethic of integrity in smaller campus communities, and second, not surprisingly, class sizes seem to be smaller at smaller schools, with fewer impersonal, large lecture classes. In larger classes, students may find it easier to justify cheating and/or to "hide" such copying, given an inadequate number of proctors

and faculty in large exam rooms, where students are sometimes seated close together. In addition, we find the 1962/1963 general versus medium/large school comparison less relevant, as *very* few schools in the Bowers sample would rival the mega-campuses that exist today. Indeed, Bowers used three thousand students or more as his largest category for campus size—hardly large by today's standards.

- Despite the fairly significant rise in self-reports of several forms of test cheating between the Bowers sample and our 1993 and 1999/2000 samples, the data for engagement in any of the nine forms of cheating studied by Bowers suggest that cheating in 1999/2000 was roughly comparable to what it was in 1962/1963, despite the self-reported decline in most forms of cheating on written work.

So far, we have not directly addressed a major issue that could provide an alternative explanation for some of our findings: the declining survey response rates over time. Though they may be important in this earlier phase of our project, they assume even greater importance as we prepare to discuss the last phase of our work: the web-based surveys that we have used on a large scale since the fall of 2002, and continue to use today. Among no-code schools, we can calculate that the rate of return for the Bowers survey was 61%. By 1990/1991, students seemed to be less willing to complete surveys, especially one that asked them to admit possible engagement in an unethical act, and the no-code school response rate was a dramatically lower 36%. This trend continued into 1993, when we observed a similar rate of 39%. But by 1999/2000, the response among no-code schools had dropped to 24%.

Web-Based Surveys

We have made some changes to the web-based survey that we introduced at the start of the 2002/2003 academic year, but they are relatively minor. A very small number of changes focused on reducing the demographic information we requested, to more adequately protect anonymity; others involved adding or deleting certain questions. Some questions were added when we thought they might help us more effectively understand changes that seemed to be taking place in the larger environment (e.g., the increasing sophistication of electronic technologies that enable new forms of "cheating" or make old ones dramatically easier). A smaller number of selected questions were deleted to satisfy our Institutional Review Board's concerns about student anonymity.

Although we have a very large dataset after eight years of web-based surveys (149,161 students in the United States and Canada, as of the end of academic year 2009/2010, including first-year students and graduate students), we think the comparability of these surveys over time provides a convincing rationale to discuss this period as a single survey, 2002–2010. However, unlike our previous surveys, this dataset includes some two-year colleges (17 in the United States and 2 in Canada, with a total of 11,673 students), making the decision to drop first-year students from our analysis more difficult. Fortunately, the majority of schools that have completed this survey since 2002 have excluded first-year students at our suggestion, and some have even administered a unique survey to this group (referred to as the "first-year survey") that attempts to understand how student attitudes and behaviors regarding cheating might change from high school to college. In the analysis here, we generally exclude first-year students, as we have done earlier, except in a limited number of cases where we are explicitly comparing two-year and four-year schools.

Another decision that needs to be made in using this dataset is how to treat participating schools from outside the United States—including the 16 four-year Canadian schools and campuses in eight other countries. However, only two of the country studies—Canada (Christensen-Hughes and McCabe 2006a, 2006b) and Lebanon (McCabe, Feghali, and Abdallah 2008)—have sufficient student populations to allow for meaningful analysis: 29,964 students at 18 schools in Canada and 1,543 students at 3 English-speaking schools in Lebanon, reduced to 1,317 after removing first-year and graduate students. (The Canadian sample includes 2,252 students at two junior colleges or two-year schools, 4,189 first-year students, 2,307 graduate students, and 4,817 students for whom we do not have class data, including 4,346 at the Canadian school that had the largest number of responding students but elected *not* to include the question on class level in its survey.) Although three schools were also surveyed in the United Arab Emirates (in 2008), those data are not included here, since only 871 useable surveys were obtained from upperclassmen, and the results were generally similar to those obtained in Lebanon. Only a single school was surveyed in each of the remaining countries. The bottom line is that we discuss results based only on the U.S. schools in our sample, unless otherwise noted.

In table 3.7 we summarize the self-reported rates of cheating found among U.S. upperclassmen in our 2002–2010 web-based surveys, added to the data presented in table 3.6. In contrast to the popular opinion often expressed in the media that cheating, especially plagiarism, is now rampant among college students, we find that—with two exceptions ("getting questions or answers from someone who has already taken the same exam" in 1990/1991 and 1993 and "working on the same homework with several students when the teacher does not allow it" in 1962/1963 and 1990/1991)—self-reported cheating recorded in the 2002–2010 web surveys is *lower* than in any previous surveys. Though we would like to believe that this is an accurate assessment of prevalence, we have several reasons to be skeptical. First, and probably most important, technology has enabled new forms of plagiarism—in particular, what we call "cut-and-paste" Internet plagiarism, in which students copy a few sentences (or more) of material without footnoting or using quotation marks. Bowers, of course, measured such cut-and-paste plagiarism from written sources only. But if we combine self-reports of cut-and-paste plagiarism from written sources with the identical activity from the Internet, we find a combined self-reported rate for these behaviors of 43% in our 2002–2010 sample. Although this level is still generally lower than in earlier years, it is in the same ballpark as the earlier range, from 41% to 54%. Not surprisingly, when asked explicitly about this in a question added to our survey in 2007, 78% of the 2,949 students indicating they had engaged in cut-and-paste plagiarism reported that their primary method for doing so was the Internet rather than written sources, and another 16% indicated they used the two forms interchangeably. Only 6% relied primarily or exclusively on written sources.

Not only has the Internet become the cut-and-paste mechanism of choice, but it seems to have helped blur students' views about whether cut-and-paste plagiarism is actually cheating. Although we cannot accurately quantify this point, we are convinced that a large number of students respond "no" to questions about engaging in cut-and-paste plagiarism for this reason. While we try to suggest to students that they should report actual engagement in this behavior regardless of whether they think it is cheating or not, students often appear not to understand, or they ignore, this request. Many students today simply do not

TABLE 3.7. Students' engagement in nine types of cheating at no-code schools, 2002–2010 survey results compared with Bowers 1962/1963 and McCabe et al. 1990/1991, 1993/1994, and 1999/2000 results (% of students reporting behavior)

Type of cheating	Bowers 1962/1963	McCabe et al.			
		1990/1991	1993/1994	1999/2000	2002–2010
Copying a few sentences of material without footnoting in a paper	53	41	54	45	36
"Padding" a few items on a bibliography	35	25	29	26	13
Plagiarized from public material on papers	36	19	26	19	6
Getting questions or answers from someone who has already taken the same exam	43	19	29	56	30
Copying from another student on a test or exam	31	31	52	34	14
Working on the same homework with several students when the teacher does not allow it	14	40	49	51	42
Turned in papers done entirely or in part by other students	20	13	14	8	6
Giving answers to other students during an exam	27	27	37	27	11
Used crib notes during an exam	21	21	27	19	8
Any of the nine behaviors	83	74	87	83	65
N	2,313	2,854	1,744	693	73,738*

*For this and subsequent analyses based on our 2002–2010 web survey data, we show an N of 73,738. This is the number of eligible students who were presented with all or most of the components of a question, and we are using this figure as a matter of convenience. In each case, the number of actual respondents is lower. For example, in this table, the actual number of respondents for each individual behavior ranges from a low of 66,681 for "padding' a few items on a bibliography" to a high of 69,944 for "getting questions or answers from someone who has already taken the same exam." For the nine-item composite, we have complete data for only 58,168 students (non-first-year undergraduates attending a four-year school).

consider cut-and-paste plagiarism from the Internet or written sources to be cheating, so when asked in a survey on "cheating" whether they have engaged in this behavior, many simply say no—even if they have. As noted earlier in the chapter, in their open-ended comments, many explain that they answered this way because, when *they* engaged in one of these behaviors, it simply wasn't cheating. In fact, only about one in four students indicated in our 2002–2010 surveys that they considered cut-and-paste plagiarism from the Internet to be serious cheating (24.4%), and a slightly lower number (22.3%) classified cut-and-paste plagiarism from written sources in a similar way.

Students' perspectives on whether cut-and-paste plagiarism is cheating may be slowly changing, however. If we examine the trend for both forms of cut-and-paste plagiarism over the eight-year period of our web-based project, we see self-reported engagement slowly but steadily *decreasing*, from 39% to 30% for plagiarism from the Internet and from 41% to 28% for plagiarism from written sources. In both cases, we also see slow but steady *increases* in the percentage of students who classify each behavior as serious cheating—from 24% to 31% in the case of Internet plagiarism and from 21% to 28% for plagiarism from written sources. This inverse relationship between engagement in a behavior and opinion on its seriousness is typical in our sample for virtually all forms of cheating. It is one of the reasons we suspect that some of our cheating statistics underestimate the actual level of cheating: students are reluctant to admit to behaviors that they acknowledge are clearly wrong, and many seem to use one of the neutralization strategies, originally identified by Sykes and Matza (1957), to explain their behavior and deflect the blame. For example, Bouville (2008) showed that students were able to rationalize cheating behavior by using instructor-based neutralizations such as "the instructor did an inadequate job" or "the instructor assigned too much material." In another study, Granitz and Loewy (2007) showed that, compared with other ethical reasoning strategies, students predominately invoke deontology, situational ethics, and Machiavellianism when defending plagiarism.

In the case of cut-and-paste plagiarism, as well as working collaboratively when told not to, students' open-ended comments in our surveys seem to suggest that, although the efforts on many campuses to address plagiarism issues are helping to convince more students that even cut-and-paste plagiarism may be cheating, students are still able to rationalize or neutralize this behavior. For example, they didn't have enough time to do the assignment and had no choice; the assignment had little learning value or was unfair; or using the Internet in this way is effective time management—a skill that will serve them well in the real world when they graduate.

Returning to the question of whether cheating is decreasing or increasing, we note that self-reported levels of cheating, using our typical indices of cheating versus those of Bowers, show results similar to the trends in cut-and-paste plagiarism. For example, in our web-based survey data, we observe decreasing levels of self-reported cheating between 2002/2003 and 2009/2010, declining from 53% to 39% for serious cheating on papers (primarily plagiarism) and from 21% to 16% for serious cheating on tests or exams. We observe a similar trend in tracking responses to a survey question that asks students how often they have seen someone cheat on a test or exam. Overall, there has been a decline of 8 percentage points in the number of students who report observing test cheating by other students—from 52% in 2002/2003 to 44% in our 2009/2010 survey. Yet in this same period, the number of faculty who say they have observed test cheating rose from 50% to 60%. As noted earlier, one potential confounding factor in such comparisons is the rate of survey response among students and faculty, both of which have declined markedly over this period—among students, from somewhat over 60% in the Bowers survey in 1962/1963 to 38% to 39% in our early 1990s studies (1990/1991 and 1993) to about 20% (on average) in our web-based surveys since the fall of 2002. (Faculty returns are generally higher but show a similar trend.) Intuitively, it seems to make sense that if students cheat more often, they will be more reluctant to complete a survey indicating that they do so. Unfortunately, in spite of all the precautions we take to satisfy the requirements of our Institutional Review Board, there is really no way we can convince a student receiving an e-mail invitation to complete a survey that his or her response will remain completely confidential. The comments offered by some students who do complete the survey suggest they have been very cautious in how they answer questions and may not have been completely forthright. We occasionally also see survey submissions that provide only an open-ended response stating the belief that, obviously, their personal data will be shared with their school and thus they are unwilling to complete the survey. Others who are skeptical do respond, but may intentionally supply false information about their own behavior, just in case. In fact, in the absence of any real incentive to do so, it's surprising that even

20% of the surveyed population bothers to respond, including some who have clearly engaged in cheating of some sort.

Cross-Cultural Surveys

An increasing number of studies have examined the prevalence of cheating in international and cross-cultural contexts. Countries studied include Russia (Lupton and Chapman 2002), Taiwan (Lin and Wen 2007), Croatia (Hrabak et al. 2004), Brazil (Rocha et al. 2007), Malaysia (Ahmad, Simun, and Mohammad 2008), Romania (Teodorescu and Andrei 2009), Lebanon (McCabe, Feghali, and Abdallah 2008), Cyprus (Zopiatis and Krambia-Kapardis 2008), India (Taylor-Bianco and Deeter-Schmelz 2007), Australia (Marsden, Carroll, and Neill 2005), Ireland (Ledwith and Risquez 2008), Japan (Diekhoff et al. 1999), and China (Bernardi et al. 2008).

This cross-cultural research indicates that cheating is a global phenomenon and a characteristic of human behavior wherever humans are found. We very briefly discuss here some data we have gathered in our work outside the United States—in Canada and Lebanon, for which we have the most data. In Canada, our effort was primarily focused on major universities, although we did survey two two-year schools whose data are excluded here. One Canadian university was surveyed in the 2001/2002 academic year, nine in 2002/2003, three in 2003/2004, one in 2004/2005, one in 2006/2007, and one in 2009/2010. Following the model we used to compare our U.S. studies, in table 3.8 we show the calculations for 2002–2010 for the United States (from table 3.7) and the calculated Canadian data for the same period. There do not seem to be any strong differences here. Self-reported engagement in cheating is 1 to 2 percentage points higher in the United States for four comparisons, and the Canadian students reported 1 to 7 percentage point higher levels of engagement for the other five items. However, for all nine behaviors combined, the Canadian self-reports of cheating are 8 percentage points higher—a statistically significant difference—although the larger differences are for behaviors that many students do not consider too serious: padding a bibliography and getting some information on a test from someone who took it earlier.

The U.S.-Canadian comparison seems to do little other than reinforce, to some degree, the basic U.S. findings. The interested reader may find a more detailed analysis of the U.S.-Canadian comparison in the

TABLE 3.8. Students' engagement in nine types of cheating at no-code schools, United States versus Canada, 2002/2003 through 2009/2010 (% of students reporting behavior)

Type of cheating	United States	Canada
Copying a few sentences of material without footnoting in a paper	36	38
"Padding" a few items on a bibliography	13	19
Plagiarized from public material on papers	6	5
Getting questions or answers from someone who has already taken the same exam	30	37
Copying from another student on a test or exam	14	13
Working on the same homework with several students when the teacher does not allow it	42	45
Turned in papers done entirely or in part by other students	6	7
Giving answers to other students during an exam	11	9
Used crib notes during an exam	8	6
Any of the nine behaviors	65	73
N	73,738	16,407

NOTE: One Canadian school completed the survey in the 2001/2002 academic year.

Canadian Journal of Higher Education (Christensen-Hughes and Mc-Cabe 2006a, 2006b).

In Lebanon, we found a dramatically different story. Working with colleagues from the American University of Beirut (McCabe, Feghali, and Abdallah 2008), we gathered data from 1,317 English-speaking students attending one of three major universities in Lebanon in the 2004/2005 academic year. The data were compared with the information provided by 12,793 students at seven large U.S. universities. The U.S. data were also collected in the 2004/2005 academic year, and the seven universities generally offered a mix of majors similar to those at the Lebanese schools. Data from the Lebanese sample were collected through an online community known as Bicharaf ("with honor" in Arabic). Students who had previously registered with Bicharaf were given the opportunity to participate in the survey, and 1,543 of the 2,384 registered members did so—1,317, after eliminating first-year and graduate students. In line with the hypotheses developed for this study, the major findings included the following: (1) Significantly higher levels of academic dishonesty were self-reported by the Lebanese students ($p < 0.001$), especially for cheating on tests and exams (66% admitting to one or more violations in Lebanon vs. 21% in the United States). (2) As in the United States, in Lebanon the perception of the behavior of one's peers with regard to academic integrity showed a very strong relationship with a student's individual decision on whether to engage in academic integrity—reinforcing, in our minds, the importance of community (peer pressure) in promoting student integrity and reducing academic dishonesty. And (3), the findings seem to suggest that the collectivist nature of Lebanese society is an important factor underlying its greater self-reported levels of student dishonesty, results that we believe "provide significant support for the view that Lebanese university students are strongly influenced by the norms of the collectivist society in which they are raised" (McCabe, Feghali, and Abdallah 2008, 464).

Much more work needs to be done, of course, to understand the differences between Western and other cultures with regard to cheating. We argue in chapter 5, in discussing honor codes, and again in chapter 9, that within a specific country, campus culture may be the most important influence on academic integrity. Even where national culture is the most important, the impact of local culture, if properly nurtured, can overcome many negative aspects of the larger culture—especially with idealistic college students who may be eager to improve the larger culture of their country.

Graduate Students

We began including graduate students in our 2002/2003 web-based study, and we have now collected data from 15,331 students identifiable as graduate students at 111 schools in the United States and from 2,307 at 14 Canadian schools. The U.S. sample has a mean of 138 graduate student respondents per school (ranging from a low of 1 to a high of 1,405), and the Canadian mean is 165 (ranging from 12 to 484). Table 3.9 shows the self-reported levels of engagement in the various cheating behaviors (studied by Bowers) for graduate students in the United States and Canada. We once again see relatively small differences between the two countries, although, unlike the undergraduate student results, we do see a pattern in the sense that graduate students in Canada report somewhat higher levels of engagement in seven of the nine behaviors evaluated, with the remaining two equal in both countries. This leads to an 11 percentage point higher overall engagement in cheating behaviors in Canada.

TABLE 3.9. Graduate students' engagement in nine types of cheating at no-code schools, United States versus Canada, 2002/2003 through 2009/2010 (% of students reporting behavior)

Type of cheating	United States	Canada
Copying a few sentences of material without footnoting in a paper	23	25
"Padding" a few items on a bibliography	5	9
Plagiarized from public material on papers	3	4
Getting questions or answers from someone who has already taken the same exam	13	17
Copying from another student on a test or exam	5	5
Working on the same homework with several students when the teacher does not allow it	23	29
Turned in papers done entirely or in part by other students	2	3
Giving answers to other students during an exam	4	4
Used crib notes during an exam	3	4
Any of the nine behaviors	41	52
N	15,331	2,307

NOTE: One Canadian school completed the survey in the 2001/2002 academic year.

Shortly before working on this section, we received a Google news alert reporting: "It may seem counter-intuitive but postgraduates are more likely to commit plagiarism than undergraduates, according to information obtained by The Independent under the Freedom of Information Act" (Rennison 2010). The London-based *Independent* was referring to data obtained at the University of Glasgow, under the U.K. Freedom of Information Act, reporting that 57% of postgraduate students were found responsible for plagiarism in the 2008/2009 academic year, compared with 26% of undergraduates. Although the absolute level of these numbers does not surprise us, they clearly are the reverse of our findings, as we have consistently found higher levels of self-reported plagiarism among undergraduates than graduate students in the United States. Even if we look at 2008/2009, the same year as the *Independent*'s data, we see the same relationship in our U.S. data as reported earlier—that is, total self-reported plagiarism by 35% of undergraduates and 27% of graduate students. In the most recent year for which we have multi-campus Canadian data, 2003/2004, we still see the same pattern: 45% of undergraduates and 31% of graduate students in Canada self-reporting some form of plagiarism. It is possible that graduate students are less likely to self-report any plagiarism and that these differences stem from differences in the types of graduate students included in our study and in the *Independent*'s data, as well as differences in how much writing of papers is required of students. For example, graduate students in technical fields tend to write fewer papers that those in the humanities and social sciences. We would need to know more about the explicit data in the *Independent*'s study before commenting further.

Seriousness of Cheating

We have made several comments about students' perceptions of the seriousness of cheating and how these perceptions seem to be changing, and it is useful to summarize some of our major findings on seriousness. Intuitively, it makes sense to expect an inverse relationship between students' ratings of seriousness and their self-reported levels of engagement for different behaviors—the more seriously students view a cheating behavior, the less likely they are to engage in it. If we examine, for both graduate and undergraduate students in the United States, the nine behaviors from the Bowers study (table 3.10), we find significant rank order correlations for the engagement and seriousness data we collected in web-based surveys in the 2002–2010 period. Only two terms show a significant deviation in these calculations: the behaviors "copying from another student's test or exam" and "turned in papers done entirely or in part by other students." In the case of copying on a test or exam, one could make the argument that this is the only behavior on the Bowers list that does not require true premeditation. Indeed, it is possible that a student could go into a test or exam with no intention of cheating and find the test to be harder than expected. In a moment of panic, the student looks at someone else's test, because it is easy to do so, even if the student knows it's wrong. Some students' open-ended comments refer to moments of such panic.

The scale used for the seriousness ratings is a four-point Likert scale: not cheating, trivial cheating, moderate cheating, and serious cheating. Unfortunately, we cannot compare our ratings of seriousness with the Bowers survey or any of our other surveys, since it wasn't until we started the web-based surveys that we moved from a three- to a four-point cheating scale, and so the results are not comparable. Of course, we do have a number of seriousness ratings for behaviors not included

TABLE 3.10. Undergraduate and graduate students' self-reports of engagement in and ratings of the seriousness of nine types of cheating at no-code schools in the United States, 2002–2010 web surveys (% of students reporting behavior or rating)

	Undergraduates		Graduate students	
Type of cheating	Reporting engagement in behavior	Rating as moderate or serious cheating	Reporting engagement in behavior	Rating as moderate or serious cheating
Copying a few sentences of material without footnoting in a paper	36	59	23	71
"Padding" a few items on a bibliography	13	59	5	76
Plagiarized from public material on papers	6	92	3	95
Getting questions or answers from someone who has already taken the same exam	30	71	13	83
Copying from another student's test or exam	14	93	5	96
Working on the same homework with several students when the teacher does not allow it	42	37	23	59
Turned in papers done entirely or in part by other students	6	91	2	94
Giving answers to other students during an exam	11	91	4	94
Used crib notes during an exam	8	90	3	95
N	73,738		15,331	

in the Bowers index. Of particular interest are ratings for various forms of cheating involving electronic technologies that were not available in Bowers's time. Not surprisingly, the self-reports of engagement and ratings of seriousness for these items tend to mirror their non-electronic counterparts. For example, if we look at using electronic versus written crib notes during a test or exam, our results are almost identical: 7% of undergraduates reported engaging in this behavior, and 95% rated the behavior as moderate or serious cheating. This compares with the values of 8% and 90% (in table 3.10) for the use of written crib notes by undergraduates. For graduate students, the values of 3% engagement and 93% seriousness (moderate or serious cheating) when describing the use of written crib notes are comparable to the 2% and 95% for the use of electronic crib notes. The results for written cut-and-paste plagiarism (36% engagement and 59% seriousness rating for undergraduates; 23% engagement and 70% seriousness rating for graduate students) are almost identical to those for Internet cut-and-paste plagiarism (37% engagement and 60% seriousness rating for undergraduates; 23% engagement and 71% seriousness rating for graduate students). Although the seriousness ratings are almost the same, one place where we see a significant difference is the self-reported level of engagement in electronic versus written collaboration. While 42% of undergraduates and 23% of graduate students acknowledge in-person collaboration, the same question focused on collaboration that occurs electronically reveals engagement reports of roughly half those levels: 24% for undergraduates and 14% for graduate students. Although much of our work shows electronic forms of cheating beginning to substitute for in-person forms, this may not be as much of a problem with the issue of collaboration. In defending collaboration in their open-ended comments in our surveys, students often suggest that they collaborate because they do not understand something and the teacher is unavailable for help or guidance. The data above may support this argument, in the sense that electronic collaboration would seem to suggest copying versus learning, in contrast to in-person collaboration, where learning could be a legitimate objective in students' minds.

Two-Year versus Four-Year Colleges

We have also examined issues of academic dishonesty at two-year versus four-year colleges and looked for meaningful differences. Our

TABLE 3.11. Students' engagement in nine types of cheating at U.S. four-year schools (no-code schools) versus two-year schools, 2002/2003 through 2009/2010 (% of students reporting behavior)

Type of cheating	Four-year school	Two-year school
Copying a few sentences of material without footnoting in a paper	36	34
"Padding" a few items on a bibliography	13	9
Plagiarized from public material on papers	6	9
Getting questions or answers from someone who has already taken the same exam	30	22
Copying from another student on a test or exam	14	14
Working on the same homework with several students when the teacher does not allow it	42	35
Turned in papers done entirely or in part by other students	6	7
Giving answers to other students during an exam	11	13
Used crib notes during an exam	8	10
Any of the nine behaviors	65	55
N	78,738	9,421

2002–2010 survey database includes data solicited from 11,673 students attending 19 two-year schools (17 in the United States and 2 in Canada). Almost all of the two-year schools in our sample have extensive programs intended to terminate in a two-year associate's degree or certificate, as well as large numbers of students who elect to do the first two years of their college work at a two-year school—often for financial reasons. Thus, our sample is not homogeneous.

If we look at the 9,421 students attending one of the 17 U.S. two-year schools in our database and compare them with our sample of four-year students, we see moderately higher levels of self-reported cheating in the four-year sample on four of the nine possible comparisons and a significant difference for the nine behaviors combined (table 3.11). For the other five comparisons, the numbers are essentially equal (within 3 percentage points). Although we have not tested any hypothesis that may explain why the difference for the sum of the nine behaviors is significant, we might suggest a hypothesis for future testing. One could argue that at least some of those pursuing a two-year vocational degree might be less committed to the academic process and feel less need to cheat, being less worried about grades. More research in this area is clearly needed.

The Impact of the Internet

Finally, we examine what impact the availability of the Internet has had on students' self-reports of cheating. As reflected in table 3.12, when we first added electronic plagiarism to our survey in 1999/2000, when the Internet was less pervasive than it is today, students self-reported only small amounts of engagement in this behavior. By the time of our 2002–2010 surveys, Internet access had become increasingly common. However, the self-report data in table 3.12 suggest that use of the Internet had not displaced "manual" plagiarism techniques but merely offered students another tool, which they were using equally. We began to question this result in our surveys, based on the extensive student comments that suggested Internet plagiarism was the new cheating tool for students. As noted earlier, we added a question to some of our surveys, beginning in 2007/2008, that asked students who self-reported any form of cut-and-paste plagiarism (a few sentences) exactly how they had accessed that information—through electronic means only, hard (paper) copy only, electronic primarily, hard copy primarily, or both sources equally. In response, 78% of the 2,949 students indicating they had engaged in cut-and-paste plagiarism reported that their primary method was the Internet rather than written sources, and another 16% reported that they used the two forms interchangeably. Only 6% relied primarily or exclusively on written sources.

But, as reflected in table 3.12, this switch to the Internet has not resulted in a dramatic increase in self-reported cheating overall. It seems to be more of a replacement phenomenon, although students certainly suggest in their open-ended comments that such cut-and-paste plagiarism is almost routine for those who do it at all, versus the occasional plagiarism that seems to have been more prevalent historically. So, even if the self-reported numbers for those who have engaged in Internet plagiarism are correct, these students seem to be engaging in cut-and-paste plagiarism far more often than did paper-driven, pre-Internet plagiarizers. In fact, if we look at the ratings of seriousness for *all* students, not just those who have engaged in Internet plagiarism, we find that 39% consider cut-and-paste plagiarism from the Internet either not cheating at all or just trivial cheating. Only 25% consider it serious cheating. If we look only at those who have engaged in the behavior, 6% consider it to be serious, and 62% label it trivial cheating or not cheating at all. Offering some support for the thesis discussed by Susan Blum

TABLE 3.12. Students' engagement in plagiarism and overall cheating at no-code schools, 1962/1963 through 2009/2010 (% of students reporting behavior)

| | Bowers | | McCabe et al. | | | |
Type of cheating	1962/1963	1990/1991	1993/1994	1999/2000	2002–2010
Copying a few sentences of material without footnoting in a paper	53	41	54	45	36
Plagiarized from public material on papers	36	19	26	19	6
Paraphrasing or copying few sentences from electronic source without footnoting them	—	—	—	14	36
Turning in a paper from a "paper mill" and claiming it as your own work	—	—	—	7	3
Any of the nine behaviors	83	74	87	83	65
N	2,313	2,854	1,744	693	73,738

(2009), students and faculty may be living in two different worlds on this issue, as 39% of faculty consider Internet cut-and-paste plagiarism to be serious cheating, and only 2% consider it not to be cheating at all.

We should make one last point about cut-and-paste plagiarism. The advent of technological advances to catch such plagiarism may have an impact on these numbers, as more professors take advantage of this anti-plagiarism software. Just as it is getting easier to cut and paste from the Internet, catching it is also getting easier. If students know that faculty will be checking—or better yet, if students are expected to do so themselves—such cut-and-paste plagiarism may decline.

Conclusion

We have provided a great many data on the prevalence of cheating in college, mostly from our own database and some previously unpublished. Any conclusions we draw about prevalence must recognize that all of these data are self-reports and are therefore subject to caveats about the validity of self-report data on a sensitive topic such as cheating (despite promises of anonymity or confidentiality). Also, more recent surveys have been conducted electronically, lowering response rates dramatically. We suspect that respondents to electronic surveys are less honest than respondents to paper surveys, because of concerns about confidentiality of the electronic data.

Keeping all of this in mind, no matter how one looks at the data, the prevalence of self-reported cheating is high enough for all of us—students, faculty, and administrators—to be seriously concerned. When more than two-thirds of college students are reporting that they have cheated, we need to pay attention. One benefit of our dataset is that it allows us to look at changes over time. Although cheating remains high, some shifts appear to be occurring as certain types of cheating are increasing and others are decreasing. This should provide us with ideas about which areas might need the most attention. We hope we have at least captured your attention with these numbers so that you will want to read on. In subsequent chapters, we focus on the personal and contextual influences on cheating that should add to our understanding of why students cheat, and we suggest some potential tools for addressing the prevalence problem.

CHAPTER FOUR

Individual Student Characteristics
That Influence Cheating

I ndividual characteristics influence students' academic integrity and dishonesty. A focus on such characteristics is consistent with the individual differences, or "bad apples," perspective, which suggests that cheating is attributable to the personal characteristics of individuals acting on the basis of predispositions or personal motives. Past research has suggested a wide variety of individual factors that influence students' cheating behavior, including gender (Genereux and McLeod 1995; Gibson, Khey, and Schreck 2008; Hendershott, Drinan, and Cross 1999; Huelsman, Piroch, and Wasieleski 2006; McCabe and Treviño 1997; Niiya et al. 2008; Taylor-Bianco and Deeter-Schmelz 2007; Tibbetts 1997, 1999; Ward and Beck 1990; Whitley, Nelson, and Jones 1999), age (Klein et al. 2007; McCabe and Treviño 1997; Mustaine and Tewksbury 2005), grade point average (Baird 1980; Davy et al. 2007; Genereux and McLeod 1995; Klein et al. 2007; McCabe and Treviño 1997; Roig and Caso 2005), type A behavior and competitive achievement-striving (Perry et al. 1990), self-esteem (Kibler 1992; Ward 1986), participation in athletics (McCabe and Treviño 1997; Mustaine and Tewksbury 2005), and membership in fraternities/sororities and other extracurricular activities (McCabe and Treviño 1997; Storch and Storch 2002).

Although much of the research in the area of individual differences has been atheoretical, scholars are increasingly employing theoretical approaches such as attribution theory (Murdock and Stephens 2007), neutralization theory (Rettinger and Kramer 2009), and social cognitive theory, goal theory, expectancy theory, and intrinsic motivation theory (e.g., Murdock and Anderman 2006) to explain relationships between individual difference factors and student cheating. Critics of the individual differences approach argue that it offers a limited number of prescriptions that are open to administrative influence. The few individual differences–based options available to administrators or faculty who are searching for methods of curbing academic cheating are limited mainly to attracting students who match a profile of desirable characteristics and engaging in psychological development and training programs to facilitate students' progression through the stages of cognitive moral development (Kohlberg 1969). Critics (including us) have also argued that individual differences have generally been shown to be weaker predictors of academic dishonesty than are situational factors, when the two types of factors are studied together (e.g., McCabe and Treviño 1997; for an exception, see Kisamore, Stone, and Jawahar 2007). Nevertheless, the individual differences approach can offer important insights into why students do or do not cheat. For that reason, we believe that it is important to address this category of influences as part of any comprehensive understanding of the drivers of academic integrity or dishonesty.

The purpose of this chapter, then, is to summarize the current state of knowledge regarding individual differences associated with higher levels of academic integrity and lower levels of student cheating. We begin by discussing the individual factors that have received the most research attention, then turn to other individual factors identified in the literature. Throughout the chapter, we highlight our own work in this area, including some unpublished data.

Major Individual Difference Factors

Although our own research has focused primarily on the role of contextual factors in influencing academic dishonesty, we have also examined relationships between individual influences and academic dishonesty. For example, in our 1997 study, we examined several individual-level variables that have received a great deal of research attention, including gender, age, academic achievement (GPA), participation in intercollegiate athletics and other extracurricular activities, and membership in fraternities or sororities (McCabe and Treviño 1997). Although we found these factors to be less important than contextual factors, they were nonetheless significant correlates of cheating among college students.

Gender

The individual factor that seems to have received the greatest amount of research attention is gender. Historically, research in this area has demonstrated that men cheat more than women (Aiken 1991; Bowers 1964; Davis et al. 1992; Kelly and Worrell 1978; Ward 1986). This relationship has been explained through socialization theory, which argues that women are more likely than men to be socialized to obey rules (Gilligan 1982). However, some studies have failed to show a difference between men and women (Baird 1980; Haines et al. 1986; Lipson and McGavern 1993; Ward and Beck 1990), and at least two studies have even reported that women cheat more than men (Antion and Michael 1983; Leming 1980). But multi-campus studies, including our own in the 1990s (McCabe and Treviño 1997) and those of Davis and colleagues (1992) and Bowers (1964), found significantly lower levels of cheating among female students. The variation in findings made the area ripe for meta-analysis, and Whitley, Nelson, and Jones's (1999) meta-analysis of gender differences in cheating attitudes and behavior among college students supports the notion that men report more favorable attitudes toward cheating and more cheating behavior. The mean effect size for attitudes was moderate (equivalent to a correlation of $r = 0.21$), but the mean effect size for behavior was quite small (equivalent to $r = 0.08$). This small effect size is consistent with a recent meta-analysis that evaluated the effect of gender on unethical decisions more generally (Kish-Gephart, Harrison, and Treviño 2010).

If we assume a socialization explanation, it is particularly interesting to note that our most recent unpublished data suggest that women have "caught up" to men in their propensity to cheat, and this may be because more women are choosing to major in areas that were formerly male-dominated. The data suggest that, within similar majors, gender differences in cheating are typically very small. And the overall data reflect a narrowing of the overall gender difference. For example, generally higher levels of cheating were found among women in engineering than among women in other majors, and women majoring in engineering reported cheating at rates comparable to those for male engineering majors. This may simply reflect the norms in these engineering classes. It may also be reflective of a perception that engineering remains a relatively male-dominated field, and women may feel a need to go by the "men's rules" to be successful in this major.

Year	Reporting test cheating (%)*		Reporting written cheating (%)[†]	
	Women	Men	Women	Men
2002/2003	19 (7,123)[‡]	24 (4,435)	54 (6,455)	52 (4,008)
2003/2004	22 (5,039)	26 (2,787)	52 (4,797)	52 (2,626)
2004/2005	20 (8,427)	23 (5,581)	50 (7,890)	49 (5,060)
2005/2006	21 (6,232)	26 (3,348)	47 (6,171)	46 (3,061)
2006/2007	19 (6,563)	22 (4,867)	45 (6,200)	45 (4,056)
2007/2008	18 (2,417)	20 (1,207)	39 (2,350)	39 (1,118)
2008/2009	18 (1,838)	19 (868)	38 (1,381)	40 (844)
2009/2010[§]	15 (1,551)	17 (1,024)	38 (1,438)	38 (922)

NOTE: The samples used for all calculations here exclude first-year students and graduate students, those attending traditional honor code schools, and those in two-year schools.

*Percentage acknowledging one or more of the following behaviors in the past year: copying from another on a test with or without that person's knowledge, the use of crib notes, or helping another to cheat.

†Percentage acknowledging one or more of the following on written work: cut-and-paste plagiarism from either written or Internet sources, taking all or most of one's paper from a written or Internet source, submitting the work of another as one's own, or falsifying a bibliography. This and the above index were first introduced in McCabe and Treviño 1993 and have become a staple in our survey work.

‡Numbers in parentheses are the number of observations in each category.

§The 2009/2010 sample was adjusted as described in the text.

If we look at our unpublished data collected from second-year through fifth-year undergraduates in the United States from academic year 2002/2003 to 2009/2010 (table 4.1), we see that by 2009/2010, men and women self-reported levels of cheating on written work that are very similar (as they are for the preceding seven years), although the differences in test and exam cheating are greater than expected. However, a closer examination of our data reveals that almost all of this difference occurred in just 2 schools in a total sample of 13 schools in 2009/2010. If we exclude these 2 schools, we find that 15% of the women at the remaining schools (N = 1,551) self-reported one or more instances of serious test/exam cheating, versus 17% of the men (N = 1,024), and 38% of both men and women self-reported one or more instances of serious cheating on written work. And this is for *all* majors, not just engineering. These data suggest two important conclusions: first, the small gender differences in self-reported cheating found in previous research seem to be disappearing, and second, the general decline in self-reported cheating seems to indicate that students are cheating less today than historically. However, as we noted in chapter 3, these declines may reflect a growing reluctance on the part of many students to acknowledge their academic dishonesty in online surveys, rather than an actual decline in cheating; or they may reflect a changing definition of what constitutes cheating in the minds of today's students, especially as it relates to a more permissive attitude toward cut-and-paste plagiarism from the Internet. Of course, our explanation also shows how sensitive our data are to specific schools when we look at smaller subsamples.

This continues a trend we first observed when comparing our 1993 and 1999/2000 surveys. In 1993 we surveyed 1,491 students at nine medium to large public institutions, and in 1999/2000, as part of a research project conducted for the Center for Academic Integrity, with the support of the John Templeton Foundation, we surveyed 2,156 students on 21 campuses. Looking at the results by gender, we observed that men cheated more than women on both test and written work, but unlike our earlier work (McCabe and Treviño 1997), the differences were not significant in the case of written cheating (65% vs. 61%, $t=1.81$, $df=1288$, $p< 0.10$) or test cheating (66% vs. 62%, $t=1.55$, $df=1284$, $p< 0.15$). The important point, however, is how these relationships had changed by the time of our 1999/2000 survey. Men and women clearly reported similar rates of test cheating in this survey (34% of men and 33% of women admitting one or more serious infractions in the past year; $t=0.26$, $df=1404$, $p=0.79$). Men reported more cheating on written work, but the effect was not statistically significant (52% vs. 49%, $t=1.60$, $df=1415$, $p=0.11$). Comparing these results with the data in table 4.1, we again see evidence of the declining rate of self-reported student cheating and a continuation of the gender trends with regard to written work. We have no solid theoretical explanation for the apparent relative decrease in test cheating among women in 2009/2010. However, it may simply underscore the sensitivity of self-reported cheating statistics to the sample of schools involved, especially when comparing data collected only a few years apart. In comparing our 1999/2000 and 2002–2010 data, we must also remember that the 1999/2000 data were gathered using written surveys, whereas the 2002–2010 data were generated using a web-based survey. However, even with this noise in our data, it does seem clear that the traditional belief that men self-report more cheating than women is no longer a supportable conclusion.

TABLE 4.2. Self-reported cheating by major and gender, 1962/1963 versus 2002–2010

	Women (%)		Men (%)	
	Enrolled	Reporting cheating	Enrolled	Reporting cheating
1962/1963 (Bowers)				
Business and engineering	4	—	26	—
Tests/exams	—	24	—	50
Written work	—	55	—	74
Other	96	—	74	—
Tests/exams	—	23	—	39
Written work	—	59	—	64
2002–2010 (McCabe et al.)				
Business and engineering	21	—	39	—
Tests/exams	—	22	—	24
Written work	—	49	—	50
Other	79	—	61	—
Tests/exams	—	19	—	22
Written work	—	47	—	45

In trying to understand this shift, we argue that the greater number of women in business and engineering majors today may provide a predominant part of the explanation. Using Bowers's (1964) data, we can evaluate this hypothesis, to some degree, by comparing his 1962/1963 data with our 2002–2010 data. We see significant gender shifts in business and engineering since Bowers's work was completed, as reflected in table 4.2.

While the findings are somewhat confusing due to the overall decline in self-reported cheating, as we discussed in chapter 3, table 4.2 does not seem to support the view that it is the substantially higher relative numbers of women majoring in business and engineering in the 2000s (21% of the total female student population in our surveys) versus 1962/1963 (only 4%) that explains why the gap between male and female cheating rates has narrowed. Table 4.2 suggests that the significant disparity that existed between men and women almost fifty years ago has been essentially erased in the case of business and engineering majors and those majoring in other areas.

In some of our earliest work, we observed that women at women's (i.e., all-female) colleges seemed to be more responsive to the dictums of honor codes and, on average, reported lower levels of academic dishonesty than either men or women at coed schools with honor codes. But

TABLE 4.3. Cheating trends by gender at 31 selected campuses
(% self-reporting one or more instances of serious cheating)

	1990/1991	1995/1996	2005/2006
Code schools			
Male students	46 (759)*	54 (527)	50 (238)
Female students on co-ed campuses	46 (820)	51 (707)	51 (366)
Female students on women's campuses	38 (898)	49 (701)	57 (345)
No-code schools			
Male students	72 (1,018)	73 (547)	59 (235)
Female students	68 (1,135)	68 (781)	63 (235)

*Numbers in parentheses are the number of observations in each category.

this no longer seems to be the case. Our surveys of a group of 31 schools in 1990/1991 and 1995/1996, which helped initiate our work, included 14 schools with traditional academic honor codes, each of which had a pledge and student judiciary. Unproctored exams and some obligation or expectation concerning the reporting of any cheating a student might observe were part of most of these codes as well. Twenty-eight of the 31 schools also agreed to participate in a follow-up student survey in 2005/2006, although only 23 (12 of our original 14 honor code schools and 11 of the original 17 no-code schools) agreed to do a written survey that would be comparable to our surveys in 1990/1991 and 1995/1996. Unfortunately, this reduced the sample to a size that precludes our establishing statistical significance, but the results remain instructive. Using total self-reported serious cheating (a combination of our serious test cheating and serious cheating on written work indices), we see further support for the conclusion that self-reported rates of cheating among women have caught up to, or surpassed, those of men (in both code and no-code environments). The data in table 4.3 also suggest that the primary trend behind this change is increased levels of cheating among women at women's colleges. (Note: Only four of our original five women's colleges are included in this analysis, as one of the original five did not participate in the 2005/2006 written survey, opting instead to survey students only electronically.)

At three of the four women's colleges in this sample, students' comments suggest their campuses have reduced the emphasis on their honor codes in the past 15 years. While women on two of these campuses were quick to write open-ended comments in the 1990/1991 survey about the strength of their campus code and the rituals surrounding it, such as elaborate honor code signing ceremonies for new students, there was a sharp reduction in the number of such comments in 1995/1996, with several students bemoaning the loss of such traditions. By 2005/2006, such comments were almost completely absent. It is possible that the elimination or diminishment of some of the rituals historically associated with the honor code on these two women's campuses may have contributed to the increases in self-reported academic dishonesty among these women.

The third campus, which also seems to have reduced its emphasis on its honor code, presents a unique and interesting case. Like many surviving women's campuses today, this campus has an affiliation and cross-registration agreement with a traditional men's school (i.e., formerly all-male campus) that is now coed and does not have an honor code. Compared with its sister schools, this women's campus has a much longer history of affiliation and cross-registration with its male "partner" and, in many ways, a stronger affiliation agreement. In spite of similar self-reported rates of cheating among women at both the women's college and on the formerly all-male campus in 1990/1991, men at the formerly all-male college did report notably higher rates of cheating than women that year, as shown in table 4.4. Several women at the women's college argued that it was this rampant cheating on the formerly all-male campus that led *them* to cheat, in an effort to remain competitive in courses they took on the affiliated campus. Several women even claimed that although they may have cheated in a course at the former men's college, they would never do so on their own campus, where they took the honor code seriously. Women at the women's college made similar claims in 1995/1996 and even in 2005/2006, even though their self-reported rates of cheating were now comparable to or higher than those of either men or women at the now coed traditional men's school. As noted earlier, we believe such competitive considerations, especially as greater numbers of women have entered previously male-dominated fields of study such as engineering, help explain the disproportionate rise in cheating among women compared with men. This does not, however, give us much insight as to why cheating seems to have risen to a greater degree on women's campuses with traditional honor codes. We may need to look to broader societal trends for such insights.

TABLE 4.4. Cheating trends by gender at two selected schools
(% self-reporting one or more instances of serious cheating)

	1990	1995	2005
Women at all-female campus	56 (117)*	65 (153)	59 (88)
At traditional male "affiliated" campus			
Women	55 (69)	56 (54)	45 (60)
Men	72 (54)	67 (42)	40 (55)

*Numbers in parentheses are the number of observations in each category.

If a relationship does exist between gender and cheating behavior, it is important to better understand the underlying mechanisms. Recent research has delved more deeply into multiple mechanisms that could be responsible for a relationship between gender and cheating attitudes and behavior, as well as for the differences between male and female students when this relationship exists. For example, Gibson, Khey, and Schreck (2008) examined how internal control mechanisms such as self-control, shame, embarrassment, and moral beliefs might account for differences between men and women in cheating behavior. Their results suggest that two internal controls, self-control and moral beliefs, help explain the gender gap, in that moral beliefs matter more for women and self-control matters more for men. Specifically, men with lower self-control were more likely to report cheating on tests than men who had more self-control, whereas there was no relationship between cheating and self-control for women. Women with stronger moral beliefs were less likely to report cheating on tests than women with weaker moral beliefs, but this relationship was not significant for men. Niiya et al. (2008) examined the issue of gender and student cheating in a laboratory setting in which a peer confederate invited participants to cheat on an academic test. Consistent with previous research, direct effects showed that male students cheated more than female students. Interaction results showed that men who base their self-worth on competition and have performance-avoidance goals were more likely to cheat, whereas men who base their self-worth on virtue were less likely to cheat. None of these factors were related to cheating for women, suggesting, again, that the mechanisms driving cheating may be different for men and women.

Taylor-Bianco and Deeter-Schmelz (2007) investigated gender effects and cultural differences in MBA students' self-reported cheating behavior in the United States and India. Their results suggested that, in the United States, men are more likely to cheat than women, but no differences were found between men and women in India. Huelsman, Piroch, and Wasieleski (2006) examined the relationship between religiosity and academic dishonesty and found that the relationship is significant for women but not for men. Tibbetts (1997, 1999) investigated gender differences in test-cheating intentions. She found that the effects of moral beliefs and grades were more pronounced in predicting women's cheating intentions, whereas men were more affected by prior cheating and friends' cheating behavior. The results also showed that higher levels of anticipated shame among women and less self-control among men accounted for most of the difference in cheating intentions between women and men.

Gender and Reporting

Hendershott, Drinan, and Cross (1999) showed that both men and women are reluctant to report instances of academic dishonesty that they witness. Although our most relevant study on reporting did not address the question of gender (McCabe, Treviño, and Butterfield 2001), we have been able to conduct such an analysis of our data in preparing this book. The data used in our 2001 article on reporting do support the observation of Hendershott and colleagues (1999) concerning the low level of reporting by both males and female students: in our survey, only 5.5% of those students responding that they had observed an incident of cheating indicated that they had reported it—6.3% of the women and 4.1% of the men. This gender difference prevailed in both the honor code schools in our survey (8.5% for women vs. 6.6% for men) and the no-code schools (4.7% vs. 3.2%). While the results show that reporting is higher at the code schools, the differences are not as great as one might predict based on the much greater prevalence of some form of reporting requirement at the code schools. At the five women's colleges in the code sample, the self-reported rate of actual reporting was 8.9%. Responses to a second set of questions on reporting—the likelihood that the respondent would report an incident of cheating of which he or she was aware, and the likelihood that the typical student on campus would do so—show a similar pattern. These data seem to support the low levels of actual reporting, with only 15% of all female respondents suggesting they would be likely or very likely to report an incident of cheating (vs. 8% of the male respondents), and only 17% (vs. 13% of males) indicating that the typical student would be likely to do so.

We replicated this 1995/1996 study in 2005/2006, and 28 of the 31 schools in the original study participated in this replication, some using web-based surveys and others using written surveys. Using the same type of calculations on these unpublished data, we see that actual reporting remained at approximately the same low levels compared with 10 years earlier: 5.9% for women and 4.7% for men. Looking at honor code versus no-code schools, we again see a pattern similar to that observed in 1995/1996: 8.1% of the women at code schools versus 4.1% at no-code schools, and 6.9% of the men at code schools versus 3.8% at no-code schools. In all cases we see a very small decline in actual reporting among women and a corresponding increase for men. This seems to support our findings that the behavior of men and women with regard to academic dishonesty is becoming more similar, although the indication of a possible increase in reporting among men seems to belie the many comments we continue to receive in our surveys that suggest students in general are opposed to reporting, with words such as "narc" and "tattletale" frequently punctuating these comments. With the exception of a few honor code schools, many students simply seem to believe it is not their place to report any cheating they might observe, and they feel strongly that they should not be expected to do so. We revisit this issue in chapter 9.

Because of the lack of relevant differences in cheating between male and female students today, we think it is time to abandon the study of gender differences. As found in other ethical decision-making arenas (Kish-Gephart, Harrison, and Treviño 2010), any existing gender differences are negligible and probably not worth pursuing further, except perhaps to attempt to understand the different underlying processes driving these behaviors in men and women.

Age

The research literature is fairly consistent in demonstrating that younger students cheat more than older students (Antion and Michael 1983; Haines et al. 1986; Lipson and McGavern 1993; Mustaine and Tewksbury 2005). Klein et al. (2007) showed that serious cheaters across all professional schools were more likely to be younger. However, it is not clear how much of this relationship reflects age rather than class rank (i.e., upperclassmen vs. lowerclassmen). These two variables are strongly correlated, and we have argued that first-year students and sophomores often find themselves in large lecture courses that are outside their primary interest area. They may see a lot of cheating in these courses, as faculty struggle to monitor all of the students. Under such circumstances, underclassmen may find it easy to cheat and to rationalize cheating. In our experience, juniors and seniors are often more enthusiastic about their courses and faculty. At smaller schools, these students talk about the personal relationships they have developed with professors in their major, often making it harder to justify cheating in those courses.

In the early phases of this project, we observed that students in their first year of college, especially those in their first semester, reported significantly lower levels of cheating than upperclassmen. Indeed, focus groups we conducted in 1998 suggested that college-bound high school seniors envisioned college as a place where it would be time to get more serious about academics and where cheating would not occur as frequently as it seemed to in high school. Open-ended student responses in our earliest surveys and from our high school focus groups suggested that most students newly arriving on campus avoided cheating, unless and until they observed cheating among others and began to feel that this was the norm or that they had no choice but to engage in cheating to maintain a competitive GPA. Unfortunately, students arriving on campus today seem more predisposed to cheating.

Academic Achievement

Academic achievement, generally operationalized as grade point average (GPA), has consistently shown a negative relationship with academic dishonesty. Previous studies have generally shown that students with higher GPAs report less cheating than students with lower GPAs (Antion and Michael 1983; Baird 1980; Bowers 1964; Haines et al. 1986; Hetherington and Feldman 1964; Klein et al. 2007; Lipson and McGavern 1993; Michaels and Miethe 1989; Roig and Caso 2005; Singhal 1982). For example, Davy et al. (2007) found higher levels of cheating behavior among business students with lower academic performance. Our own research has confirmed this general finding (McCabe and Treviño 1997). As discussed by Leming (1980), it is possible that students with lower academic achievement have more to gain and less to lose by cheating and are therefore more likely to take the risk.

One exception to this general finding occurred several years ago, when the measure of GPA we employed had more divisions than our current measure and it was possible to differentiate the very best students on a campus from the very good students. In this unpublished research, we found a U-shaped relationship between GPA and self-reported cheating. Students at the very top seemed to be ultra-competitive for grades and to self-report more cheating than their peers. This effect appeared to be somewhat more pronounced at campuses that were more selective in their admissions policies, but the relationship existed on most campuses. Some students seemed to be cheating at above average rates in order to thrive, while a greater number, those with low GPAs, were cheating to survive—to maintain a financial aid award that required some minimum GPA, to remain eligible for athletics, to keep their parents "off their backs," or for any number of reasons.

When a student decides he or she needs a certain grade in a course, situational ethics seems to be important in the student's decision-making process. A good illustration of this phenomenon is distribution requirements that students have to fulfill. Consider, for example, a student majoring in science or engineering who, to graduate, might be required to take a course in the social sciences or a language. Students completing our surveys have argued (in open-ended comments) that taking shortcuts such as handing in copied homework or downloading small amounts of information from the Internet is not really cheating, since they shouldn't have to take that course anyway—yet another example of how easily students can "justify" cheating in different situations.

Extracurricular Involvement

Research has also found higher levels of cheating among students who participate in various extracurricular activities (Mustaine and Tewksbury 2005). In our 1997 study, we measured extracurricular involvement by using a composite of extracurricular activities (intramural athletics, political and cultural organizations, student government, musical groups, religious organizations, and college publications) (McCabe and Treviño 1997). Our findings were consistent with those of Bowers (1964) and Haines and colleagues (1986), who showed that students who are more involved in extracurricular activities are more likely to report higher levels of academic dishonesty. In our unpublished data, we have also found evidence that students who must care for children or aging parents at home self-report higher levels of academic dishonesty. We speculate that the time commitment associated with these various non-academic activities is part of the problem. As students are required to reduce the number of hours available for school (e.g., because of the need to work to pay their tuition or support their family), or as they elect to do so (to engage in some extracurricular activity such as social activities), the motivation to cheat and the ability to "justify" cheating seem to increase.

Athletic and Fraternity or Sorority Involvement

Two extracurricular activities that have been studied extensively are membership in fraternities or sororities (Storch and Storch 2002; A. E. Williams and Janosik 2007) and participation in intercollegiate athletics (Mustaine and Tewksbury 2005), with research consistently showing that students involved in these activities are more likely to cheat. For example, A. E. Williams and Janosik (2007) examined academic dishonesty among sorority and non-sorority women. Their results showed that incoming women with an interest in sorority involvement and junior and senior women already in a sorority reported significantly higher levels of cheating behaviors than women with no interest in being a member of a sorority in these two groups. Incoming women with an interest in sororities reported the highest level of cheating among the four groups.

In our 1997 study, we viewed fraternity/sorority membership as a contextual variable, because it can provide access to people and resources (e.g., test files) that facilitate cheating and may represent an environment where norms, values, and skills associated with cheating are more easily transmitted (e.g., Stannard and Bowers 1970). However, there may also be particular characteristics of individuals who are attracted to the emphasis on social life generally associated with fraternity/sorority life. As such, membership in a fraternity or sorority can also be viewed as an individual difference factor, and we treat it as such in this chapter. Consistent with previous studies, we found a strong relationship suggesting higher levels of self-reported cheating among fraternity and sorority members than among independent students (Baird 1980; Bonjean and

McGee 1965; Haines et al. 1986; Harp and Taietz 1966; Kirkvliet 1994; Stannard and Bowers 1970).

We also found a significant positive correlation between participation in intercollegiate athletics and cheating behavior in our unpublished data. This is consistent with Bowers (1964) and Haines and colleagues (1986), who reported that students' involvement in intercollegiate athletics is associated with higher levels of academic dishonesty. Haines and colleagues examined both intramural and intercollegiate athletics and found participation in either was associated with higher levels of cheating, with intramural athletics demonstrating a stronger relationship. Overall, we speculate that those who are more committed to extracurricular pursuits may be less able to devote time to academic pursuits. Engaging in these activities, in general, creates greater demands on students' time, which in turn leads students to take various shortcuts to remain competitive in their course work.

Compounding this for many students, in our view, is the "burden" associated with participation in intercollegiate athletics—especially for those who are recruited by a school because of their athletic rather than their academic abilities. For example, in the case of Division 1 football and basketball players (men and women), it is not unusual to hear about schools that make admissions concessions for an individual student they believe will enhance the performance of a major athletic team. In many cases, the school is accepting students who may not have the ability to be truly competitive in the classroom, then giving them the equivalent of a full-time job and expecting them to perform in the classroom. It is an almost self-fulfilling prophesy that they will be unable to do so. Many schools, in an effort to "help" such individuals, offer extensive tutoring services and other study assistance. Without getting into the age-old argument of whether such assistance sometimes crosses the line and becomes cheating, we note that at many schools with prestigious athletic programs, the comments offered by more than a trivial number of non-athletes suggest a level of resentment, even anger, on the part of students as a whole that such services are available to athletes but not to them. Perhaps more important, athletes are one of three groups that are consistently singled out by other students as the most common cheaters on campus—the other two being fraternity/sorority members and business majors.

Social Class

Another stream receiving attention within the individual differences area pertains to the effect of social class, as measured by factors such as family income, parents' occupation, and parents' education. In our 1997 study, we examined parents' level of education as a potential influence on cheating behavior (McCabe and Treviño 1997). Although the result was not significant, the logic connecting these factors is consistent with Kirkvliet (1994) and Bowers (1964), who argued that social class may have an impact on academic dishonesty. This argument is driven by the belief that children from higher social class backgrounds may be better prepared for college work through better secondary schooling and, perhaps, a more encouraging environment for academic achievement at home, and thus they have a higher commitment to further education. Both researchers found weak but significant relationships, but Bowers found an inverse relationship (i.e., children of more highly educated parents are less likely to cheat in college), whereas Kirkvliet found a positive relationship. We view Kirkvliet's results with caution, however, as his sample included students in a single course at a single university, whereas Bowers's sample included 99 academic institutions.

Risk Taking

Yet another stream within the individual differences area involves the relationship between cheating and other risky and/or problematic behaviors (e.g., drinking, partying, excitement seeking). The idea here is that students who engage in cheating are driven by the same risk-taking propensity that drives other risky behaviors. For example, de Bruin and Rudnick (2007) showed that low conscientiousness and a predisposition toward excitement seeking are related to self-reported premeditated cheating in tests and exams among university students. Zimny, Robertson, and Bartoszek (2008), examining academic as well as personal dishonesty among college students, showed that academic dishonesty was related to personal dishonesty, propensity for impression management, and partying behavior. Mustaine and Tewksbury (2005) showed that men who cheat academically are more likely than women to be involved in other risky or problematic behaviors (e.g., skipping class, alcohol and drug use). This suggests that cheating may be part of a larger orientation toward problem behavior, especially for men. In an examination of the relationship between binge drinking and student cheating, Bichler and Tibbetts (2003) showed that low self-control had a stronger correlation with students' cheating behaviors for those who were heavy binge drinkers than for those who were non-binge drinkers.

Ethically Desirable Traits

Some studies have approached the issue of integrity and cheating through a more "positive" lens, examining negative relationships between academic dishonesty and various ethically desirable traits. Bloodgood, Turnley, and Mudrack (2008) and Rettinger and Jordan (2005) found a significant negative relationship between students' religiosity and cheating behavior. Results of Bloodgood and colleagues' study also showed interactions among religiosity, taking a business ethics course, and intelligence. Students who were highly religious were unlikely to cheat, whether or not they had taken a business ethics course, whereas students who were not highly religious cheated less if they had taken a business ethics course. In addition, the extent of cheating among highly intelligent students was significantly reduced if such students had taken a course in business ethics. Individuals who were highly intelligent displayed significantly less cheating if they were also highly religious.

Schlenker (2008) showed that integrity, operationalized as a principled ideology, is negatively associated with cheating behavior. Staats, Hupp, and Hagley (2008) found that courage, empathy, and honesty are predictors of academic honesty and are negatively related to students' future intent to cheat. In an examination of relationships among academic cheating, moral identity, and sensitivity to social evaluation, Wowra (2007) showed that students are less likely to cheat when they place greater emphasis on their moral identity and are less sensitive to social evaluation. Lucas and Friedrich (2005) found that workplace integrity test scores were moderate to strong negative correlates of self-reported academic cheating. Bolin's (2004) results revealed that low self-control is related to more positive attitudes toward academic dishonesty, which is related to more cheating. Finally, research has found a relationship between students' level of cognitive moral development (Kohlberg 1969) and cheating behavior. For example, Malinowski and Smith (1985) found that the higher the moral reasoning scores, as measured by Rest's (1986) Defining Issues Test, the less students cheated in a laboratory study.

Other Individual Difference Factors

Other studies have demonstrated relationships between cheating behavior and a wide variety of attitudes, behaviors, and other personal characteristics. An interesting study by Mazar, Amir, and Ariely examined a theory of self-concept maintenance, suggesting that "a little bit of dishonesty gives a taste of profit without spoiling a positive self-view" (2008, 633). The results of a series of experiments suggested that two mechanisms, inattention to moral standards and categorization malleability, allowed the maintenance of a positive self-concept despite engaging in minor acts of dishonesty.

Other interesting work includes that of Greenberger et al. (2008), who examined "academic entitlement," a construct that includes individual students' expectations of high grades for modest effort and demanding attitudes toward teachers. Results showed that students who were higher on academic entitlement were more likely to engage in academic dishonesty.

Other individual difference factors shown to be positively related to cheating behavior include extrinsic, as opposed to intrinsic, motivation (Jordan 2001; Rettinger and Kramer 2009), psychopathy (Nathanson, Paulhus, and Williams 2006; K. M. Williams 2007), neutralizing attitudes (Rettinger and Kramer 2009), poorly developed value systems (Kibler 1992; Kibler and Kibler 1993), and having moderate expectations of success, having cheated in the past, and holding positive attitudes toward cheating (Whitley 1998). Research on the Big 5 personality factors has generally not supported connections to cheating behavior (e.g., Nathanson, Paulhus, and Williams 2006).

Conclusion

We have outlined here what we know about the influence of individual differences on student cheating. Although we know quite a bit, we often don't have enough high-quality research to make strong claims about such relationships. Clearly, more studies are needed. And, when enough studies do exist, we need more meta-analyses (beyond gender) to help us understand the results.

So far, most of the attention to individual differences has focused on demographics such as gender or age rather than on stable psychological predispositions. We were surprised by the lack of attention to such predispositions, since at least several have been related to ethical decision making more broadly. For example, future research may want to focus more on cognitive moral development (particularly important during the college years), locus of control, ethical decision styles, Machiavellianism (Kish-Gephart, Harrison, and Treviño 2010), and moral disengagement (Detert, Treviño, and Sweitzer 2008). It will be important to include multiple individual differences in a single study, so that we can better understand which ones are the main drivers of behavior. Because these individual differences in predisposition are theoretically related to thinking and conduct in ethics-related situations, they could help us get beyond the atheoretical approach taken by much of the research to date. Thus far, little agreement exists about the most important theories driving an individual differences approach. More work will also be required to identify the most important underlying theories and the mechanisms driving these relationships.

Despite the limitations of the research, it does seem that individual differences matter enough that faculty and administrators should consider the meaning of the findings we do have. For example, students could be considered to have different "risk profiles" with reference to cheating, and programs could be designed to address those at the highest risk. Rather than targeting men, for example, the research suggests that it makes more sense to focus on students in certain majors, with programs that might reduce the opportunity to cheat or create a more ethical classroom environment. Students with lower GPAs and/or those involved in fraternities, sororities, or athletics might also be good candidates for special attention.

Finally, few studies have combined individual differences with contextual factors in the same study. When they have done so, contextual factors appear to be more influential. Clearly, more research in this vein would be extremely helpful.

CHAPTER FIVE

Institutional Factors That Influence Academic Integrity

The Role of Honor Codes

M cCabe and Treviño began conducting research on academic integrity in part because of their own experiences attending undergraduate institutions with strong academic honor codes. Those experiences convinced us that participation in a strong honor code community can play a powerful role in reducing dishonest behavior and promoting lifelong integrity. As we discussed in chapter 1, a traditional honor code environment, as defined by Melendez (1985), includes one or more of the following elements: (1) unproctored exams, (2) the use of a written pledge in which students affirm that they have not cheated on a particular exam or assignment, (3) a judicial or hearing body in which students play a major role (e.g., a student serves as chairperson, students constitute a majority of the panel, or student consent is needed to change the constitution of this body), and (4) an expectation that students should report any violations of the code they may observe. In our work, we have used a stronger definition by requiring that a traditional code include at least two of these characteristics and elements of a third, and most of the schools we have identified as traditional honor code schools contain some elements of all four characteristics. The reporting requirement is missing from many code environments today, as students are very reluctant to engage in such reporting and often ignore the requirement if it exists. As a result, many codes that once contained this reporting requirement no longer do. But many of these schools still encourage student reporting, and their codes are still considered traditional codes.

In this chapter, we review the historical insights on honor codes found in the work of Bill Bowers, then we review the current state of knowledge on honor codes and their ability to influence important outcomes. As in other chapters, we discuss our own work in this area as well as other significant contributions.

Insights from the Bowers Data

Much can be learned from the data collected by Bill Bowers almost fifty years ago (Bowers 1964). Although the Bowers data on the impact of honor codes have not been published in much depth, we are able to discuss this work here, thanks to Bowers's generosity in sharing his original data with us. One of the many interesting findings that Bowers did not discuss in detail in his 1964 publication involved a question on his survey that asked respondents whether their school had an honor code. We were able to use this question to sort the Bowers sample of 99 schools into 32 code schools and 64 no-code schools. Three schools were eliminated from the analysis due to lack of clarity about whether their campus had a formal honor code or not. We also eliminated first-year students from this analysis, as we normally do. The results of our analysis are shown in table 5.1. The table summarizes the percentage of students engaging in each of the nine cheating behaviors that we have been using from Bowers's original work. The table presents data both for the Bowers study and for our 1990/1991 study. We focus here on the results at the honor code schools versus the no-code schools.

Although the data in table 5.1 support the effectiveness of honor codes, that power is perhaps even more evident in our 1990/1991 data if we look only at those test cheating behaviors that students consider the most obvious forms of cheating: copying from someone else's test and using unauthorized crib or cheat notes. For example, for test copying, we find that more than twice as many no-code students (31%) as code students (13%) acknowledge engaging in the behavior. Of course, one must wonder whether students attending an honor code school would be willing to admit to cheating. In other words, would a student attending a code school be more reluctant to admit any transgressions? While we cannot answer this question for certain, we do have at least two pieces of information that seem to support the validity of our findings. First, and most important, we included a question on our 1990/1991 survey that asked students what percentage of their classmates they thought "have cheated on a test, exam or paper while at [school X]." At no-code schools, more than 45% of respondents said that more than one in five of their classmates had done so, while at code schools, only a little

TABLE 5.1. Students' self-reports of engagement in nine types of cheating at campuses with and without honor codes, Bowers 1962/1963 and McCabe and Treviño 1990/1991 surveys (% of students reporting behavior)

Type of cheating	Bowers 1962/1963		McCabe and Treviño 1990/1991	
	Code	No code	Code	No code
Copying a few sentences of material without footnoting in a paper	38	53	24	41
"Padding" a few items on a bibliography	32	35	14	25
Plagiarized from public material on papers	23	36	7	19
Getting questions or answers from someone who has already taken the same exam	16	42	12	19
Copying from another student on a test or exam	11	31	13	31
Working on the same home-work with several students when the teacher does not allow it	10	14	20	40
Turned in papers done entirely or in part by other students	8	20	3	13
Giving answers to other students during an exam	5	27	8	27
Used crib notes during an exam	7	20	9	21
Any of the nine behaviors	63	83	48	74
N	1,398	2,313	2,923	2,854

over 10% indicated such a high level of perceived classmate cheating. Second, we have been struck by the fact that, when we have compared code and no-code schools in our surveys, the response rate at the code schools is always notably higher. For example, in our 1990/1991 survey we had a response rate of 41.4% at code schools versus 35.7% at no-code schools (McCabe and Treviño 1993)—a statistically significant difference. It seems reasonable to suggest that the lower response rate at no-code schools may, to at least some degree, reflect an unwillingness to admit cheating on the part of these students (for fear of detection through the survey process, if for no other reason) and that, if we had comparable return rates, the no-code students might be reporting cheating at an even higher rate than the code students.

1995/1996 McCabe, Treviño, and Butterfield Survey

While our work after the 1990/1991 survey began to focus more on no-code schools, our ongoing curiosity about the effect of honor codes encouraged us to try to replicate our 1990/1991 survey. Therefore, in the 1995/1996 academic year, we once again contacted the original 31 schools. Eventually, all 31 agreed to participate in this second survey. Although our agreement with these 31 schools, and all the schools that have participated in this project, does not allow us to thank them by name, this whole project has depended on their cooperation, for which we are most grateful. Imagine sitting in your office one day when someone you never heard of calls and asks you to allow him to survey your campus on such a sensitive topic as cheating. It took some courage and trust on the part of all of our participating schools to join this effort—especially the earliest pioneers who joined on almost blind faith. At least for schools participating after 1990/1991, we could show them the type of work we intended to publish, which has always protected the anonymity of any school desiring it.

In table 5.2 we show the code and no-code school results for both our 1990/1991 and 1995/1996 surveys. The same 31 schools participated in each survey and the same protocol was used in each. An envelope containing a letter outlining the purpose of the survey was sent to each student, and included in the envelope was a survey that the student was asked to complete and return. In 1990/1991, typically 500 randomly selected juniors and seniors were contacted on each campus, and in 1995/1996 this number was reduced to 400 to help control costs. Return rates were fairly comparable—36% and 41%, respectively, at our no-code and code schools in 1990/1991, compared with 39% and 41% in the 1995/1996 survey. The most notable difference between the two surveys is that, in 1995/1996, we broadened our interest beyond primarily seniors and surveyed a large number of sophomores and juniors as well. While 92% of the 1990/1991 respondents were seniors, and the vast majority of the balance were juniors, in 1995/1996 only 51% of the respondents were seniors, with 25% sophomores and 24% juniors. Based on analysis over all of our surveys, we would expect this to have a very minor impact—perhaps inflating the 1995/1996 numbers by a percentage point or two, as we have seen some tendency for seniors to report slightly lower rates of cheating than juniors.

Several conclusions are supported by the data in table 5.2.

TABLE 5.2. Students' engagement in nine types of cheating at selected campuses with and without honor codes, McCabe et al. 1990/1991 and 1995/1996 surveys (% of students reporting behavior)

Type of cheating	McCabe et al. 1990/1991		McCabe et al. 1995/1996	
	Code	No code	Code	No code
Copying a few sentences of material without footnoting in a paper	24	41	31	42
"Padding" a few items on a bibliography	14	25	15	27
Plagiarized from public material on papers	7	19	9	19
Getting questions or answers from someone who has already taken the same exam	12	19	20	45
Copying from another student on a test or exam	13	31	19	32
Working on the same homework with several students when the teacher does not allow it	20	40	26	47
Turned in papers done entirely or in part by other students	3	13	4	11
Giving answers to other students during an exam	8	27	10	22
Used crib notes during an exam	9	21	11	16
Any of the nine behaviors	48	74	60	82
N	2,923	2,954	2,244	1,912

- We once again see the power of honor codes. Every possible comparison of code versus no-code students favors the code schools (lower levels of self-reported cheating), and the difference is significant for each individual behavior. Not surprisingly, the difference is strongly significant ($p < 0.0001$) for the composite measure of all nine behaviors as well ($t = 15.62$, $df = 4154$).
- For both code and no-code schools, we see an increase from 1990/1991 to 1995/1996 in the percentage of students self-reporting engagement in one of the nine cheating behaviors. In the case of code schools, we see an increase in four of the nine behaviors, while five are relatively stable (a 1 or 2 percentage point

change). For no-code schools, we also see an increase overall, as well as more substantive changes in four of the nine behaviors. However, in the case of no-code schools, we begin to see the first signs of erosion in self-reported cheating, as two of these four substantive changes are decreases: 5 percentage point decreases in both "giving answers to other students during an exam" and "used crib notes during an exam."

- Although the change in "getting questions or answers from someone who has already taken the same exam" for no-code schools is by far the most dramatic shift seen in table 5.2, its removal from the analysis does not change the basic relationships in the table; it just lowers the composite index of test cheating for no-code schools in 1995/1996 to 78%.

Even more interesting aspects of our longitudinal honor code study begin to appear in 2005/2006, to which we now turn our attention.

2005/2006 McCabe, Treviño, and Butterfield Survey

Although similar in many ways to the two previous surveys in our honor code project, our 2005/2006 study differs in several potentially important points. Probably the most important difference is that some of the schools were not willing to do a written survey, arguing that they had eliminated all written surveying of students in favor of online surveys. We attempted to turn this into an asset by asking schools to do two surveys—one web-based and one written. We expected to see the same basic relationship in both, but we hypothesized that the written survey would have a somewhat higher rate of response due to students' anonymity concerns. Even more important, we thought these anonymity concerns would result in a higher level of self-reported cheating on the written survey. Although we asked all 31 schools to consider this dual survey option, only 19 agreed to do so (9 code and 8 no-code schools, in addition to 2 schools we classified as modified honor code schools, to be explained shortly). Four schools (1 code and 3 no-code) elected a web survey only, and 5 schools (3 code and 2 no-code) chose a written survey only. In total, then, we had web-based survey data from 23 schools (10 code schools, 2 modified code schools, and 11 no-code schools) and written data from 22 schools (12 code schools and 10 no-code schools).

TABLE 5.3. Calculated survey return rates, 1990/1991 through 2005/2006
(% of surveys returned)

Type of school	1990/1991 written survey	1995/1996 written survey	2005/2006 written survey	2005/2006 web survey
No honor code	41	41	14	18
Honor code	36	39	18	25
Modified honor code	—	—	17	25

We should note some further points here. First, our total sample included only 28 of the original 31 schools, as we were unable to convince one honor code school and two no-code schools to allow us to conduct a third survey on their campus. Second, we were able to exercise less researcher "control" in this survey than we normally had. At a number of schools, we were dealing with the same people (faculty, administrators) for a second or third time, and some thought they could implement the survey without our assistance. This generally proved uneventful, with some exceptions. For example, at one school we raised a question about the very low response rate. Our contact "admitted" that more than 20% of the surveys never made it into student hands, because some were never mailed and others were not mailed to valid student addresses. Third, we had some technical problems of our own, with our mainframe computer malfunctioning at one point and not recording students' responses at two schools for several hours one day during the survey period. This seemed to have a dramatic impact at only one school. We also had mailing problems with our paper surveys, which may also have reduced our response rate slightly. Fourth, there was consensus among almost all of our school contacts that many (most?) students were now less willing to complete surveys at all. Finally, at least four of the schools sent a small number of surveys to first-year students, in spite of our request that they not do so. Although these problems may be important, especially in the aggregate, we have no reasonable method of incorporating their impact into our calculation of return rates, which have dropped dramatically since our earlier surveys in this project, as shown in table 5.3.

In spite of all these potential "excuses" to explain the lower response rates, we believe the single most important factor is a growing student unwillingness to complete surveys, just as the many student and judicial affairs personnel we worked with in administering this 2005/2006 survey had predicted. We should also note that we cannot provide an accurate test of any hypothesis about return rates, because each campus doing a web-based survey used at least one reminder, and most used two, to promote higher response rates; for the written surveys, no reminders were used, due to the cost of a second mailing. Although subject to some researcher interpretation, it appears that the web response rates before the first reminder were "slightly" lower than the written response rate with only the single mailing. However, we don't know how many students who responded after the first or second reminder would have done so in the absence of a reminder.

The modified code group in table 5.3 represents two schools that began in our no-code group in 1990/1991 (and 1995/1996) but by 2005 had adopted a "modified" form of honor code. Although there is no single definition of what constitutes a modified honor code, two strategies (and often some combination of the two) are typically involved (e.g., McCabe and Pavela 2000). One strategy is to utilize culture-building mechanisms such as integrity rallies, presidential involvement, and integrity seminars to focus a campus's attention on the issue of academic dishonesty and clearly communicate to students that integrity is an institutional priority and something to be valued. The second strategy is to give students a significant role in the judicial or hearing body on campus and in developing programs to inform other students about the code, including its purpose, its major components, and methods of enforcement. Thus, modified codes emphasize students' responsibility for academic integrity, just as traditional honor codes do, but without the reporting requirement. In certain cases, schools using modified codes also allow the possibility of unproctored exams and/or the use of an affirmation pledge, at the instructor's discretion, but these are generally not mandated, as they are at almost all honor code schools.

The primary reason for not classifying the two modified code schools as code schools in table 5.3 was that they did not have unproctored exams and did not require students to report any cheating they might observe, although they often encouraged such reporting. As the reader can see, on average, the survey response rates for these two modified code schools are between those for the code and no-code schools, and we have observed similar results in our general survey as well. The reader should also observe in the table 5.3 data that, in 2005/2006, the response rate for students at honor code schools once again was higher than the rate for students at no-code schools.

In table 5.4 we have added students' self-reported rates of cheating for both the no-code and traditional code schools from the 2005/2006 surveys to our earlier data (table 5.2), and we see several important results—including, once again, the significant impact of an honor code, as rates of self-reported engagement in all nine behaviors are higher for students at no-code schools. (Note: For this analysis, we combined the results of the 2005/2006 web-based and written surveys. The basic relationships were very similar; the primary difference was that self-reported cheating was higher in the written survey, as we expected. For the nine individual behaviors, students responding on the web self-reported rates ranging from essentially equal, such as for "used crib notes during an exam," up to differences of 8 percentage points for "working on the same homework with several students when the teacher does not allow it" [27% in the written survey and 22% in the web survey for the code group; 50% and 42%, respectively, for the no-code group]. For the nine-behavior composite measure, we find a 48% self-reported rate among code students on the web survey vs. 60% on the written survey—a difference significant at $p < 0.0001$. For the no-code group, the respective rates are 64% and 70%, also significant.)

The data in table 5.4 support some important insights from the 2005/2006 phase of our longitudinal study on honor codes.

- In the honor code environment, we see a U-shaped longitudinal relationship—with the nine-item self-reported measure of cheating increasing from 48% to 60% in the early 1990s, then dropping to 50%, or essentially back to 1990/1991 levels. If we look only at the written survey responses for 2005/2006, we see an increase from 48% in 1990/1991 to 60% in 2005/2006.
- In the no-code environment, self-reported cheating increased from 74% to 82% in the 1990s, then dropped back to 68% in 2005/2006 (64% in the written survey–only segment).

Although we do not have a ready explanation, these data suggest that self-reported cheating stabilized or decreased in the no-code environment and stabilized or increased in the code environment between 1990/1991 and 2005/2006.

TABLE 5.4. Students' engagement in nine types of cheating at selected campuses with and without honor codes, McCabe et al. surveys 1990/1991 through 2005/2006 (% of students reporting behavior)

Type of cheating	1990/1991		1995/1996		2005/2006	
	Code	No code	Code	No code	Code	No code
Copying a few sentences of material without footnoting in a paper	24	41	31	42	30	36
"Padding" a few items on a bibliography	14	25	15	27	9	13
Plagiarized from public material on papers	7	19	9	19	2	4
Getting questions or answers from someone who has already taken the same exam	12	19	20	45	9	24
Copying from another student on a test or exam	13	31	19	32	8	14
Working on the same homework with several students when the teacher does not allow it	20	40	26	47	24	48
Turned in papers done entirely or in part by other students	3	13	4	11	2	4
Giving answers to other students during an exam	8	27	10	22	5	9
Used crib notes during an exam	9	21	11	16	5	7
Any of the nine behaviors	48	74	60	82	50	68
N	2,923	2,954	2,244	1,912	2,162	1,553

Reporting of Violations

The effectiveness of traditional honor codes partly depends on students' willingness to report any cheating they observe. Because students often tell us of their frustration with others' cheating, we have always been a bit surprised by responses to a series of questions, posed on our surveys, concerning the reporting of cheating that a student might observe. In our most recent (2005/2006) honor code survey, only 2% of students in a no-code environment and 7% in a code environment indicated that they would be likely to report a *friend* who had cheated—not much of a deterrent, especially when you realize that at least some of these students might like to think they would report cheating but would have difficulty doing so when actually faced with the decision. All of our surveys have generated frequent open-ended comments from respondents about how students learned as children not to be a "narc," a "rat," a "tattletale," and so on. In our 1990/1991 survey, these two values for reporting were exactly the same (2% in no-code and 7% in code schools) as in 2005/2006, suggesting that little has changed. Students' comments do suggest, however, that they would be more likely to report someone who was not a friend, and especially in courses that are graded on the curve, where a successful cheater might have an impact on the potential reporter's own grade.

Our 1995/1996 study of 31 colleges and universities, 14 of which had traditional academic honor codes, revealed that the percentage of code students who had reported a peer (7.9%) was nearly twice as large as the percentage of no-code students who had done so (4.0%). This suggests that the rate of peer reporting is low at honor code as well as no-code schools. The 1995/1996 data also showed that 13.8% of respondents at no-code schools indicated that they were likely or very likely to report cheating, compared with 43.4% of the students at code schools. As we noted, "The fact that almost half of the code students in this survey said they were likely to report an incident of cheating, yet less than one in twelve actually has, suggests that even code students have difficulty with reportage requirements" (McCabe, Treviño, and Butterfield 2001, 40). Nevertheless, the perception that fellow students would be more likely to report in an honor code environment may help to keep cheating at lower rates.

So, What Do We Know about Honor Code Effectiveness?

Examining the efficacy of honor codes has been a major goal of the surveys we have conducted over the past twenty years. These surveys have involved about two hundred academic institutions, varying in size, selectivity, public versus private, primarily residential versus nonresidential, and other important dimensions. Among the major conclusions from this research are that honor codes are effective in promoting integrity and reducing cheating and that effective honor codes (those that promote integrity and reduce cheating) are more than mere "window dressing." They affect faculty attitudes and behavior and can have an enduring effect, and modified honor codes can be a somewhat effective alternative to traditional honor codes—especially at larger schools. We review our findings in each area below, along with significant contributions from other studies.

Honor Codes Are Effective in Promoting Integrity and Reducing Cheating

Recent research (e.g., Engler, Landau, and Epstein 2008), including our own survey results, outlined in detail above (McCabe and Treviño 1993, 1997; McCabe, Treviño, and Butterfield 1996, 1999, 2002; Treviño, Butterfield, and McCabe 1998), supports Bowers's (1964) conclusion that academic dishonesty is significantly lower in honor code environments. Desplaces et al. (2007) have also shown that honor codes are positively related to students' moral development and affect students' perceptions of the ethical nature of the university culture.

Although almost all of the research has been survey research, recent laboratory work in behavioral economics has the potential to affect our understanding of student cheating. Some of this work is highlighted in the best seller *Predictably Irrational: The Hidden Forces That Shape Our Decisions* (Ariely 2008). Ariely and his colleagues (Ariely 2008; Mazar, Amir, and Ariely 2008) have conducted a series of laboratory studies in which participants, who are assumed to be generally honest, are "tempted" to cheat in a controlled experiment. In the series of experiments of greatest interest to us, participants are college students who are asked to complete a simple written test under varying conditions. After completing this basic test, some students are given the opportunity to cheat, either by exposing them to the correct answers in some way or by allowing them to self-report their own scores on the test. Ariely reports on a set of experiments in which the experimenters organized two groups of students who would be given the opportunity to cheat, in addition to a control group, not given an opportunity to cheat (Mazar, Amir, and Ariely 2008). Immediately before taking their tests, one of these two groups was asked to write down the titles of 10 books they had read in high school, and the second group was asked to write down the Ten Commandments. The group recalling their readings from high school cheated at a statistically greater rate (i.e., their test scores were higher) than the control group, but the group asked to record the Ten Commandments did not cheat at all. Even those students who could recall only one or two commandments seemed to be equally affected by this experiment, and thus the researchers concluded that it may have been "the mere contemplation of a moral benchmark of some kind" that was the causative factor here and wondered whether "nonreligious benchmarks" (Ariely 2008, 285) might work in a similar way—such as a professional oath or, more germane to our interest, an honor code.

At the heart of Ariely and colleagues' explanation for their initial results is "the theory of self-concept maintenance," or the belief that "people are often torn between two competing motivations: gaining from cheating versus maintaining a positive self-concept as honest" (Ariely 2008, 634). The researchers suggest that most people resolve this dilemma by looking for some degree of balance between these two competing actions—making individual decisions about how much they can gain through cheating without affecting their self-concept too negatively. The result is a range of behaviors that we might argue objectively are "cheating" but may not be viewed as so egregious that they adversely affect the individual's self-concept. Of course, one problem with this formulation, as we have discovered in our work, is that behaviors that some might classify as cheating are viewed by others as acceptable. For example, one student might take every provision of his or her school's honor code or academic integrity policy quite literally, while another sees the code or policy only as an expression of "suggested" behaviors, which he or she will live up to *except* when the cost of doing so is perceived to exceed the need to obey that standard. Such a view helps to explain the apparent dichotomy we often see in our data, where someone makes a strong open-ended statement about the evils of cheating yet engages in a variety of behaviors that many would consider questionable and others would classify as cheating.

Mazar, Amir, and Ariely (2008) also reported another experiment of interest to us. Using the type of manipulation described above, but substituting a brief honor code statement that students had to sign in lieu of the Ten Commandments exercise, the researchers reported that the honor code intervention eliminated cheating. Test scores in the honor code condition where students had the opportunity to cheat were the same as (or slightly lower than) the scores achieved in the control group, and both were significantly lower than the scores reported by students in the group that was given the opportunity to cheat and had not been exposed to the honor code statement. The authors raise some interesting questions when they note that "the two institutions in which we conducted this experiment did not have an honor code system at the time, and therefore, objectively, the honor code had no implications of external punishment. When we replicated the experiment in an institution that had a strict honor code, the results were identical, suggesting that it is not the honor code per se and its implied external punishment but rather the reminder of morality that was at play" (Ariely 2008, 637).

Although this laboratory work has enormous potential to tease out the effects of specific aspects of the social context and to investigate how they may work in combination, it does not address the question of what happens over time with honor codes and other morality reminders in the real world. For example, how would the results of these experiments change if students were asked to repeat them several times? Would the apparent power of an honor code erode if students concluded, over repeated testing, that the chances of getting caught cheating truly were minimal?

We gained some insights into students' thinking in our 1990/1991 study of 31 colleges and universities, approximately half of which employed a traditional honor code (McCabe and Treviño 1993). Because many students took advantage of the opportunity to write open-ended comments on the surveys, we were able to look in a systematic way at the different perspectives of code and no-code students about honor and integrity in the classroom by studying their open-ended comments. A typical comment from students on campuses with honor codes was: *I don't think that cheating is a problem on this campus; we are on the honor system and I think students take that seriously.* In contrast, a more typical comment at schools that did not have a code was: *There is very little sense of personal responsibility, honesty, or integrity w/ respect to cheating.*

In a systematic analysis of open-ended comments on a follow-up survey we conducted at these same 31 survey schools in the 1995/1996 academic year (McCabe, Treviño, and Butterfield 1999), the results confirmed that students at honor code schools view academic integrity in very different ways from students at no-code institutions. In addition to being less likely to cheat, students at honor code institutions were less likely to rationalize or justify any cheating behavior that they admitted to, and they were more likely to talk about the importance of integrity and how an ethical community can minimize cheating. For example, the following comment from a student at a no-code school reflects how risk-reward calculations sometimes overwhelm one's sense of honesty.

The stakes are higher in college [vs. high school] as well as penalties. The greater workload, pressures, financial scholarships, and future employment induces immeasurably high levels of stress and tension that causes many students to do things once thought unthinkable. This seems to offset the penalties—as great as they are.

Such sentiments are heard with much greater frequency at schools that do not have honor codes than at those that do. In contrast, the following is a more typical comment heard on campuses with well-established honor codes:

[The] Academic Honor Code at [my school] is tremendous! Students appreciate it and live up to it.

Although our surveys suggest that honor code students generally feel the same pressures to cheat as students at no-code schools, the difference seems to be that code students are less likely to act on those pressures or to use them as a rationalization or justification for cheating. As we reported for the 1995/1996 study, "clearly, code students sense that they are part of a special community that demands compliance with certain standards in exchange for the many privileges associated with honor codes" (McCabe, Treviño, and Butterfield 1999, 230).

Traditional honor codes probably increase academic integrity and reduce cheating by defining expectations of academic integrity as part of an "ethical community." Support for the connection between honor codes and building ethical communities can be found in the large body of research emanating from Kohlberg's (1969, 1985) work on moral development, in particular his research on just communities (Power, Higgins, and Kohlberg 1989). Power and colleagues argued that the just communities envisioned by Kohlberg provide conditions that are necessary to and encourage moral behavior—in particular, increased student participation in establishing community norms and values. In discussing an application of Kohlberg's just community approach to a college residential setting, Ignelzi suggested that it "holds promise as a useful companion to more traditional methods of ethical education in the formal curriculum" (1990, 197). According to Ignelzi, student participation in a just community, as well as the participatory role that students play in the resolution of ethical dilemmas in such a community, "is potentially a powerful intervention for addressing both the ethical and citizenship education of college undergraduates" (1990, 197). Treviño and McCabe (1994) made a similar argument in relation to the implementation of honor codes in business schools.

Students' participation in just communities includes giving students privileges such as unproctored exams and placing a significant share of the responsibility for maintaining academic honesty on the students rather than on faculty and/or administrators. Honor code environments generally allow students to play a participatory role in dispute resolution, including the adjudication of alleged violations of the honor code. In some cases, students are in complete control of the campus judicial system. In return for such trust and privileges, traditional honor code communities create an expectation that community members will bear responsibility for holding each other accountable to shared norms and policies (Treviño and McCabe 1994). Many students seek to maintain these privileges by taking seriously their responsibility not to cheat. However, as noted earlier, students' willingness to accept responsibility for community integrity often does not rise to the level of being willing to report violations they observe among their peers. This issue remains a challenge for those wishing to implement a traditional honor code (which includes a reporting requirement), because it suggests that students are not willing to take "full" responsibility for creating and maintaining a community of trust. They prefer to rely on the authority structure (faculty and/or proctors) to identify cheating when it occurs.

To Be Effective, Honor Codes Must Be More than Window Dressing

One difficulty of determining the effectiveness of honor codes is that not all codes are equal, nor do they produce the same results. Some are much more clearly an integral part of a strong campus culture of integrity, while others can be viewed as little more than window dressing. In fact, our 1990/1991 study uncovered a particularly interesting finding (McCabe and Treviño 1993). One of the lowest levels of self-reported cheating occurred at a college that lacked an honor code, and one of the highest levels occurred at a school that had a hundred-year-old honor code tradition. A closer examination revealed a possible explanation for this apparent paradox. Despite having a long-standing honor code, the code school was no longer adequately communicating the essence of its code to students, and the code had become less influential in the overall campus culture. In contrast, the no-code school strongly encouraged academic integrity without instituting a formal code, by developing a culture that mirrors many of the important elements typically found at effective honor code institutions. Administrators and faculty clearly conveyed their beliefs about the seriousness of cheating, communicated their expectations regarding high standards of integrity, and encouraged students to know and abide by rules of proper conduct. This finding led us to an important insight: it is not the mere existence of an honor code that is important in supporting academic integrity and deterring college cheating. An effective honor code must be more than window dressing; a truly effective code must be well implemented and strongly embedded in the campus culture.

The finding was also supported in our 1996 study that looked at the influence of codes of conduct in the workplace (the authors are professors at business schools) (McCabe, Treviño, and Butterfield 1996). In U.S. workplaces, codes of conduct have become ubiquitous. While this can be seen as a positive development, research suggests that these codes often have little influence on employees' behavior. For example, our research revealed that dishonest behavior in the workplace is reduced only when corporate codes of conduct are well implemented and strongly embedded in the organizational culture. In the 1996 study, unethical behavior was reduced when managers communicated their commitment to the corporate code, when organizations communicated the code to employees and ensured compliance, and when the code was understood and accepted by employees and guided their day-to-day interactions and activities. This result is supported in a more recent meta-analysis (Kish-Gephart, Harrison, and Treviño 2010). The simple existence of codes was found to have no significant influence on ethical behavior in the workplace. Only a strongly enforced code had an effect. Such findings make it clear that simply implementing a code is not enough, whether on campus or in the workplace. The code must be part of a strong campus or corporate culture focused on integrity.

Faculty Attitudes and Behaviors Differ in Honor Code and No-Code Environments

Our research has also shown that the attitudes and behaviors of faculty members are different in honor code and no-code environments. Anecdotal comments from students and faculty, supported by empirical data collected from more than eighteen thousand faculty members, point to the reluctance of many college faculty, especially those at no-code schools, to follow existing academic integrity policies when they observe a student cheating. Instead, many faculty members prefer to deal with such issues directly with the students, outside any formal process, or not deal with them at all (Jendrek 1989; McCabe, Butterfield, and Treviño 2003; Nuss 1984). Such faculty generally tend to be more lenient than the school's formal judicial policy, and any penalty they mete out generally does not appear on a student's academic record. This is an important consideration for most students and why they are often willing to agree with a faculty member's accusation of cheating rather than contesting it in the formal judicial system, where a record would be created if they were found responsible. As a result, faculty's lack of acceptance of and adherence to the institution's policy can lead to more cheating. As noted by Dalton (1985), moral example is among the most powerful influences on students' ethical development. In the classroom, faculty members are important role models, and the messages they communicate about acceptance of the institution's policies and norms regarding academic integrity can be a strong influence on students' behavior.

A study of eight hundred faculty members at 16 U.S. colleges and universities investigated their views of academic integrity policies and how these views differed across code and no-code schools (McCabe 1993). The study showed that faculty at code schools rated their schools higher than faculty at no-code schools on factors such as students' understanding of academic integrity policies, faculty support of these policies, and overall effectiveness of the institution's policy. Faculty at code schools were also more likely to believe that students should play a significant role in the adjudication process associated with academic cheating.

Our 2003 study suggested that faculty who have experienced an honor code, either as a faculty member or as a student, generally have more positive attitudes about honor codes than faculty who lack such experience (McCabe, Butterfield, and Treviño 2003). The results also indicated that faculty members who have personal experience with an honor code are more willing to share cheating-related responsibilities with students. These findings are important because faculty members are on the front lines in dealing with academic integrity and cheating issues, and academic institutions depend on their cooperation. Although some faculty choose to disregard their institutions' policies and deal with cheating on their own, those with honor code experience are more likely to reinforce and support the institutional policy. These faculty members are more motivated to support changes to a campus's academic integrity policies that incorporate the basic philosophy of an honor code, especially greater student involvement in the judicial process. As we argued in our 2003 study, administrators who are considering moving toward an honor code system might turn to such faculty for assistance.

Collegiate Honor Codes Can Have an Enduring Effect

Given our own experiences with honor codes and their lasting effect in our lives, we wondered whether we could demonstrate such a lasting effect for others (McCabe, Treviño, and Butterfield 1996). In a survey focused on 318 alumni of two private liberal arts colleges who graduated between 1962 and 1989, we aimed to examine the long-term effects of collegiate honor codes and the effect of codes of ethics at respondents' current work organizations.

We did not find a direct effect of honor code experiences in college on current ethical/unethical behavior. However, we did find a statistical interaction effect such that unethical behavior in the workplace was lowest for participants who had experienced an honor code environment in college and who currently worked in an organization with a strongly implemented code of ethics. This suggests that participation in multiple honor code communities can play a part in reducing dishonest behavior. We speculated that individuals who experience a strong undergraduate honor code and later find themselves in a strong ethical environment at work will recognize the value of such an environment and will be inclined to follow its principles.

Modified Honor Codes Can Be an Effective Alternative to Traditional Honor Codes

Given the effectiveness of traditional honor codes, one might wonder why they have not been adopted by more schools. One of the most important reasons, we believe, is that few campuses have a strong enough academic integrity culture in place to support the provisions of a traditional code, such as unproctored exams and peer reporting requirements. Additionally, moving to a traditional honor code typically requires years of preparation and continuing hard work to maintain its effectiveness. This may help explain why, with some notable exceptions such as the University of Virginia and the College of William and Mary, traditional honor codes are generally found only in smaller, residential institutions. On such campuses, it may be easier to build a strong sense of campus community around an issue such as academic integrity. As noted by McCabe and Pavela, "Conventional wisdom suggests it is more difficult to develop and nurture a strong sense of campus community at large universities—an important foundation on which an honor code tradition can be built" (2000, 34).

Therefore, in recent years, some large, public universities have begun to adopt modified honor codes (McCabe and Pavela 2000; Roig and Marks 2006). As is the case with traditional honor codes, research has not uniformly supported the efficacy of modified codes. For example, Roig and Marks (2006) examined students' attitudes toward cheating before and after implementation of a modified honor code. Their results showed that attitudes were virtually unchanged after the code's implementation. However, the majority of studies suggest that modified codes are associated with reduced cheating behavior. Langone (2007) discussed how a modified code at a community college has enabled faculty to monitor the integrity status of the nursing program and establish policy protocols for unethical behaviors among nursing students. In our own study of 21 institutions, we examined the relationship between modified honor codes and academic dishonesty (McCabe, Treviño, and Butterfield 2002). We found that modified codes had a moderate impact on academic dishonesty. Levels of self-reported cheating at schools with modified codes were greater than the levels at the typical school with a traditional code but lower than at the typical school with no honor code. We concluded that modified honor codes can significantly reduce cheating on college campuses and may be especially useful at large schools where implementing a traditional code is generally more difficult. This has important implications for higher education.

Conclusion

After the Bowers study, there began a long, persistent decline in the number of schools with honor code traditions (although some have now reintroduced codes on their campuses). Some of these codes may have been casualties of the student unrest of the late 1960s and early 1970s, as students rejected codes along with a host of other campus traditions. Some schools weathered this early student resistance, only to watch their codes erode in influence later. We know of a few schools that have had campus honor codes in effect since the 1800s and are currently struggling to reinvigorate them. But we have also observed a recent surge of interest in honor codes, especially as a number of schools have adopted some variation of the modified honor code concept described above.

Based on our own longitudinal results and our experience in the field, we speculate that it is becoming more difficult to promote traditional honor codes to today's college students, who are so focused on grades and GPA as the primary sorting device for graduate school acceptance, or even for the recruitment process for a first job. And if they feel or know that other students have achieved their educational or career goals through cheating, they may feel compelled to do the same. Leveling the playing field is a justification we have heard from many students when rationalizing or justifying their cheating. This may help explain the apparent decrease in self-reported cheating. Although we ask students to indicate how often, if at all, they have engaged in various specific cheating behaviors, such as the nine behaviors we have been tracking, it is clear that they are also making judgments about whether or not what they have done is actually cheating. Perceptions and definitions of what cheating is are changing, and we must all keep this in mind as we think about creating and/or nurturing honor codes and as we continue to conduct research in this arena.

The low levels of reporting of observed cheating and students' resistance to having this obligation placed on them, even in honor code environments, raise questions about whether schools should try to implement a reporting requirement as part of a new honor code effort. We have seen it succeed in some smaller environments. But, in our experience, when schools have not been able to generate student support for the introduction of some form of honor code, the battle has generally been over the reporting requirement. Many students are willing to be bound by the basic principles of an honor code themselves—but not by a reporting requirement. They feel that it is the faculty's job to monitor cheating, not a student's responsibility. The lack of a reporting requirement shifts the responsibility for surveillance back to the faculty, however, and generally means that the "benefit" of unproctored exams must generally be abandoned.

Despite the apparent challenges in our contemporary environment, we remain believers in the power of strongly implemented and well-run honor codes to influence students' behavior with regard to academic integrity. At the same time, our surveys point to some erosion in the effectiveness of a traditional honor code, especially if the code is not deeply embedded in the campus culture. In short, the power of an honor code today appears to be directly related to how effectively students are oriented into this tradition and how much effort and resources a campus is willing to expend in working with faculty and students to institutionalize a code within its culture and keep it alive over time.

CHAPTER SIX

Institutional Factors That Influence Academic Integrity

Other Contextual Influences

I n chapter 4, we noted that much of the research conducted on academic integrity over the past five decades has studied the role of personal characteristics. In chapter 5, we focused on academic honor codes as a contextual strategy to promote academic integrity in educational institutions. Here we shift our focus to other contextual influences found to be related to the promotion of academic integrity.

Research on academic integrity, including Bowers's (1964) seminal study, has consistently demonstrated that contextual factors are as important as personal characteristics in influencing academic integrity (e.g., McCabe and Treviño 1997; for an exception, see Kisamore, Stone, and Jawahar 2007). Indeed, the primacy of the institutional context was supported by a study we conducted that explicitly compared various contextual and personal factors (McCabe and Treviño 1997). The results showed that such contextual factors as peers' cheating behavior, peers' disapproval of cheating, a student's perception of the culture of academic integrity on campus, and the perceived severity of penalties for cheating were more strongly related to the level of academic integrity among students than were personal characteristics such as age, gender, GPA, and participation in extracurricular activities. Further, these contextual factors seem particularly important because faculty and administrators can influence them to some degree. A subsequent investigation of a more diverse set of academic institutions supported this conclusion and suggested that students' perceptions of peer behavior were the most influential contextual factor, followed by the perceived certainty of being reported, and then by the existence of an honor code (McCabe, Treviño, and Butterfield 2002). Also found to be important, but less so, were students' perceived understanding and acceptance of campus academic integrity policies and the perceived severity of penalties for violations of those expectations.

The purpose of this chapter is to provide a comprehensive review of the current state of knowledge on the major contextual influences, other than honor codes, associated with higher levels of academic integrity and lower levels of student cheating. Much of our own work falls into this category, and we use our research to provide an overall structure for the chapter, while also summarizing the significant contributions of others. We begin by discussing the contextual factor that research has identified as the most influential: the influence of one's peers. We then turn our attention to other contextual factors that have been identified as influential.

Peer Influence

Our two-decade-long journey into the issue of student cheating originally focused on honor codes. So we were somewhat surprised to discover that peer influence exhibits a stronger relationship with academic integrity than does the presence or absence of an honor code. We know that peer influence is related to honor codes, because research such as that of Bowers (1964) has shown that students behave differently (i.e., they cheat less) in honor code environments. But peer influence is conceptually distinct and broader, because it operates in all academic settings, regardless of whether a campus has an honor code. Bowers's landmark study was the first major multi-campus investigation of contextual influences on student cheating in college. Of the many personal and contextual influences that he studied, Bowers concluded that peer disapproval, an obvious form of peer influence, was "the most important determinant of changes in cheating behavior between high school and college" (1964, 196). Students were much less likely to cheat in college if they perceived that their peers would disapprove.

Since beginning our work on student dishonesty in 1990, we have at various times examined the relationship between academic dishonesty and three possible sources of peer influence. Like Bowers, we have studied the approval or disapproval of academic dishonesty voiced by peers and the perception of peers' actual behavior. We have also constructed a measure of the general environment of academic integrity on a campus, using a four-item scale that includes measures of students' and faculty's acceptance and understanding of campus integrity policy, faculty support of that policy, and the policy's perceived effectiveness. We have referred to this third variable as "understanding of policy" (McCabe and Treviño 1993). In general, we have found that fewer students cheat when they perceive that peers more strongly disapprove of cheating, when they perceive that the overall level of academic dishonesty among all students is low, and when they perceive that the campus community more strongly understands campus integrity policies and supports an environment of academic integrity. Peers do influence students' behavior, and based on anecdotal comments from our research, we believe this effect can be particularly strong in first-year students as they look to their peers for clues about acceptable behavior in their new environment.

Two theoretical perspectives have generally been used to explain the relationship between peer influence and students' cheating behavior: social learning theory and differential association theory. Social learning theory emphasizes that much of human behavior is learned through the influence of example (Bandura 1986). From this perspective, if students see their peers cheating, they are more likely to cheat. However, positive behavior can also be learned from peers. If students observe their peers disavowing cheating, behaving with honesty and integrity, and educating other students about the importance of academic integrity, then students learn from positive role models rather than negative ones. The implication for colleges seeking to promote academic integrity and reduce cheating is clear: they must ensure that peer influence on their campuses is pointing students in the right direction. We offer some suggestions on how to do this in chapter 9.

Differential association theory (Sutherland, Cressey, and Luckenbill 1992) has also been used to explain the role of peer influence. According to this theory, students learn techniques, rationalizations, motives, and attitudes favorable to cheating through close association with others. Students become more willing and able to neutralize or rationalize their cheating behavior when their associations with dishonest peers are greater in duration, intensity, frequency, and priority. According to Michaels and Miethe (1989), the "novice deviant" will develop positive attitudes toward the deviant behavior through association with those who engage in it, support it, or reinforce it. Research has supported differential association theory, suggesting that successful peer cheating behavior increases the tendency of other students to behave in similar ways (Vowell and Chen 2004).

The three peer-related factors we have identified as important in our work are clearly interrelated, and their influence can be explained using either differential association or social learning theory. For example, it makes intuitive sense that achieving a positive culture of academic integrity on campus (as evidenced by a greater level of student and faculty understanding, acceptance, and support of these policies) would lead to greater levels of peer disapproval of cheating and therefore to lower levels of cheating on campus. Thus, although it is difficult to discuss any one of these factors without referencing one or both of the others, we organize our discussion into three parts. We first discuss peer disapproval, then perception of peer behavior (which has received strong support in our own work), and finally, student and faculty understanding and acceptance of campus policies concerning academic dishonesty and student perceptions of how effectively the policy works (what we refer to as understanding of policy).

Peer Disapproval

As noted earlier, Bowers found peer disapproval to be "the most important determinant of changes in cheating behavior between high school and college" (1964, 196), with students being much less likely to self-report cheating in college if they perceived that their peers would disapprove. Using Bowers's original data, we can look closely at the basis of this conclusion. One of the questions Bowers asked students was to rate how strongly different individuals would disapprove if they knew the student had cheated. He offered his respondents four response choices: very strongly, fairly strongly, not very strongly, and not at all. The "different individuals" included a close friend, one of the students you go around with, a faculty member, and your parents. Bowers quickly concluded that "since there is little variation in the amount of disapproval students perceive from their parents and from faculty, disapproval from these sources cannot account for much of the variation in academic dishonesty" (1964, 145–46). Noting that "the situation is different when it comes to perceived disapproval from peers" (1964, 146), Bowers constructed an index based jointly on the perceived disapproval from "a close friend" and from "a student you go around with." Although Bowers does not detail the exact calculations he used to do this, he does provide enough detail to allow us to construct a similar index for students we surveyed in our own work, from the fall of 2007 through the spring of

TABLE 6.1. Students' self-reported cheating by perceived peer group disapproval, 1962/1963 versus 2007–2010 (% of students reporting)

Index of peer disapproval	Bowers 1962/1963	McCabe et al. 2007–2010
Very strong	26 (1,352)*	35 (2,605)
Fairly strong	41 (657)	49 (2,064)
Moderate	49 (1,318)	56 (3,439)
Fairly weak	59 (443)	65 (2,973)
Very weak	71 (1,532)	73 (5,720)

*Numbers in parentheses are the number of responses in each category.

2010. (We added questions on peer disapproval back into our standard survey in the fall of 2007.) Bowers "combined students' responses to the questions dealing with both groups of peers—close friends and students they go around with—to form a measure of peer group disapproval" (1964, 146), using a five-point scale ranging from very strong (score = 1) to very weak (score = 5). He explicitly stated that his "very strong" category included only those respondents who classified the perceived disapproval of both close friends and students they go around with as very strong. His "very weak" category included students who felt both peer groups would disapprove "not very strongly" or "not at all." Although he did not explicitly state how his three intermediate categories were constructed, most of the choices are fairly easy to make. And as shown in table 6.1, after about forty-five years, Bowers's original findings are still powerfully supported.

Although the relationship between perceived peer disapproval and reduced cheating is clear, the overall level of cheating appears to be higher in our 2007–2010 surveys, even though the surveys are not directly comparable. The Bowers index is based on 13 different behaviors ranging from such serious items as "having another student take an exam for you" to less egregious behaviors such as "getting questions or answers from someone who has already taken the same exam." In contrast, the index in our research covers only 10 behaviors—4 related to tests and exams and 6 related to written work—ranging from submitting a paper downloaded from a term-paper mill or website as your own to copying a few sentences of material from some source without citing it, an offense also included in the Bowers index. In addition, the Bowers data include first-year students, who have been excluded from our data. This lack of direct comparability, however, does not negate the obvious conclusion concerning the nature of the relationship between peer group disapproval and self-reported levels of cheating. The relationship is inverse and strong in both samples. And the overall climate of peer disapproval has declined over time. Another way to put this is that peer approval of cheating has risen dramatically. Those rating the climate of peer disapproval as either fairly or very weak in the Bowers sample amounted to 37% of respondents. In our 2007–2010 sample, this number rose to 52%.

Peer Behavior

We did not include a measure of peer disapproval in our earliest work, and we reported that the perception of peer behavior was the most significant variable in our regression of five independent contextual variables on the level of academic dishonesty self-reported by respondents (McCabe and Treviño 1993). This first study was a survey of more than six thousand students at 31 academic institutions, and, like the Bowers (1964) study, it was one of the few large-scale, multi-campus investigations of contextual variables associated with academic dishonesty. The results were compatible with Bowers's work and suggested that, of the various contextual variables included in the survey, the strongest influence was perception of peer behavior—a measure of how students perceive other students are actually behaving with regard to academic dishonesty. We had hypothesized this relationship based on social learning theory, so a significant result was not surprising. What was surprising, however, was the strength of the finding. We concluded that not only is academic dishonesty learned from observing the behavior of peers, but peer behavior can also provide a kind of normative support for cheating. In addition, the knowledge that others are cheating may leave non-cheaters feeling that they are at a disadvantage. Cheating may come to be viewed as a necessary and, ultimately, acceptable way of getting and staying ahead, or at least not falling behind. Cognitive neutralization strategies appear to play a major role in this relationship, as students seem to find it rather easy to convince themselves that, if others are cheating and the institution or its faculty members are not doing much about it, they must do the same (McCabe 1992). Many students feel that it is not fair that their grades should suffer because others are being allowed to cheat. Similar explanations have been discussed by Bowers (1964) and McCabe, Treviño, and Butterfield (1999).

TABLE 6.2. Pearson correlation coefficients for the Bowers sample, self-reported academic dishonesty (dependent variable), and peer disapproval and perceived peer behavior

	Bowers's measure of peer disapproval	Perceived cheating by peers	Self-reported test cheating index
Bowers's peer disapproval	1.000 N = 5,303	−0.335 N = 5,270 $p < 0.001$	−0.382 N = 5,205 $p < 0.001$
Perceived cheating by peers	−0.335 N = 5,270 $p < 0.001$	1.000 N = 5,385	0.471 N = 5,282 $p < 0.001$
Self-reported test cheating	−0.382 N = 5,205 $p < 0.001$	0.471 N = 5,282 $p < 0.001$	1.000 N = 5,312

We can illustrate the essence of our point here by using the original Bowers dataset to look at the correlations between self-reported academic dishonesty (the dependent variable) and both perceived peer behavior (using a five-point scale that asked students how often they felt test cheating occurred on their campus, with response choices ranging from 1 = very seldom to 5 = very often) and Bowers's peer disapproval measure (table 6.2). (Note: For ease of presentation, in tables 6.2 and 6.3 and the associated discussions, we have reversed Bowers's measure of peer disapproval so that 1 = very weak and 5 = very strong on his five-point scale.) Simple correlation calculations show that our measure explains more variance, but more important is that both results are in the same direction, both highly significant ($p < 0.001$), and are roughly comparable in size, suggesting that peer disapproval and perceived peer behavior have had a similar effect on an individual student's decision to cheat or not.

We would argue that the fact that the correlation between perceived peer behavior and peer disapproval is not stronger suggests that, although they have similar effects, the mechanisms by which they operate may be slightly different. It could be that peer disapproval is best explained by differential association theory (Sutherland, Cressey, and Luckenbill 1992), with its emphasis on trying to conform to the norms of groups that an individual associates with or wishes to be part of, while

TABLE 6.3. Pearson correlation coefficients for the McCabe et al. 2006–2010 data, self-reported academic dishonesty (dependent variable), and peer disapproval and perceived peer behavior

	Bowers's measure of peer disapproval	Perceived cheating by peers	Self-reported test cheating index
Bowers's peer disapproval	1.000 N=20,944	−0.258 N=20,935 p<0.001	−0.298 N=16,801 p<0.001
Perceived cheating by peers	−0.258 N=20,935 p<0.001	1.000 N=20,935	0.306 N=16,762 p<0.001
Self-reported test cheating	−0.298 N=16,801 p<0.001	0.306 N=16,762 p<0.001	1.000 N=16,801

the influence of peer behavior is better explained through social learning theory (Bandura 1986), with its focus on learning from observing others' behavior. If one perceives a high level of cheating in the general student population on campus, one is more likely to cheat. This argument is supported to some degree by a stepwise regression model that, in this case, forces the variable explaining the greatest amount of variance in self-reported cheating to enter first, then evaluates whether the second variable adds significantly to the explanatory value of the model. Not surprisingly, based on the results above, the perceived cheating by peers variable enters the model first, explaining 22.5% of the variance ($F=1505.82$, $p< 0.0001$). The peer disapproval measure enters on the second step and explains an additional 5.7% of the variance in self-reported cheating ($F=407.63$, $p<0.0001$).

Using the Bowers methodology to calculate the peer disapproval variable, we observe a similar result when we examine our data for the years 2006/2007 to 2009/2010 (table 6.3). (Again, we have reversed Bowers's original measure of peer disapproval for ease of presentation, so that it ranges from 1=very weak to 5=very strong.) Although the correlations are modest, we observe with interest how longitudinally robust Bowers's analysis is. We again observe a significant contribution from the peer disapproval variable ($p< 0.0001$) in a stepwise regression, as it explains an additional 5.2% of the variance in the self-reported cheating index after perceived cheating by peers is already in the regression model accounting for 9.3% of the variance. The final model thus accounts for 14.5% of the variance in the self-reported cheating index ($F = 1422.06, p < 0.001$).

Two of our other studies further corroborate our finding that perceived peer behavior is a significant influence on students' decisions to cheat. In an investigation of almost eighteen hundred students at nine medium to large universities (McCabe and Treviño 1997), peer-related factors once again emerged as the most significant influence on cheating behavior. We later reexamined this relationship, using data from a more diverse set of academic institutions (McCabe, Treviño, and Butterfield 2002), and once again, students' perception of peer behavior was clearly the most influential factor.

Others' research has also strongly supported the importance of peer influence (Bonjean and McGee 1965; Broeckelman-Post 2008; Carrell, Malmstrom, and West 2008; Liska 1978; Passow et al. 2006; Whitley 1998). For example, Whitley (1998) reviewed 107 studies of factors associated with cheating among college students, published between 1970 and 1996. Students' perception that social norms support cheating was among the contextual factors that showed the strongest relationship with self-reported cheating. Carrell, Malmstrom, and West (2008) studied cheating behavior at the three major U.S. military service academies and found a strong positive relationship between levels of peer cheating and the probability that observers of that cheating will also cheat. They used these data to calculate a social multiplier effect: one additional college cheater drives approximately 0.61 to 0.75 additional college students to cheat. Broeckelman-Post (2008) showed that, of the variables in her study, students' belief that their peers are engaging in academic dishonesty was the strongest positive influence on academic dishonesty. All of these findings strongly support the importance of peer influence on cheating behavior.

Understanding and Acceptance of Policy

In our own work, we have also examined students' perceptions of how well others on campus (both peers and faculty) understand and accept campus integrity policies, how effective they perceive these policies to be in reducing the cheating of others, and how well the policies are supported by faculty. While this is not strictly a measure of peer influence, it is an important related measure that is not easily categorized. We discuss it here because it measures students' perceptions of how well their peers, along with faculty, understand and accept campus integrity policies and how effective those policies are.

We first identified this significant relationship in our initial study of student academic honesty conducted in the 1990/1991 academic year (McCabe and Treviño 1993). In that study, this four-item variable exhibited a strong, positive relationship with self-reported cheating. Yet this relationship did not remain statistically significant in a multiple regression of all the other independent contextual variables on self-reported academic dishonesty. However, in subsequent analysis of the factors influencing perceived peer behavior, understanding of policy exhibited the strongest influence, suggesting that the impact of perceived policy understanding on the self-reported cheating of individual students may occur through the relationship between perceived policy understanding and perception of peer behavior. A reasonable hypothesis is that a campus that works hard to achieve a high level of understanding and acceptance of its academic integrity policies among both students and faculty will significantly affect the behavior of students. As we suggested in chapter 5, this is why schools either with or without honor codes can have high levels of academic integrity as long as they are willing to expend the resources and do the hard work necessary to orient students into an environment in which students and faculty understand and accept the academic integrity policy and are willing to sustain this effort over time.

Rewards and Deterrence-Based Factors

Rewards and deterrence-based factors, such as the perceived certainty of being caught and punished, represent another important contextual influence on academic integrity and misconduct. Three theoretical perspectives have been used to explain how these factors influence students' cheating behavior: learning theory, social learning theory, and deterrence theory. Classic learning theory, such as operant conditioning, suggests that learning and behavior are a function of consequences (Skinner 1969). Cheating is more likely when it is rewarded and less likely when it is punished. As discussed above, social learning theory argues that people also learn what behaviors are rewarded and punished through observation of others' behavior, a process known as role modeling (Bandura 1976, 1986). From this perspective, cheating is learned vicariously from observing others and is more likely when positive outcomes are observed and less likely when negative outcomes are observed.

Deterrence theory (Gibbs 1975) argues that "for misconduct to be inhibited, wrongdoers must perceive, first, that they will be caught and second, that severe penalties will be imposed for the misconduct" (McCabe and Treviño 1993, 526). The deterrence approach is based on the power discrepancy between students and faculty/administrators and assumes that students are self-interested, rational, and compliant (McCabe, Treviño, and Butterfield 2001). Administrators and faculty who use this approach emphasize exercising authority and imposing rules and sanctions. The reasoning underlying this approach is that cheating can be reduced by convincing students that, if they cheat, they will be caught and punished severely. The greater the severity of the penalties for a particular act of cheating, the less likely individuals will be to engage in that act; the potential consequences simply outweigh the potential reward (Zimring and Hawkins 1973). For example, university officials might publicize cases in which students have been caught and punished for academic dishonesty.

Our research has shown that academic dishonesty is negatively associated with the perceived certainty of being reported and the perceived severity of penalties (McCabe, Treviño, and Butterfield 2002). We have argued that these findings may reflect the fact that students are operating at a preconventional level of moral development (Kohlberg 1969). In other words, they may simply be obeying rules to avoid punishment, not considering the rights of others or exhibiting some higher level of principled thinking (Evans, Forney, and Guido-DiBrito 1998; McCabe and Treviño 1993, 1997). Our qualitative work also suggests that students are affected by deterrence methods, particularly the use of harsh penalties (McCabe, Treviño, and Butterfield 1999).

Others' research shows that cheating behavior is also influenced by perceived rewards, the perceived certainty that cheaters will be caught and punished, and the perceived severity of penalties (Bisping, Patron, and Roskelley 2008; Gire and Williams 2007; Leming 1980; Michaels and Miethe 1989; Stern and Havlicek 1986; Tittle and Rowe 1973). For example, Bisping and colleagues' (2008) study of student misconduct in introductory economics courses indicated that cheating is less likely when students believe their actions truly constitute cheating and when there is a high perceived likelihood of being caught. Their results also suggest that students may perceive the embarrassment of being caught as the most important cost of engaging in academic misconduct. Gire and Williams (2007) examined the effect of perceived severity of punishment in two honor code contexts. Their study showed that students at a military school, who face a severe threat of punishment for honor code violations, were less likely to engage in dishonest behavior in a public setting than in a private setting. Students in a nonmilitary context, who face only a mild threat of punishment, showed no such difference. Passow et al. (2006) examined several factors pertaining to perceived costs and benefits of cheating among engineering students. Their findings suggest that students are more likely to cheat on exams when cheating leads to positive consequences, including maintaining financial assistance, avoiding failing, and avoiding letting their family down, or when it prevents negative consequences. Whitley's (1998) review also showed that anticipating a large reward for successful cheating was among the strongest contextual influences that increased self-reported cheating.

Ariely and colleagues have conducted a series of laboratory experiments relevant to rewards, deterrence, and cheating. In one condition, students' self-reports of their test scores dictate the level of monetary "reward" they will receive for their efforts. Ariely summarized two notable conclusions from these preliminary experiments: first, "when given the opportunity, many honest people will cheat," and second, "once tempted to cheat, the participants didn't seem to be as influenced by the risk of being caught as one might think" (2008, 201). This latter conclusion is based on the finding that those in the test group, given the opportunity to shred their original work and to avoid any possibility of detection, cheated at "about the same level" as the group that did not have this opportunity. However, both of these groups reported 10% more correct answers than the control group, meaning that they cheated more in a condition where cheating was rewarded.

We have not tested this hypothesis directly, but we have collected data that are suggestive. As indicated in chapter 2, at several of the schools we surveyed over the past two decades, especially in the fall semester, we had to decide how to handle first-year students, who have little or no real experience with the exam and testing environment in college. In some cases, we simply excluded these students from our survey process. In others, we included them and looked at their data separately. And in the final group (albeit small), we administered a special first-year survey that attempts to understand how first-year students approach the question of academic dishonesty in college, based on their high school experiences. The open-ended comments supplied by respondents to these first-year surveys suggest that students expect the issue of cheating to be quite different in college than it was in high school. Students seem to look at college more seriously and view learning in college as more important than it was in high school. The following comments are selected from those collected at five large universities that participated in our first-year survey in the 2004/2005 academic year. The students appear to be more cautious, perhaps afraid, when they first arrive on campus and are fairly conservative when it comes to obeying the school's academic integrity policy.

High school's more about friends and people and having fun than working and studying. A lot of times I would cheat because I didn't have enough time to prepare for a test because I was out with friends. Nobody in high school stays home at night because they have a test the next day.

I didn't care in high school as much as I do now. I am in university to learn, and I like it, but I hated high school, and I just wanted to get out.

Paraphrasing from other sources was generally accepted in my high school as long as it wasn't word for word. I was motivated to do this because a lot of the other students in my school were cheating and plagiarizing and it was almost as if you were at a disadvantage if you didn't.

Plagiarism is not really discussed in high school classes but discussed repeatedly in universities and colleges.

The points made in these comments are supported by two focus groups we conducted with college-bound high school seniors in New Jersey in April 1998, with support from the Educational Testing Services. Relevant to the current discussion, there was little question that the participating students, who came from several different high school settings, generally characterized cheating in high school as pervasive, inconsequential, and often ignored by teachers. Almost to a person, however, they talked about how they expected college to be different—more serious, more relevant, with more severe consequences for cheating, and, in general, a more meaningful experience where cheating would have both short-term (stronger sanctions) and long-term (lack of needed knowledge) repercussions. As we discuss in chapter 9, we think many colleges are missing an opportunity by not working harder with incoming students to reinforce the message that college is, and indeed should be, different. Unfortunately, in recent surveys, it is fairly clear that self-reported cheating among first-year students at most colleges quickly reaches the same level as in other classes. Fortunately, both levels are noticeably below the levels reported by high school students, but as demonstrated in chapter 3, both are still high.

Comparison of Campus Contextual Factors

In our 2002 survey, we examined the relative contribution of the three major contextual factors—campus culture of integrity, peer influence, and rewards and deterrence-based factors—across surveys we conducted in the 1990/1991, 1993/1994, and 2000/2001 academic years. The combined results show that each of these factors made significant contributions to the total variance explained. Overall, consistent evidence supports the influence of these contextual variables on academic integrity, and although each factor is important, students' perception of peer behavior remained the single most important influence, as noted above.

In terms of the implications of these findings, it is important that each of these contextual factors influences students' behavior and is open to administrative influence. However, many questions remain about how these factors work together and how positive messages about honor and integrity can be balanced with accountability messages about peer reporting and punishment for rule violation to create the strongest campus integrity culture. In chapter 9, we offer our ideas for faculty and administrators, based on our research and practical experience.

The Classroom Factor: Opportunity and Classroom Context

Our focus so far has been on the campus-wide context. But research also suggests that individual faculty members can influence the environment of academic integrity in their classrooms by adopting practices that reduce the opportunity to cheat or that promote integrity. In a replication of our original study, conducted at the same 31 highly selective institutions in the 1995/1996 academic year, we learned that perceived "opportunity to cheat" was also influential. More than seventeen hundred of the more than five thousand students participating in this study provided us with open-ended comments that we analyzed in an attempt to generate additional insight into influences on academic integrity and dishonesty (McCabe, Treviño, and Butterfield 1999). Many comments suggested that individual faculty members can decrease cheating in their classes by reducing perceived opportunity. Strategies suggested by students mirror many of the approaches found in the literature on cheating, including monitoring tests, ensuring that there is ample space between test takers, replacing incompetent or apathetic teaching assistants, and having multiple versions of the exam and scrambling the questions on these versions (Bernardi et al. 2008).

Other studies have also supported faculty efforts explicitly aimed at reducing the opportunity to cheat. Broeckelman-Post (2008) indicated that instructors who employ safeguards against academic dishonesty and discuss plagiarism, collaboration, and source attribution are more likely to detect these problems when they occur. She also found that when instructors spend time discussing their expectations regarding plagiarism and source attribution, students are less likely to report engaging in serious plagiarism and are more likely to believe that copying sentences without attribution is a serious form of cheating. Ledwith and Risquez (2008) examined first-year students at an Irish university after their first exposure to anti-plagiarism software. The results showed that faculty's use of anti-plagiarism software led to a decrease in Internet plagiarism. Scanlan (2006) argued that methods useful in preventing cheating behavior among students include testing/assignment preventive strategies, including honor pledges and honesty declarations. In Genereux and McLeod's (1995) study, factors rated most likely to increase cheating included low instructor vigilance, unfair exams, and an instructor who does not care about cheating. Factors rated most likely to decrease cheating were high instructor vigilance, fair exams, high punishment for getting caught, essay exams, widely spaced exam seating, and valuable course material. Pulvers and Diekhoff (1999) found that perceptions of the classroom environment are related to students' cheating behavior and attitudes. Cheaters described their classes as significantly less personalized, satisfying, and task-oriented than students who did not cheat. Stern and Havlicek (1986) reported that faculty and students cited smaller classes and closer proctoring as techniques that can reduce cheating.

Other research has focused on pedagogical concerns. Murdock, Miller, and Goetzinger (2007) found that poor pedagogy and goal structures based on performance (rather than learning) are associated with more teacher blame, less student blame, and a perception that cheating is more acceptable and more likely. Jordan (2003) showed that a climate of dishonesty is positively related to a teaching pedagogy that emphasizes information delivery. Levy and Rakovski (2006) found that a zero tolerance policy with regard to cheating will keep dishonest students away, but at a price—it will also keep many honest students away.

Although we don't doubt the usefulness of these approaches to curb cheating in particular classrooms, especially in environments where cheating is currently rampant, these approaches rely on very different assumptions than our preferred approach. The basic assumption that drives these classroom efforts to reduce opportunities for cheating is the belief that students will cheat if given the opportunity and thus individual faculty must strictly control behavior to reduce cheating. By contrast, the ethical community-building approach that we favor assumes that it is ultimately possible to create an "honorable community" (Treviño and McCabe 1994), one where students will control their impulses and adhere to positive standards because they value the creation and maintenance of a community of trust.

We also wonder whether these two approaches can work together or whether too much focus on reducing opportunities to cheat (through increased proctoring, the use of plagiarism detection software, etc.) shifts the responsibility back too much to faculty (and away from students). If so, students will be more likely to think it is a faculty member's role to catch them cheating and will feel less responsibility to control their own impulses or hold their peers accountable. Certainly, we believe that faculty behaviors that reduce opportunity are preferable to doing nothing at all. But faculty and administrators who are considering opportunity reduction approaches may want to think hard about the message they are sending and whether it is consistent with the broader message they wish to create. Some control measures may simply convey the message that the faculty member takes academic integrity seriously. But the balance between aspirational approaches and faculty control is a delicate one that must be constantly assessed.

Conclusion

These findings, in the aggregate, reinforce the idea that contextual approaches to promoting academic integrity are extremely important. Students' perceptions of peer disapproval and honest behavior contribute the most to creating a strong normative environment that supports academic integrity and disapproves of cheating. Also important are students' perceptions that academic integrity policies (whether embodied in a formal honor code or not) are understood and accepted among students and faculty and that cheating is taken seriously and is punished when it does occur. Although honor codes can be an extremely effective strategy for moving academic communities in the direction of academic integrity, no-code colleges can also create a strong environment of academic integrity by attending to the contextual factors discussed in this chapter. In general, we believe that broad, campus-wide efforts to create a positive normative environment are required to combat the perceptions of widespread cheating that students bring with them from high school. But, in the absence of a campus-wide effort, individual faculty members can address cheating in their classrooms by reducing the opportunity to cheat, in a variety of ways.

CHAPTER SEVEN

The Faculty Role in Creating a Strong Environment of Academic Integrity

A key conclusion from our discussion, in chapters 5 and 6, of the role of honor codes and other contextual factors in reducing student cheating and promoting academic integrity in university environments is that formal honor codes are not the only way to promote academic integrity. It is not honor codes, per se, that matter, but rather the strong ethical environment they can help create. Because we are convinced that faculty should be and need to be an essential part of creating a strong environment of academic integrity, in this chapter we examine data on faculty perceptions of and responses (or lack of responses) to student cheating, in building a case for why the faculty role is essential. We also offer an initial discussion of actions that faculty members can take to contribute to an environment of academic integrity (we give a more detailed treatment in chapter 9).

What Faculty Say about Cheating

We begin by examining the frequency with which faculty say they observe different forms of questionable behavior among their students. Although the specific behaviors studied in our survey research have changed slightly over the years, certain core questions have remained constant, ranging from such serious behaviors as copying from others during a test or exam to behaviors that both students and faculty members consider less serious—for example, collaborating on assignments with other students when specifically asked for individual work.

Table 7.1 summarizes the frequency with which faculty report observing many of these behaviors, and table 7.2 includes data on the percentage of faculty who consider each behavior to be serious cheating. The seriousness ratings in table 7.2 were generated by asking faculty

TABLE 7.1. Faculty reporting that they have observed various cheating behaviors at schools in the United States, McCabe et al. 2002–2010 web surveys (% of faculty observing behavior)

Behavior	Never observing	Observing once	Observing more than once	N
Cut-and-paste plagiarism from written source	22	8	70	15,324
Cut-and-paste plagiarism from Internet source	30	9	61	15,155
Significant plagiarism from written source	40	18	43	15,664
Significant plagiarism from Internet source	71	11	18	14,366
Any form of plagiarism	18	4	78	13,458
Student copying from another without other's knowledge	56	15	29	16,068
Student copying from another with other's knowledge	66	13	21	15,897
Student helping other cheat on test/exam	68	12	20	15,827
Student using unpermitted crib notes in test/exam	72	12	16	15,132
Any of these nine test cheating behaviors	45	17	38	13,775
Students collaborating on individual assignments	39	10	51	14,819
Students sharing information about test others have not yet taken	62	9	29	15,278

members how serious each of the behaviors is, using a four-point scale: not cheating, trivial cheating, moderate cheating, and serious cheating. In each case, we include all faculty surveyed in the United States since the fall of 2002, using our web-based survey. The total number is 19,080, but many faculty members (as many as 30% in one case) either did not answer a question at all or indicated that a particular behavior was not relevant in their courses. In tables 7.1 and 7.2 we show the number (N) on which the results indicated for each individual behavior or rating of seriousness are based—ranging from a low of 13,458 faculty in the case of the rate of engagement in any form of plagiarism to a high of 16,105 for the ratings of seriousness for "cut-and-paste" plagiarism from a written source.

TABLE 7.2. Faculty's perceptions of seriousness of different cheating behaviors at schools in the United States, McCabe et al. 2002–2010 web surveys (% of faculty giving rating)

Behavior	Not cheating	Trivial cheating	Moderate cheating	Serious cheating	N
Cut-and-paste plagiarism from written source	2	14	49	36	16,105
Cut-and-paste plagiarism from Internet source	2	13	46	39	15,877
Significant plagiarism from written source	1	<1	9	90	15,917
Significant plagiarism from Internet source	1	1	7	92	15,020
Student copying from another without other's knowledge	1	1	9	90	15,674
Student copying from another with other's knowledge	1	1	7	91	15,383
Student helping other cheat on test/exam	1	1	12	86	15,286
Student using unpermitted crib notes in test/exam	1	1	11	87	14,906
Students collaborating on individual assignments	3	14	52	32	15,690
Students sharing information about test others have not yet taken	2	4	18	75	15,384

Two particular concerns are reflected in the data in table 7.1: first, faculty members say they have observed a significant amount of cheating in their classes, and second, they observed a very high level of plagiarism. In table 7.2, although most faculty (90%) do rate "significant plagiarism" as serious cheating, a relatively low percentage of faculty (36% to 39%) rate cut-and-paste plagiarism as "serious cheating," suggesting that at least some faculty may be implicitly condoning such forms of plagiarism. Numerous open-ended comments on our faculty surveys seem to support this position. And at a time when many people believe we need to do more to help students improve their writing skills, an even more serious outcome of such high levels of cheating may be captured in the comments of a faculty member from a large public university on the West Coast: "I quit assigning papers because I was unable to control the plagiarism." A faculty member at a liberal arts college in the Midwest raises another concern about how some colleagues address the issue: "Some faculty members here actually assign research papers that don't require citation. This is unconscionable."

Faculty Responses to Cheating

Research shows that faculty members respond to students' cheating in many ways, some of which can undermine the broader ethical environment. Faculty members frequently disregard or circumvent their institution's formal policies, deal with cheating on their own, and/or fail to report cheating to a central authority, as many systems require (Graham et al. 1994; McCabe 1993). For example, Singhal (1982) found that although 65% of faculty respondents observed students cheating, only 21% reported the student to a dean or other administrator. Wright and Kelly (1974) found that only 15% of faculty respondents said they had reported a student who had cheated to the academic dean or other administrators. Nuss (1984) reported that only 34% of faculty respondents said they would report a case of cheating to the appropriate authorities. Another 34% said they would respond by lowering the student's grade, after discussing the matter with the student, and 26% said they would only give the student a warning. One percent said they would simply ignore the matter or lower the student's grade without even discussing the incident with the student. In Jendrek's (1989) study, 60% of faculty respondents said they had observed cheating on examinations. However, only 33% of this group said they followed the official campus policy, which required the faculty member to report the suspected student to the department chair. Eight percent said they simply ignored the incident. Sixty-five percent directly penalized the cheater in some way, generally by reducing the grade on the given examination. Graham et al. (1994) found that of the 79% of faculty in their sample who observed cheating, only 9% penalized the student in some way.

Our own research has produced similarly discouraging results. McCabe's (1993) survey of 789 faculty at 16 U.S. institutions uncovered a variety of reasons that faculty members prefer to bypass university policy and handle cheating incidents one on one. These included a lack of confidence in the judicial system, a belief that gathering proof is difficult or impossible and that pursuing official channels requires too much time and effort, a perception that the penalties given to offenders are often inappropriately harsh or lenient, and a belief that they, not the accused student, are the ones who end up being "on trial."

The data collected from faculty in our surveys from 2002 to 2010 are similar. For example, 40% of all faculty in the United States responding to a question about whether they had ever ignored an incident of cheating in their course indicated that they had. And 51% reported that they had *never* referred an incident of cheating to anyone else—either handling it themselves or ignoring it. The primary reason offered for ignoring a possible incident was a lack of proof. Also important was a desire not to have to deal with such issues. We should note that exact values in this case are not directly comparable because, by the choice of different participating schools, the same selection of reasons for ignoring suspected cheating was not available on each school's survey. Clearly, however, lack of adequate proof was cited by an overwhelming number of faculty who suspected cheating in their courses (estimated to be in excess of three-fourths of all respondents; a second major factor was a desire not to have to deal with such incidents—cited by roughly one in four respondents). Also significant may be the fact that 37% of those who had referred an incident to someone else were not satisfied with the outcome, and 19% were actually dissatisfied. For many of these faculty, the issue was their perception that the system either let the student off or imposed what the faculty member considered to be too lenient a punishment.

In spite of the number of faculty who admit they've ignored cheating, the good news is that slightly less than 1% selected the choice "do nothing about the incident" when asked how they would react if they "were convinced . . . that a student had cheated on a test or assignment in [their] course." This suggests that the large majority of faculty members believe they have some responsibility to address cheating. Reporting the incident to the appropriate authority on campus was selected by only 19% of the responding faculty, but a greater number (64%) said they would "fail the student on the test or assignment." Other popular faculty responses to student cheating include giving a reprimand or warning (selected by 38% of our respondents), requiring the student to retake the test or redo the assignment (19%), and lowering the student's grade in the course (18%). These responses suggest that faculty members are addressing cheating but are doing so outside formal channels. (Note: Faculty were allowed to offer multiple responses to this question, so percentages total more than 100%. Also, these latter calculations concerning faculty reactions are based only on the last two and a half years of data collection, since the survey composition was relatively static at all schools over this period. In this case, $N = 1,814$.)

While faculty members on many campuses are given the freedom to address cheating on their own with academic sanctions, these systems often require reporting of the case to a central authority so that problem students can be identified. Within these systems, some students complain that they have felt coerced into accepting a failure on the test or assignment, or even in the course. These students report that some faculty members threaten to report the incident to the appropriate authority and to seek a greater penalty if the student does not agree to their proposed resolution. Accused students are often willing to agree to a faculty member's proposal, because they are concerned that the incident will be recorded on their college record or transcript if it is referred to the campus judicial system.

As a growing number of schools introduce systems that permit faculty to take direct action, to give them more power and to encourage them not to ignore cheating when it occurs, we believe it is important that these schools utilize appropriate strategies to also encourage faculty to report these cases. If faculty members do not report incidents to a centralized office, the deterrent value is reduced and there is no opportunity to track repeat offenders, as the following faculty comments suggest. (Even though such systems are typically being adopted at the urging of faculty, because they often expand faculty power, many faculty still fail to report incidents—if they even address them at all.)

Faculty members each deal with cheating in their own way. The problem is that most cheaters cheat in several classes and the penalties should escalate but they don't due to lack of knowledge of previous incidents. Only a central source like Judicial Affairs can make sure that penalties escalate. (faculty member at a large public university on the West Coast)

A system that tracks offenses would help students and faculty take incidents of academic dishonesty more seriously. (faculty member at a small private university in the Midwest)

Although an increasing number of campuses seem to be adopting policies that mandate some form of centralized reporting, faculty often do not know about or use these campus-wide record-keeping systems. Campuses need to do a much better job of communicating to faculty (and students) the existence and importance of these systems. A record-keeping system is of little value if faculty members do not report the cheating they observe.

The fact remains that when faculty are asked what they actually do in the face of suspected cheating (rather than what they might do), about half of the respondents reveal that they ignore cheating or handle incidents on their own, bypassing the established judicial mechanisms on campus. As we have already indicated, to some extent this may be driven by their dissatisfaction with the way suspected instances of cheating have been handled in the past—in particular, concern about the failure of their campus to deal strongly with proven cheating, as suggested by these comments from faculty members at a large state university in the Southwest.

A student had submitted a paper taken from a Web site. She changed only the name of the paper. She also plagiarized substantially on another project. Despite having copies of both the student's submitted work and the originals from the Web, pressure from the department director and academic adviser was to only fail the student for the assignment, which failed her for the course, and place a warning in the student's file. Their reasoning was that the student was a senior and, therefore, shouldn't be expelled from school.

Although the student was found to have cheated, my punishment was overruled and the student was given a Withdrawal from my course. It was as if the incident never happened!

Similar concerns are voiced by faculty on many of the campuses surveyed in our ongoing research. One of the unfortunate outcomes of this perceived lack of support is faculty members who become convinced that there is no point in pursuing suspected cases of cheating within the system. Witness the comment of a faculty member at a large state university on the West Coast:

> The [Judicial Affairs Office] needs to be supportive of faculty who report academic dishonesty. [It] has not supported faculty decisions regarding plagiarism even when faced with DEFINITE, UNDENIABLE PROOF of plagiarism. Because of this, I (and other faculty) am extremely hesitant to report any cases of academic dishonesty.

The power of personal experience and social learning to affect faculty attitudes and behaviors is obvious. Faculty members either experience the system themselves or hear stories from faculty colleagues and decide what to do as a result. Faculty comments on our surveys frequently suggest that some faculty members have made the decision not to use the recommended, typically required, judicial system on campus because of the negative experiences of their colleagues. These stories often take on "urban legend" status, as the purported "horrors" of the experience get exaggerated in the repeated telling. The story of one really bad experience can travel far and wide among the faculty and have a huge impact as it travels through social networks. The following comments demonstrate the problem:

> From discussions with colleagues, the current system of dealing with cheating allegations is so complex and cheating is so difficult to prove that most who have gone through the process would not do it again. (faculty member at a large public university in the Southeast)

> I know from a colleague who caught a student cheating that the process for her (in terms of documenting etc.) was extremely stressful. She often felt like she was the one who was under suspicion even though it was the student who was cheating. (faculty member at a state university in the Midwest)

> Many faculty are unwilling to put in the necessary time to process cases of cheating. The hearing boards vary dramatically in their evaluations. There was [a] recent case of a student who forged his transcript, letters of recommendation from his advisor and THE

COLLEGE DEAN and he only got a one semester suspension with no notation on his transcript and nothing passed on to his subsequent employer . . . It is this sort of outcome that makes faculty unwilling to put in the effort to prosecute [academic integrity] cases. (faculty member at a private university in the Northeast)

I have heard stories of faculty catching students cheating on exams . . . The faculty member took the situation to the "authorities" and bottom line, nothing was done to the student and the student was allowed to remain in the class. This is a terrible inconsistency with [our] policies when the final authority in charge (administration) virtually condones cheating in the classroom. (faculty member at a public university in the Midwest)

I was once a member of the University Grade Appeal Committee. During one case, a student admitted to cheating on multiple homework assignments, and aiding to distribute the solutions to others in the class. The instructor found out about this and reduced the percentage of the final course grade that went to the homework. The student then filed a complaint to the Committee, since because of the reduced number of points that went to homework, he did not receive the grade that he wished. His defense? "Everyone did it." Rather than reporting the student for academic misconduct, the board unbelievably awarded the student the higher grade. I was absolutely appalled. (faculty member at a large public university in the Southeast)

Yet another problem is faculty members who say they don't have the time needed to report and follow up on suspected cheating, especially when they feel the system is heavily weighted in the students' favor. The following comments from faculty members at multiple types of universities are representative:

Make it easier for faculty to report cheating. The way it is now it is like the faculty member is on trial.

The time and bureaucracy involved discourages faculty from reporting suspected violations of academic integrity.

It takes a large amount of time to build a solid case against a student. When that is combined with the lack of administrative support, as well as the high risk of an undesirable outcome (parental involvement, potential complaints to the chair, dean, provost, etc.) it makes pursuit of the cheater seem like a fool's errand.

The rights of the students are important. However, they have become so important that a faculty member has too much work to do and too many hoops to jump through to make reporting academic dishonesty something they will do. It is now that the student's word is taken over the instructor's word almost always . . . there are too many other time-consuming career-oriented pressures related to promotion/ tenure, that faculty feel it is counterproductive to take the necessary time for reporting academic dishonesty.

I was told early on that it is a big hassle to follow through with cheaters. There is no reward for taking the time, effort and energy. It is not as if a case can even be used to scare other students. Why make the effort? For me—it means more work. For them—will it really make a difference in their personality or life? I doubt it.

It seems clear that faculty members at many schools perceive that the effort required to pursue a case through established channels is just not worth it. Again, this is worrisome and should send up huge red flags for those who are responsible for designing and administering these systems.

Perhaps even more worrisome, we have learned that some faculty members do little or nothing in the face of suspected student cheating because of the perceived impact such reports might have on the faculty member's chances for promotion and tenure, or perhaps even retention in the case of adjunct faculty. Such faculty concerns are expressed in the following comments from our surveys:

Proving cheating, even copying, is difficult—takes time and you get nasty parent letters—admin finds "the teacher" is the "problem"—as non-tenured you always have a problem—for the pay we should give such time to this????? and as adjuncts we teach the BIG courses (500 to 700 students each semester) give us a break—nasty parent letters make us vulnerable to have our contracts terminated and students give us bad evaluation—all can mean we can no longer teach!!!! (adjunct faculty member at a large state university in the East)

On multiple occasions, I have heard it expressed that it is best to not address those [suspected cheating] situations because of potential reprisals on student course evaluations. Students have gotten the upper hand, and it should not be a surprise that cheating in high schools and colleges has been on a rapid increase because untenured faculty members know that their job security is at risk. (faculty member at a private university in the South)

As a non-tenured faculty, one incidence of plagiarism/cheating was serious enough to warrant dismissal of the student but the major professor wanted to keep him so I failed him and he retook the course. Making an unpopular decision would have impacted my tenure process. This student is now completing a PhD and does not deserve it. (faculty member at a large state university in the Southwest)

Another faculty "justification" for not taking action in the face of suspected cheating, which we have heard with some frequency, is a belief that it is not necessary to report or deal with students who are not performing well anyway. As the following comments suggest, some faculty members feel that no added value in the penalty is likely to result if the cheating were reported:

Student was failing so even if they received a better grade on test it would not help them. (faculty member at a state university on the West Coast)

Student failed the test anyway. (faculty member at a private university in the Southeast)

Faculty members offer many other reasons for not reporting suspected cheating, and it is simply impossible to discuss them all here. We conclude our discussion of faculty responses to cheating by offering some abbreviated faculty comments on three additional issues: (1) issues related to adjunct faculty, (2) the question of whether faculty have any obligation to address moral or ethical issues in their courses, and (3) the influence of parents on faculty reactions to cheating.

As more and more institutions hire adjunct faculty to teach courses in a fiscally difficult environment, it is problematic if these faculty are not fully in the loop and committed to academic integrity policies. Note the following comment:

Adjunct faculty are often left out of the loop on policies and procedures at [school X]. It would be helpful if we were reminded of the policies regarding academic integrity. (adjunct faculty member at a two-year technical college in the Midwest)

Then, on the second point, there is the idea that faculty members should be free to do as they please in this arena, including doing nothing. The following comment is not an isolated one:

> I think this [reporting suspected cheating] is totally up to the individual faculty members. Frankly, I do not think it is our responsibility. My view is that if a student cheats, he or she is cheating themselves, wasting their money, etc. If they are concerned with their bottom line grade rather than actually learning something, then they have missed the whole point of college and I feel sorry for them, but it is not my job to change their value orientation in that regard. (faculty member at a private university in the South)

Finally, concerning the role of parents, it often seems to be the case that parents *only* involvement comes when they wish to defend their own child against a charge of cheating, no matter what the evidence suggests.

> [Pursuing this incident] pitted the prof against the parents who did everything possible to get the child off. It was actually a sad experience to watch what the parent did in front of his child. In the future, I'll find other ways to deal with someone who is cheating. (faculty member at a liberal arts college in the South)

These comments uncover several important issues. First, adjunct faculty handle increasingly large teaching loads on many campuses and, as such, are on the front lines when it comes to witnessing and dealing with academic dishonesty. They may also be responsible for many of the large introductory courses that give students their first experience of the environment of academic integrity on campus and ample opportunity to cheat, unless precautions are taken. Our experience suggests, however, that many adjunct faculty members are given little academic integrity training or support and have little incentive to address academic integrity or to report cheating incidents through proper channels.

The second comment, on faculty members' freedom to do as they please, illustrates a sentiment among a minority but not trivial number of faculty that dealing with issues of student integrity is not part of the faculty role. We could not disagree more. We contend that the entire campus benefits when faculty take part in developing students' character and sense of honor and integrity, especially as an essential part of a campus-wide process of developing a climate of responsibility and integrity (e.g., McCabe, Treviño, and Butterfield 1999).

Finally, the third comment, on pressure from parents, speaks to one of the many disincentives that serve to reduce the likelihood that faculty will report cheating behavior. Many faculty members perceive that administrators and judicial bodies succumb all too easily to pressure from aggressive parents, who often threaten legal action, making it more likely that faculty will handle cheating incidents by themselves or not at all. It takes a strong faculty member, backed up by administrative support, to stand up to such threats. In our experience, these threats usually go nowhere, because judges are not interested in intervening in campus integrity violations. But, having heard a horror story or two, faculty members are hesitant to get involved. While this is definitely a problem among faculty, it really is indicative of what seems to be a larger phenomenon, with each major constituency blaming someone else for what it sees as the deteriorating ethics of students—parents blaming the school in general, students blaming faculty, faculty complaining about parents and the administration, and the administration blaming faculty and students, and even, on occasion, parents for the way they have raised the current generation of students. Unfortunately, the outcome often is a failure on the part of any one group to do anything. We hear a continuing chorus of "ain't it awful" when adults discuss the current generation of students, but we see very few action programs at the school level (with only a modest number of exceptions) that are substantive enough to have a measurable impact, versus many programs that seem to be more cosmetic and designed to please one or more of a school's major stakeholders.

So, how can we expect students to believe that cheating is a serious issue when faculty and others are reluctant to deal with cheaters, when they shun the established system, when cheating receives only minor consequences, and, worst of all, when faculty simply look the other way? If faculty members turn a blind eye to cheating and/or refuse to work within established channels, we shouldn't be surprised if students decide that no one really cares about cheating—that it is accepted in the campus environment. By any measure, the general faculty response to cheating is disturbing. If nothing else, those who fail to take action become known to students, and our student surveys suggest that some students even consider such information when making course and instructor choices—preferring faculty who have a reputation of not pursuing such incidents.

A different problem is presented by faculty members who overemphasize the maintenance of law and order through fear and retribution. As we have discussed (McCabe, Treviño, and Butterfield 2004), the strict "deterrence approach" taken by some faculty members begins with the assumption that students will cheat and that only fear of serious penalties for breaking rules will reduce cheating. Although we believe that clear rules and sanctions for rule breaking must play a key role in any approach designed to support academic integrity, we also believe that this approach should take a back seat to a broader and more aspirational focus on developing a culture of integrity (we say much more about this in chapter 9). Some faculty members find deterrence approaches appealing because they can easily be applied in their own courses, and many claim that these techniques are necessary in the battle against cheating. In our opinion, such approaches have little long-term impact and can be counterproductive. In the long term, what happens when the deterrence mechanisms (e.g., proctors) are removed? Students have not internalized ethical standards that can guide their behavior. Further, deterrence approaches deal only with reducing cheating behavior and have little or no impact on broader aspirational goals, such as promoting a sense of trust and integrity in the environment. In addition, if other faculty members are not doing so, the faculty member who engages only in a deterrence approach may experience a backlash from students who expect to be trusted and react negatively to a more "police state" environment in that particular classroom.

Of course, aspirational and deterrence-based approaches are not mutually exclusive. Deterrence focuses on convincing students that, if they cheat, they will be caught and severely punished. Effective ethical community-building approaches do not eliminate the need for sanctions. In fact, as we discuss further in chapter 9, effective aspirational approaches are always backed up by accountability systems. The difference is one of emphasis, with the emphasis in aspirational approaches being placed more on trust, respect, and promoting honesty and integrity. If the rules are breached, that is when accountability systems kick in.

Before we leave the question of how faculty respond to suspected incidents of cheating in their courses, we should note that our sense is that faculty, to at least some degree, may be exaggerating what is actually happening "on the ground." Indeed, a number of faculty may be reporting how they respond to *significant* breaches of academic integrity, or how they think they would respond *if* they were to experience such a breach. In reality, we believe, faculty often "convince" themselves that a breach was not serious enough to warrant a formal response and ignore it, when, in fact, the breach was serious or would present an opportunity to educate students on questions of academic integrity. In short, we are concerned that at least some faculty think they are doing the right thing when, arguably, they are not, throwing at least some of their survey responses into question. Of even greater concern would be faculty who are simply indicating that they follow the policy on their campus when they do not. Certainly, the small number of cases processed on any campus each year suggests that the number of faculty who would ignore an incident of cheating in their classroom is probably much greater than the 1% who selected this option in our survey. Any failure by faculty members to address cheating they observe may undermine campus policy. The same is true when faculty members address cheating in ways that are inconsistent with the institution's academic integrity policies.

So, What Can Faculty and Administrators Do?

Administrators and faculty need to realize that action and leadership on their part is essential, because, along with students, they play a critical role in establishing and supporting a culture that supports academic integrity. We believe that the data presented in this chapter should serve as an alarm bell to administrators who may be feeling complacent about the systems they have put in place. At a minimum, they should be surveying their faculty to learn about their attitudes toward the system and whether it is being utilized as designed. If it is not, administrators need to understand why and to address the problems. Are faculty members (at all levels, including adjunct faculty) familiar with the system? If so, are they satisfied with its effectiveness? If not, what are the problems and potential solutions?

As faculty, we need to collectively look in the mirror and realize that we probably contribute to the cheating problem, and therefore we are at least partially responsible for fixing it. Faculty members are clearly a key to the success of any efforts toward achieving academic integrity, because they are in the classrooms and dealing with students every day. For faculty, contributing to the ethical culture is about taking an active role in the day-to-day work required to promote the culture and keep it alive. Faculty members should ask themselves, "What am I doing right now to support the campus's ethical culture?" The classroom is where principles of academic integrity are translated into actual attitudes and behavior. Faculty cannot assume that students are familiar with codes or policies, definitions of plagiarism or other forms of cheating, and the importance of academic integrity. Students must be taught about these issues, and we strongly encourage faculty to take the time to regularly promote students' awareness and understanding of academic integrity. We have seen some of our own colleagues shrink from explicitly addressing these issues, because they think they will be unpopular with students if they do so. Our experience is quite different: faculty members who explicitly discuss these issues and create an environment supportive of academic integrity in their classrooms and beyond earn increased respect from the majority of their students.

Faculty members can also contribute to building a strong environment of academic integrity if they make sure that students understand what the requirements for academic integrity are in their particular class and especially in relation to specific assignments. Faculty need to make clear their policies on collaboration and other potential cheating behaviors and explain the reasons for these policies. If it is relevant, they should ensure that students know what plagiarism is and how to avoid it. And if their school has an honor code, faculty should engage students in discussions about the code, its application in the particular course, and its importance to the culture of integrity.

Faculty often do not realize that they need to address these issues explicitly because their colleagues may have very different expectations and standards, and these differences can be confusing to students. For example, one faculty member may allow collaboration on homework, while another doesn't. If you're the one who doesn't, you should explain the reason in a way that makes sense to students and that they accept. We advise faculty and administrators to be conscious of potential discrepancies in defining what constitutes cheating and to communicate standards of acceptable and unacceptable behavior to students in a clear, explicit, and unambiguous manner.

Thus far we have assumed that reasonable academic integrity policies exist at a faculty member's institution. But that may not always be the case. In the absence of campus integrity policies that work, we do think it is important for faculty to develop classroom strategies that, at a minimum, make it clear to students that the faculty member cares about academic integrity and is taking action to reduce cheating. How faculty members represent this to students can be important. Faculty can reduce the opportunity to cheat in a variety of ways, as different faculty members have suggested in the course of our surveys. For example, they might use multiple versions of an exam or monitor the exam environment more closely. Alternatively, they might spend more time worrying about how students are seated in preparation for taking the examination. For other examples, see Whitley and Keith-Spiegel (2002).

Although it may seem risky, faculty members can also take a more aspirational approach on their own. We know of at least one circumstance in which a faculty member discussed academic integrity at length with students and then instituted unproctored exams (a practice unheard of in the undergraduate program at this institution), getting students to agree to hold each other accountable for monitoring and reporting any violations. And it worked! The students gave the professor some of the highest student evaluation ratings ever, perhaps in part because of the trust created in that class. And the grades suggest that no cheating occurred.

As we have noted elsewhere in this book, we are fans of honor codes, but we have tried to make clear that we are not promoting honor codes as the only approach that works or an approach that will always work in every environment. Honor codes involve much hard work and preparation within a community. Nevertheless, faculty should know that they can benefit from honor code environments. For example, honor codes place responsibilities and obligations on students, not just on faculty, to prevent cheating. The underlying thrust is to address the issue of student cheating through the development of strong community standards and the significant involvement of students in the formation and implementation of these standards. As such, honor codes reduce uncertainty and ethical "gray areas" (McCabe, Treviño, and Butterfield 1999), and they shift the locus of responsibility, at least somewhat, from faculty to students. Our research shows that faculty benefit from honor codes (McCabe, Butterfield, and Treviño 2003), primarily by reducing the burden on faculty members to monitor and enforce regulations concerning cheating. At institutions that lack codes, faculty members perceive themselves as "shouldering the burden" when it comes to cheating, and their institutions depend on their cooperation to catch and report cheating incidents. However, faculty at such institutions are at least as likely to disregard their institution's policy, to ignore cheating, or to deal with it on their own as to support the institutional policy. In contrast, faculty members at honor code institutions are more likely to support the institution's academic integrity system and to view it as fair and effective (McCabe, Butterfield, and Treviño 2003). Faculty at code schools are also more willing to share responsibility with students for monitoring academic dishonesty and adjudicating suspected cases of cheating, and therefore they have less responsibility for catching and dealing with cheaters. Institutions without formal honor codes have to work harder to demonstrate to their faculty the fairness and effectiveness of their policies and to encourage faculty to follow designated policies and procedures.

Conclusion

Academic dishonesty represents both a challenge and an opportunity for faculty. One challenge is that cheating clearly exists and probably is not going away. So we could easily throw up our hands in despair, as some have done. But we can't contribute to students' moral character if we are unwilling to address unethical behavior inside our schools and classrooms. We believe strongly that this is part of our faculty obligation. Our institutions have undergraduate students for four years, during a crucial time for their moral development, and herein lies our opportunity to have an impact. We have an obligation and an opportunity because we are an essential part of our academic communities, and our role in building an environment that supports academic integrity is essential. In chapter 9, we will talk much more generally about what it takes to create an institutional culture of academic integrity and how students, faculty, and administrators must work together to do so.

CHAPTER EIGHT

Academic Integrity in Business and Professional Schools

Thus far we have focused primarily on academic integrity among undergraduates. In this chapter, we shift our attention primarily to graduate students and particularly to academic integrity in business and professional schools. Our own research and the research of others suggests that cheating in graduate professional schools is widespread—among medical students, law students, pharmacy students, dental students, and others. Perhaps we shouldn't be surprised. The stakes are high in professional schools, and the requirements are often difficult to meet, creating pressure that students sometimes address by taking shortcuts, at least some of which devolve into cheating. While this may not be a surprise, it is disappointing that students entering some of our most respected professions—such as law and medicine—engage in such behaviors at roughly the same high rates as their peers in other professions or occupations.

Our discussion here includes data we have collected, both previously published and unpublished, and we review what we have learned from a search of the research literature and media accounts. We then focus on academic integrity in business schools, especially MBA programs, where we have conducted the most research and have the greatest amount of personal experience.

Law Students

In our surveys, law students, at least occasionally, report significantly lower levels of engagement in academic dishonesty than other graduate students. They generally have not been the subject of articles in the popular press detailing cheating scandals. Indeed, in a precursor study to our twenty-year survey project (McCabe, Dukerich, and Dutton 1991), law students reported substantially lower intentions to cheat in a hypothetical dilemma involving an opportunity to cheat on the licensing exam relevant to students' chosen profession—the bar exam for law students, the CPA exam for business students (including all majors, not just accounting), and the state licensing exams for medical and dental students. Significantly more business (54%), medical (63%), and dental (57%) students than law students (24%) chose one of the unethical alternatives available in this scenario. This survey was administered to students on their first day of orientation and registration at each school. The sample included 55 dental students, 82 medical students, 318 business students (two schools), and 481 law students (two schools). These samples accounted for close to half or more of the incoming class in each case, with the medical student sample unfortunately reduced by a call for students to check in for their required physical exams while many were still completing the optional survey.

The stated intentions of the law students seem admirable, but are somewhat open to question when we consider other research evidence. For example, we collected data in the 2002/2003 academic year as part of the undergraduate surveys described in earlier chapters. A total of 908 of the 12,177 undergraduate students surveyed in 2002/2003 answered all nine elements in the Bowers cheating index and also supplied information on their intended occupation; 7.5% selected law as their intended profession. Of this group of intended future lawyers, 68% self-reported one or more of Bowers's nine offenses while an undergraduate, compared with 66% of the students intending to pursue other professions. (Note: In this chapter we include first-year students in our analyses, since we are more interested in relative than absolute comparisons here, and the sample size we have to work with is low in some cases.) This statistically nonsignificant difference (68% vs. 66%) is contrary to the notably lower results for the stated intentions of incoming law students in the study described above. We have no way of knowing how many of the 7.5% of students intending to go to law school actually entered a law school. But we can say that we found no difference in cheating behavior (compared with other students) among undergraduates intending to do so.

A third (and probably the best) way of evaluating cheating among law school students is to look at actual self-reports of cheating among graduate students. In our data, we had responses from only 496 law students in the United States with sufficient data to be included in this analysis. Of these law students, 30% self-reported one or more cheating behaviors on the Bowers index, compared with 39% of the total graduate student sample (N = 3,823) attending one of the 13 schools in our sample that had a law school. While law students self-reported significantly less cheating ($p < 0.01$), this difference is much smaller than the difference in intent to cheat observed in our first study. Also, we note that nearly one-third of these students did admit to cheating—a high and distressing number for those about to enter the legal profession.

With regard to media attention to academic dishonesty, law students have not been completely spared the scrutiny of the press (e.g., Crissey 1997). But in general, fewer incidents have been reported than for some other professional schools. We speculate that this has a lot to do with the bar exam and the need for applicants to present a "near perfect" record to be admitted to the bar, and some law schools are inclined to keep cheating problems quiet, even if they exist. Something of a competition exists among law schools, based on rates of successful admission to the bar by their recent graduates. Thus it is possible that law schools are reluctant to record an incident of academic dishonesty on student records, for fear that this will reduce the rate of bar admission for their students and ultimately affect the number of future applicants to the school. We also have reason to believe, based on surveys of faculty and discussions that McCabe has had with law school administrators and faculty, that many are unwilling to report suspected cheating unless they are absolutely certain of a student's guilt, for fear that they may be wrong, and the accusation alone might adversely affect a student's chance of admission to the bar. For example, we know of at least one state university where no suspected cases of cheating have been reported at the law school in recent years, because such reports in this particular state would require creating a notation on the student's record (even if the student was later judged not responsible for the behavior). This record is consulted during the bar admission process. No faculty member in more than five years has been willing to enter such a report. Although possible, we consider it highly unlikely that not a single faculty member over that period has observed an incident that at least raised some suspicion. So, while the numbers suggest that law students cheat less than their peers in other professional programs, and the popular press has reported little in the way of cheating scandals at law schools, we are not completely convinced that law students are truly that different. The students themselves may be more reluctant to self-report cheating, because the stakes are so high and they don't trust the anonymity of the survey process. If that is the case, our data would underreport the amount of actual cheating. Alternatively, law students may indeed cheat less than their peers, because they know that, if caught, they will be ineligible to sit for the bar exam, ruining their chances for a successful legal career.

Medical Students

Medical students also present some conflicting evidence. Although, in our original study of undergraduates (2002/2003), described above, medical students expressed the highest intention to cheat, an analysis of graduate medical students again raises doubts. For example, 38% of the graduate medical students self-reported cheating (N = 320), compared with 39% of the graduate students in other majors at the same schools (N = 2,553). This nonsignificant difference is inconsistent with the finding that medical students in our hypothetical dilemma study (McCabe, Dukerich, and Dutton 1991) reported notably higher levels of intent to cheat than their professional peers in law, business, and dentistry. (Note: We have erred on the side of caution here to make sure that we have included *only* medical students in this comparison. We excluded 57 responses from students whose reports of their majors made it unclear whether they were indeed medical students.)

Unfortunately, we can't replicate the analysis by intended occupation that we conducted for intended law students, because in our earliest surveys, the information we collected on intended occupation had the general category "medicine," which doesn't allow us to confidently isolate prospective medical students. This category also included students aspiring to careers in the health sciences (e.g., physical therapy and nursing). If we include all health science majors, however, we see that 67% of these students, as a group (N = 1,545), self-reported one or more incidents of cheating on the Bowers scale, compared with 66% of the "other" student group (N = 10,632)—a nonsignificant difference supportive of the finding for graduate medical students described above.

Other studies have raised concerns about dishonesty among medical students. A survey of 428 American medical students at two medical schools in 1980 found that 58% reported cheating during medical school (Sierles, Hendrickx, and Circle 1980). Baldwin et al. (1996) surveyed 3,975 medical students and received 2,459 responses (62%) from second-year students at 31 medical schools. They found that although slightly less than 5% of medical students self-reported cheating during their first two years at medical school, 39% reported witnessing some type of cheating among classmates during these first two years. This study also found that male medical students were more likely to report cheating than female students.

Our literature search for cheating scandals among medical students yielded a paucity of incidents. We did find one disturbing report. This study, conducted in 1991 at the University of New Mexico School of Medicine, was undertaken following "an episode of cheating involving three second-year medical students" and concluded: "According to both faculty and students, there was a significant incidence ($\geq$10% of the respondents) of unethical behavior at the school of medicine, most commonly in relation to cheating on examinations" (Anderson and Obenshain 1994, 323). However, this result was based on a summary of cheating that students and faculty had observed among others. This level of cheating is not very different from the self-reported levels among graduate students in general that we describe in chapter 3 (see table 3.10). Indeed, if we combine the various forms of test cheating among graduate students shown in table 3.10, we arrive at an estimate of actual self-reported cheating on tests of 14% (N = 13,047). We would expect this number to be somewhat higher, since its major component ("getting questions or answers from someone who has already taken the same exam") was not part of the Anderson and Obenshain index. Excluding this component from our calculation, we find that only 6.8% of the general graduate school population (N = 13,374) self-reported cheating, a number similar to the estimates for other students, as reported by Anderson and Obenshain. This estimate again suggests that medical students look much like their peers with regard to academic cheating. In Baldwin et al.'s (1996) study of 3,975 second-year medical students at 31 schools, described above, only 4.7% self-reported cheating in medical school, even though 16.5% self-reported cheating as undergraduates in college. In that survey, students were first presented with a series of behaviors and asked about cheating by others, but with regard to their own cheating, they were simply asked whether or not they had cheated, without any explicit definition of "cheating"—only the implication that it consisted of the same elements as those specified for judging the behavior of others. This, along with the very low estimate of cheating in college compared with the results we have found when detailing the cheating elements to be included, makes us somewhat suspicious of the low levels reported in the Baldwin et al. study.

In our experience, pre-med students have been known to distinguish themselves as undergraduates by the occasional extremes they seem willing to pursue to ensure they are among the "chosen few" when medical school acceptances arrive in the mail. At one school we have worked with over the years, which has a large pre-med program, students have even given the type of competition they encounter in the pre-med program a nickname: "throating," which explicitly derives from the cutthroat nature of competition in the program. "Throaters" have been known to foul the lab experiments of others, to remove study materials from the reserve collection in the library so that others will not have easy access to them, and so on. We find it hard to believe that such students cheat less than others or that they change their stripes dramatically when they enter medical school. The bottom line is that medical students, in spite of what one might consider their idealistic pursuit of a profession that serves others, are probably much like everyone else when it comes to cheating. Many seem to be willing to do whatever is necessary to gain an advantage over others or to help ensure their own progress through their academic programs. And as in law, although perhaps for more student-centered reasons, medical faculty are probably reluctant to accuse someone of cheating. Most likely, they especially struggle with the question of whether they are willing to possibly "ruin" someone's career unless they have explicit evidence of cheating.

Pharmacy Students

Our discussion of the pharmacy profession is necessarily brief because we have complete data for only 137 graduate students enrolled in a pharmacy program at seven schools. In this case we see quite a large and significant difference in self-reported cheating among graduate students majoring in pharmacy (N=137), with 53% reporting one or more instances of cheating, compared with only 38% of their graduate school peers (N=1,506) at the same seven institutions—a significant difference ($p < 0.001$). At least some of the programs included among these seven schools have the new six-year PharmD program, which one might think would help socialize students into pharmacy as a profession, and one would hope to see fewer instances of behaviors such as academic dishonesty. But our data suggest this is not the case and seem to indicate the need for a greater effort on the part of schools of pharmacy to promote ethical behavior among their students. Of some interest is the observation that the big disparity between pharmacy students and others concerns collaborative work (although the pharmacy students also self-report higher levels of cheating on most of the behaviors studied). This may help schools of pharmacy decide where to attack the cheating issue.

The *American Journal of Pharmaceutical Education* reports several studies of academic dishonesty among pharmacy students, but none published in the past five years provide a comparison group of non-pharmacy students, so direct comparisons between pharmacy and non-pharmacy students are not possible. In addition, most of the emphasis of this research is on pre-pharmacy students. Perhaps not surprisingly, these studies generally show high levels of cheating. For example, a study of four Canadian pharmacy schools showed that more than 80% of pre-pharmacy students indicated they had engaged in one or more forms of academic dishonesty (Austin et al. 2006).

A graduate-level study by Rabi et al. (2006) is of particular interest. It reports that approximately 74% of the students surveyed (N = 296 third-year students in PharmD programs at four schools) "admitted that either they or their classmates had worked on an individual assignment with a friend" (Rabi et al. 2006) This seems to support our own finding that pharmacy students engage in more collaborative cheating than their peers. Again, this may be a good point of attack for any pharmacy school wishing to address academic dishonesty and promote greater integrity. Another article provides some interesting data on students' perceptions of plagiarism and academic honesty, concluding that students do not view plagiarism as a serious issue (Ryan et al. 2009). However, these results are less useful to us, because the students surveyed were primarily undergraduates and were students in Australia, raising some question about comparability with our U.S. sample. The study does help confirm, however, that plagiarism is not a uniquely American phenomenon.

Dental Students

As with pharmacy students, we don't have a lot of data to review on dental students, although the data we do have raise concerns. This was the group with the second highest level of less than ethical choices in the hypothetical dilemma we described earlier (57% for dental students vs. 63% for medical students) (McCabe, Dukerich, and Dutton 1991). In addition, 56% of the 88 students we can explicitly identify as dental students among the graduate and professional students we have surveyed in the past eight years (at five schools) reported engaging in at least one form of academic dishonesty, compared with 39% of the non-dental graduate and professional students at those same five schools. This highly significant difference ($p < 0.001$), in spite of the small sample size, clearly suggests dental students cheat more often, or at least self-report more cheating. Unlike in the case of pharmacy students, we cannot identify one specific type of cheating where the two groups differ drastically, and thus we cannot offer a specific recommendation on the type of cheating that dental schools might target for improvement. Indeed, if we compare the nine components of the Bowers index for dental students versus non-dental students, we find strong and significant differences between the two groups on eight items. Unfortunately, this suggests that dental schools have a broad-based problem of academic dishonesty that they need to address.

A search of the literature seems to support our contention that cheating among dental students is notably more common than cheating among some other professional school students. A quick review of the literature—both the popular media and academic journals—uncovered several related articles. Prominent among these are reports about cheating "scandals" in dental schools at the University of Indiana (Rudavsky 2007) and University of Nevada, Las Vegas (Mower 2006), among other examples. In the academic literature, we found that 43% of the students at the Iowa College of Dentistry admitted cheating (in a questionnaire survey), and 94% believed cheating was occurring at the school (Fuller and Killip 1979). Survey research by Muhney and Campbell (2010) and Andrews et al. (2007) suggests that the majority of dental school educators have witnessed or otherwise had experience with cheating incidents among their students. We also found reports of a cheating incident involving 13 students at the University of California, Los Angeles, School of Dentistry (Genova 2008) and the denial of an appeal filed by a student dismissed from New York University's dental school for "glancing" at another student's test paper (Rubenstein 2010). As noted above, our own data suggest this is a troubling phenomenon in dental schools and will require a broad-based strategy to address.

Business School Students

As faculty members in business schools, we have always had a strong interest in the survey results obtained from business students, and we have made some effort over the years to emphasize business students in our work (McCabe, Butterfield, and Treviño 2006; McCabe, Dukerich, and Dutton 1991, 1994; McCabe and Treviño 1995; McCabe, Treviño, and Butterfield 1996; Treviño, Butterfield, and McCabe 1998; Treviño and McCabe 1994). Those familiar with our work know that one consistent theme has been the general finding that business students self-report more cheating than their peers in most other disciplines, at both the undergraduate and graduate levels.

Indeed, a great deal of attention has been paid to the prevalence of cheating behaviors across the different majors or areas of study within universities at the undergraduate level. We addressed this topic briefly in chapter 4, and here we discuss it further before moving on to our work on graduate business students.

A small number of studies have found that business school students self-report less, or at least no more, cheating than students in other majors (e.g., Klein et al. 2007). In a relatively small study (two southern universities), Eastman, Eastman, and Iyer (2008) found that non-business students self-reported that they were more likely to engage in academic dishonesty than business students. In both cases, both the samples and the comparison groups were small to modest in size.

Beginning with the seminal work of Bowers (1964), however, the majority of research has shown that business and engineering undergraduates cheat the most (e.g., Harding, Finelli, and Carpenter 2006), or at least self-report the most cheating. Rettinger and Jordan's (2005) natural experiment involving business and liberal arts students showed that business students reported more cheating than their liberal arts counterparts, even when taking the same courses. Their results suggest that business students have less critical attitudes toward cheating and a greater orientation toward grades. Smyth and Davis (2004) examined attitudes toward cheating among two-year college students and found that business students were generally more unethical than non-business majors in both behavior and attitudes. These findings are consistent with our own work, which suggests that undergraduate business and engineering students engage in academic dishonesty at above average rates (e.g., McCabe 1997).

Researchers have also examined differences in cheating across majors within business schools. Chapman et al. (2004) found that marketing majors cheated significantly more than students majoring in other business disciplines. Eastman, Eastman, and Iyer (2008) showed that insurance students were more likely to cheat than students from other business majors. They also found that the motivation for academic dishonesty differed between insurance students and other business students.

Research on business and engineering majors has examined why cheating is so prevalent within these disciplines. Passow et al. (2006) examined engineering majors at 11 institutions and found that students were less likely to cheat on exams and homework when they held a strong conviction that cheating is wrong, no matter what the circumstances, and they were more likely to cheat when they believed they were cheating to alleviate stressful situations. Research by Premeaux (2005) compared tier 1 business students (ranked by the Association to Advance Collegiate Schools of Business accrediting body) with tier 2 students and found that tier 1 students were more likely to cheat on written assignments, to believe that sanctions affect cheating, and to believe that a stigma is attached to cheaters. Tier 2 students were more likely to cheat on exams and to accept the notion that moral and ethical people cheat.

Before turning our attention to graduate business students in MBA programs, we also looked at differences between business school undergraduates and their counterparts. We first considered those undergraduates attending one of the 73 institutions included in our graduate student analysis (the seventy-fourth was a graduate student–only institution) and, second, considered students attending any institution in our database with an undergraduate business program—a total of 108 schools surveyed between 2002/2003 and 2009/2010. The additional 35 schools did not have an MBA program and in, many cases, did not have any significant graduate programs. In both cases, however, our sample included only four-year programs and excluded first-year students.

In the first group, business undergraduates (N = 9,016) self-reported more cheating behaviors than their non-business peers (N = 30,885), not only on the full Bowers index ($p < 0.001$) but also on all of the individual components ($p < 0.001$) except for "padding a few items on a bibliography," where there was no statistically significant difference between the two groups. In the second group, students attending an institution with an undergraduate but no MBA program, business students (N = 12,298) self-reported statistically greater levels of cheating for the full Bowers index ($p < 0.001$), as well as for seven of the individual behaviors ($p < 0.001$): collaboration, "copying a few sentences of material without footnoting it in a paper," "giving answers to other students during an exam," "plagiarized from published material on papers," "copying from another student on a test or exam," "padding a few items on a bibliography," and "getting questions or answers from someone who has already taken the same exam," or getting pretest information ($p < 0.01$). The behaviors "turned in papers done entirely or in part by other students" and "used crib notes during an exam" were statistically equivalent. These results raise the question, why do undergraduate business school students cheat more than their peers in other majors? The answer is that we don't know for sure. It may be something about the types of people who are drawn to business programs. Different students are attracted to different majors, and it is possible that students who are predisposed to cheating select themselves into business schools at a higher rate because of preexisting attitudes and characteristics, such as a "bottom-line mentality," a value for being financially well off, and competitiveness with regard to grades (McCabe, Butterfield, and Treviño 2006; McCabe and Treviño 1995). Research has shown that business school students' personal characteristics do make a difference. For example, Davy et al. (2007) showed that business students who are extrinsically motivated are more likely to cheat than students who are intrinsically motivated. It is also possible that the training being provided to business school students leads them to behave in self-interested and unethical ways (Ghoshal 2005). As we discussed in our 2006 article, students who are immersed in business schools may be exposed to the "get it done at all costs" culture found in many corporate workplaces, and business school curricula (e.g., economic theories, free market philosophy, self-interest perspectives) may contribute to these differences (McCabe, Butterfield, and Treviño 2006, 295):

> Students may be learning something in business school that leads
> them to have such attitudes. In support of the learning explanation,
> Ghoshal (2005) argued that the economic theories and free market
> philosophy that form the foundation of much of the business school
> curriculum have a harmful impact on business students' values,
> attitudes, and behavior. Ghoshal (2005, 76) claimed that "by

propagating ideologically inspired amoral theories, business schools have actively freed their students from any sense of moral responsibility." Business school curricula generally emphasize the maximization of shareholder wealth, without equal attention to other societal stakeholders.

Another issue that may lead business students to cheat more is ambiguity about collaboration (McCabe, Butterfield, and Treviño 2006). Business students are commonly taught that teamwork is a valuable skill, highly desirable in modern corporations, and business faculty often assign students to teams and ask them to collaborate on team projects. However, these students are also frequently asked to perform certain tasks and projects by themselves, with no outside assistance. For some students, this is a confusing mixed message: if corporations and business faculty place such a high value on collaboration, why do instructors demand that certain assignments be done without any assistance? Some students respond to this confusion by simply ignoring directives against collaboration, sometimes reasoning that, even when prohibited, collaboration is appropriate training for the workplace (McCabe, Butterfield, and Treviño 2006).

We now move on to the topic of cheating in graduate MBA programs. Some business practitioners and academics consider MBA programs to be "professional" training for business executives. However, unlike the practice of other professions—which requires a licensure exam on an agreed upon body of knowledge, self-policing according to accepted standards of practice, and widely acknowledged responsibilities to society (e.g., law, medicine)—one can generally practice business without formal training or certification, and self-policing is absent. Therefore, with some exceptions (e.g., CPAs), business schools do not train "professionals" in a similar sense. Recent attention has been paid to this issue, with some members of the business school community pushing for a more "professional" approach. For example, in a *Harvard Business Review* article, Khurana and Nohria (2008) proposed a "Hippocratic Oath for Managers." Some students at the Harvard Business School began a campaign to have students take the oath before graduating. They created a website (mbaoath.org) and claim to have developed a broad coalition of supporters across many business schools. Nevertheless, the oath remains voluntary, meaning that MBAs are not "professionals."

Although business students are not professionals, we compare graduate business students with other graduate professional school students here. The question we wish to address is how levels of academic dishonesty in graduate business schools compare with those in the more traditional professional schools of law, medicine, pharmacy, and dentistry. Our first major foray into this question was an article we published in 2006 in the journal *Academy of Management Learning & Education* (McCabe, Butterfield, and Treviño 2006). In this study, "we collected data from more than 5,000 business (mostly M.B.A.) and non-business graduate students at 32 colleges and universities in the U.S. and Canada during the 2002–2003 and 2003–2004 academic years to test a series of hypotheses regarding the prevalence of graduate business student cheating and reasons why these students cheat." The finding that generated the most attention, especially in the media, was "that graduate business students cheat more than their non business-student peers" (McCabe, Butterfield, and Treviño 2006, 294).

We have not published anything further on this question since then, but we were able go back and perform a similar set of calculations for all graduate business students who have taken our surveys since the fall of 2002. Although at some schools we can't explicitly differentiate between doctoral candidates in business and those pursuing an MBA, it is clear that more than 95% of the graduate business students were pursuing an MBA and, as a matter of convenience, we refer to this entire group as MBA students. In addition to studying this group, we offer some comments about undergraduate business students. In these undergraduate analyses, we once again eliminated first-year students.

Table 8.1 shows a global summary of self-reported cheating among MBA students compared with other selected professions. In addition to showing health sciences as one group, we show the relevant data for medical (those we can explicitly identify as studying for an MD), dentistry, and pharmacy students as separate categories, to "evaluate," to some degree, our earlier conclusions covering these professions. We also show law students separately. However, we suggest caution in interpreting the results of our analyses concerning medical, dental, and pharmacy students, given the small sample sizes.

The surprises in table 8.1, compared with our earlier finding (McCabe, Butterfield, and Treviño 2006), are, first, the statistical equivalency of self-reported cheating for business students and those in the arts and health sciences and, second, the extraordinarily high rates of

TABLE 8.1. Self-reported cheating among graduate students by major or professional group, McCabe et al. web surveys, 2002–2010

Group	N	Self-reporting cheating (%)	Comparison with business group
Business	2,018	46	—
Health sciences	1,232	45	No significant difference
Medicine	265	38	Business greater ($p < 0.02$)
Pharmacy	61	61	Pharmacy greater ($p < 0.03$)
Dentistry	88	56	Dentistry greater ($p < 0.10$)
Law	496	30	Business greater ($p < 0.001$)
Arts	239	45	No significant difference
Engineering	741	44	No significant difference
Natural sciences	831	41	Business greater ($p < 0.01$)
Social sciences and humanities	2,477	39	Business greater ($p < 0.001$)
Education	1,495	39	Business greater ($p < 0.001$)
Communications	289	39	Business greater ($p < 0.03$)

cheating in dentistry and pharmacy. In the past, we have observed and reported statistically higher levels of self-reported cheating among business students than among all other groups except engineering students (McCabe 1997). For the high level of cheating among arts students evident in table 8.1, we have no explanation. In the case of health sciences, we are not as surprised, based on our earlier analysis of cheating among both dental and pharmacy students. Of course, it is also possible that some of the difference is due to the difference in composition of the Bowers index used here and the index used in our earlier work (McCabe, Butterfield, and Treviño 2006), which included behaviors related to Internet plagiarism.

We also were able to conduct a somewhat more detailed analysis of business students compared with an aggregate of all non-business students by studying the individual components of the Bowers index for the business versus non-business students. Looking first at total self-reported cheating in the two groups, we see the expected result: 46% of the MBA students self-reported engagement in one or more of the nine components of the Bowers index, compared with 40% of the non-business students. (This analysis was conducted using the 10,973 graduate students at schools with MBA programs [N = 74] who answered all nine components of the Bowers cheating scale and supplied information about their major.) The difference between business and non-business self-reported engagement in the components of Bowers's cheating scale was highly significant ($p < 0.001$) for the full scale, as well as for two components: "working on the same homework with several students when the teacher does not allow it," or collaboration, and "copying a few sentences of material without footnoting it in a paper." But self-report rates for two other components were significantly larger for the non-business students: "getting questions or answers from someone who has already taken the same exam," or getting pretest information ($p < 0.01$), and "giving answers to other students during an exam" ($p < 0.05$). Four of the nine behaviors were statistically equivalent: "plagiarized from published material on papers," "copying from another student on a test or exam," "turned in papers done entirely or in part by other students" or turned in the work of another, and "used crib notes during an exam." And the final behavior, "padding a few items on a bibliography," was self-reported more often by the non-business students ($p < 0.01$).

Trying to make some sense out of these data, it seems clear that business students, on average, generally self-report more cheating than many of their peers—at both the graduate student and undergraduate level. Among graduate students, dental and pharmacy students appear to be an exception to this general conclusion, but larger sample sizes are needed to validate such a conclusion, and the question of how pharmacy students perceive collaborative work must be addressed as well. It also seems clear that as ethical scandals have become more commonplace in business, the average citizen expects more and is beginning to demand more from business executives and from business schools. In chapter 9, we offer advice on what those concerned about this serious issue might do to address it, based on our research and experience.

Conclusion

The picture is not good when it comes to academic integrity in professional schools, although not much research is available and much more needs to be done. Some of our data suggest somewhat lower levels of cheating at law schools than at other professional schools, but we have raised the possibility that this may simply be a reflection of how concerned students, faculty, and administrators are about the bar admission process and how reluctant (fearful) students (and faculty and administrators) are to admit, even anonymously, to anything that might affect successful admission to the bar. If fear of the bar process reduces the level of student cheating, this is good for law schools. But the question remains, once the bar process has been successfully negotiated, what is to encourage newly minted lawyers to behave with integrity? Schools of pharmacy and dentistry should also be seriously concerned about the levels of cheating. And as business school professors, we have a special interest in and concern about the relatively high level of academic dishonesty in business schools.

Given evidence that creating a culture of integrity does reduce cheating, we hope that professional school faculty and administrators are thinking about the best ways to create such cultures in their environments. We know little about the percentage of professional schools that have engaged in such efforts. This is an area ripe for future research.

CHAPTER NINE

Creating a Culture of Integrity

Practical Advice for Faculty and Administrators

B ased on the research cited in this book and our experience in the field, we can state with certainty that an academic dishonesty problem exists in our educational institutions. Research has found unacceptable levels of cheating in high school, college, and even professional school environments. Where longitudinal data exist, we have learned that while some types of cheating appear to have declined (e.g., some kinds of test cheating), other types have increased with changes in technology (e.g., more Internet-based cut-and-paste plagiarism) and changes in society (e.g., more collaboration-based cheating). As a reminder, almost all (if not all) of the multi-campus studies of cheating are based on self-reports. And recent studies have been conducted online, leading to lower response rates. These methodological issues, along with the open-ended comments offered by students and faculty in our surveys, suggest that the prevalence of cheating is probably even higher than reported in these studies. Cheating also seems to be rampant in the broader culture, where scandals have emerged in every sector of society, from sports to religious institutions, nonprofits, and business. All of this might cause us, like some of the faculty and students we have surveyed, to conclude that cheating is simply part of human nature and that nothing can or needs to be done about it. But, as should be evident by now, we believe strongly that something can and must be done, and we have some ideas about how we might approach the problem. We do not profess to have easy or foolproof answers. It has taken a long time to arrive at the current state, and it will take time and much hard work to reverse the trends. Commitment, patience, and persistence will be the keys to success.

Before we get to our ideas, you might ask, as we did earlier, why we or anyone else should take this problem on. Shouldn't ethical training and development be the responsibility of parents and religious institutions? And, if they're failing, isn't college too late to do anything about the problem? As we said at the beginning of this book, we don't think so. First, many if not most students attend college far from these earlier influences. We know from work discussed in earlier chapters that contextual influences are important, and for most undergraduate students, especially those living on campus, the college environment represents their most influential context for four or more years. That's a lot of time given to us, as educators, to have an impact on their thinking and actions. And it is certainly not too late. Research tells us that the college years are crucial to ongoing moral development and that such development continues at least into early adulthood (Feldman and Newcomb 1969; Rest and Thoma 1986). According to the most prominent moral psychology research, in the Kohlbergian tradition of cognitive moral development (Kohlberg 1969), young people at this life stage are continuing to develop their cognitive capacity to reason about ethical issues (Rest and Thoma 1986). College is a time of questioning and realigning values and beliefs before heading out into the "real world," and it is typically a time of continuing moral development. According to Kohlberg's theory, individuals advance in cognitive moral development by having their current way of thinking challenged, either through hypothetical moral dilemmas or, better yet, by engaging in discussion of real dilemmas that they face. Educators have many opportunities to challenge students' thinking both inside and outside the classroom.

We believe strongly that, as educators, we should take on this responsibility, because (as we noted in chapter 1) we are educating the leaders, managers, and professionals of tomorrow. We have a moral obligation to teach our students that it is possible and preferable to live and operate in an environment of trust and integrity where cheating is simply unacceptable.

Is such an environment really possible? It is hard for many to believe that one could experience four years of college without observing *any* cheating. But one of us who attended a traditional honor code institution actually had that experience (albeit a long time ago). Even today, ask students attending a college with a strong honor code environment about cheating, and you'll probably be surprised at the experience they relate and the pride with which they relate it.

Admittedly, our studies suggest that such reactions seem to be waning somewhat. In our 1990/1991 honor code survey, it was common for students attending institutions with traditional honor codes to talk about how they would be "socially embarrassed" if their peers knew they had cheated. Not only would cheating risk the continued existence of a system most students viewed as a privilege worth protecting, but it would suggest some students were taking an unfair advantage of their peers as well. We saw lots of evidence of this type of open-ended comment in our 1990/1991 survey, but such comments are harder to find in our more recent honor code studies. So, we recognize that traditional honor codes have become a harder "sell" to the current generation of students, many of whom seem to place more emphasis on individual success than on community norms and seem to feel more emboldened than prior generations to question the legitimacy of testing and grades. As some students tell us, getting their degree with good grades is what counts; how they do it is less important. In some cases, they note what they perceive to be the mantra of society today: achieving the bottom line, being admitted to their first-choice graduate school and program, or getting a job with the right firm at maximum salary. And following the example they think they see in the older generation, how they achieve their goals seems less important to many of these students than actually achieving them. What these changing attitudes mean to us is that, if we're going to do something, now is the time to do it. Action is needed before it's too late.

Beyond our moral obligation as educators, there is a more instrumental reason to address the issue. Many of our "customers," the private and public organizations that hire our students, care more about issues of integrity now than ever before. The best of them are addressing concerns about integrity through offices of ethics and compliance, where they develop codes of conduct, training programs, telephone lines for asking questions and reporting observed misconduct, and systems for investigating reports of code violations and imposing sanctions. Some of this is required by regulation, but not all. Given the transparency in today's environment, organizations are realizing that they simply can't afford the costs of the next scandal. So they are investing heavily in these systems, and they are looking to higher education to help by sending them graduates who are familiar with and have experience living in similar systems. A student who has lived in a strong environment of academic integrity, for example, should feel quite comfortable answering integrity-related interview questions and then entering a private or public organization that has an ethics code and expectations for appropriate behavior. One important finding of our research is that students from colleges with traditional honor codes who join work organizations with strongly embedded ethical environments are less likely to engage in unethical behavior later in their careers (McCabe, Treviño, and Butterfield 1996). So, by focusing on these issues, we hope we are better preparing our students to work in, and one day to lead, the best organizations.

Building a Culture of Integrity

We continue to believe that traditional honor code environments can have a significant impact on academic integrity, but we have observed numerous times that it is not the existence of a "code," per se, that makes the difference. What makes the difference is that the institution's environment encourages the development and maintenance of an ethical community—what we are calling a culture of integrity. Some traditional honor code schools and no-code schools have done this well. Others have not. We take an ethical culture approach to understanding the difference.

A number of scholars have emphasized the role of culture in either supporting or preventing cheating, as in Callahan's (2004) treatment of the general cheating culture in the United States and in several recent books and articles that discuss the importance of building a campus culture of honesty and integrity (Bertram-Gallant 2008; Lathrop and Foss 2005; Scanlan 2006; Whitley and Keith-Spiegel 2001). For example, Scanlan argued that promoting academic integrity and reducing cheating requires a "comprehensive strategy that promotes an institutional culture of academic integrity" (2006, 179). In Scanlan's view, such a strategy must combine efforts to detect and deter academic misconduct, a system of enforcement that emphasizes clear, consistent, and fair application of sanctions for those who violate standards, academic integrity training coupled with reinforcement in the classroom (e.g., honor pledges), faculty role modeling, and strong and visible support from administrators for upholding standards of academic integrity. In his case study of a major public university implementing an academic honor code, Dufresne (2004, 201) argued as follows:

> Previous research concerning academic honor codes and other ethics codes highlight the importance of enacting a more ethical organizational culture as well as involving many organizational members in the process . . . the design and implementation of ethics codes can help

effect change in the ethical culture by instilling and reinforcing the values of honesty and integrity . . . codes must be designed with full acknowledgement of the traditions and culture present in the student body, with the involvement of virtually all organization members, to elicit a full understanding of the ethical culture system.

We agree with these authors. But, going beyond their recommendations, we would like to offer a systematic ethical culture perspective to illustrate why a cultural approach is so important. To a large extent, the ethical culture perspective we outline here is consistent with the ethical community-building approach we have discussed elsewhere (McCabe, Treviño, and Butterfield 2002, 2004; Trevino and McCabe 1994). Ethical community building is an integrated approach to promoting academic integrity and curbing cheating, one that involves cooperation among faculty, administrators, and students, as well as broader institutional and programmatic efforts. Ethical community building emphasizes moral education, the socialization of members into an aspirational community, the creation of normative pressures, the development of mutual respect between students and faculty, and the promotion and development of a commitment to prosocial values such as mutual trust, respect, and supportiveness (McCabe, Treviño, and Butterfield 2001).

Our approach to understanding how to build a culture of integrity at a higher education institution borrows from this earlier work on ethical community building and from Treviño's work on developing and maintaining an ethical culture that was originally developed to apply to work organizations (Treviño 1990; Treviño and Nelson 2011). Think of culture as representing an organization's "personality." It is what differentiates one organization from another. When people describe an organization's culture, they're describing "how we do things around here" and how we think about what we do.

According to Treviño, an organization's ethical (or unethical) culture represents "how we do things" in relation to ethical and unethical behavior. The ethical culture can best be understood as a complex interplay among various formal and informal cultural systems that can promote either ethical or unethical behavior. Formal cultural systems include formal communication by senior administrators, selection systems, values, policies and codes, orientation and training programs, authority structures, reward systems, and decision-making processes. Informal systems include the organization's heroes and role models, rituals, the

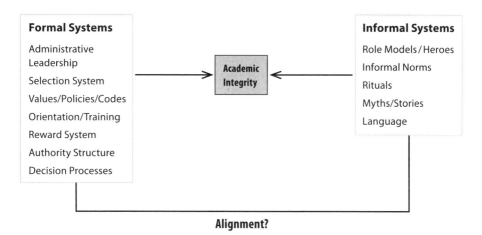

FIGURE 9.1.   Creating a culture of academic integrity: a multisystem approach. From L. K. Treviño and K. A. Nelson, *Managing Business Ethics: Straight Talk about How to Do It Right*, 5th ed. (New York: John Wiley & Sons, 2011). Used with permission of John Wiley & Sons, Inc.

use of ethical language, and behavioral norms that support integrity and discourage dishonesty. Figure 9.1 shows the visual model that has guided this work (Treviño and Nelson 2011).

If we move, step by step, through the model, we can better understand how it can help create a strong culture of academic integrity in a higher education institution and can reduce cheating. It's important to recognize that this model can also be used to understand how a school might develop a strong cheating culture, or how its culture might end up sending mixed signals because of misalignments among components of the cultural system.

Formal Systems

Let's assume that the goal is to create a strong culture of academic integrity, and let's begin with formal systems.

Administrative Leadership

Administrative leadership plays a large role, because executive leaders (in our case, senior administrators) have a lot of power to influence the integrity culture. Top-level administrative (particularly presidential) involvement sends a clear message to students and faculty that academic integrity is a major institutional priority. Senior administrators can communicate a strong and aspirational integrity message (perhaps during orientations and at various events throughout the year) and, of considerable importance, can provide resources to support ongoing integrity-related staff and activities. The message should be primarily values-based and aspirational, with the understanding that the aspirations are backed up by just procedures that hold students accountable for violations of the academic integrity policy. One challenge is the short terms of many of today's administrators. If one has a dean who cares deeply about academic integrity and conveys this in regular messages, what happens when that dean leaves and a new one arrives on the scene? If integrity is already embedded in the culture, one hopes that candidates for dean will be selected in part based on their commitment to it. But, given the importance of fundraising for today's higher education administrators, we suspect that commitment to an ethical culture may take a back seat to other commitments and skills. That's why it becomes so important to institutionalize integrity as much as possible into multiple cultural systems. Also, because most senior administrators are extraordinarily busy, we are convinced that development and/or maintenance of a culture of academic integrity must be a significant portion of some administrator's job in every college. The best approach is to name an academic integrity officer (preferably reporting to the senior administrator), similar to the ethics officers in many businesses, and this individual can provide continuing executive leadership in integrity, backed by the senior administrator. This person's job description should include a mandate to regularly assess the ethical culture and to keep the culture of academic integrity, among faculty, students, and administrators, alive and well in the institution. Some background in student development as well as in organizational development and change, and even in communications and marketing, would be helpful for such an individual. Indeed, student development experience is probably essential; we believe that no attempt to change the culture will occur without the support, and involvement of students.

The Selection System

The selection system is also important, so that the institution selects students who understand—before they even choose to apply—that a strong culture of academic integrity exists at the school. For example, for the University of Virginia (UVA), most Virginia high school students have heard about its honor code. Schools might utilize recruitment materials that include information about the academic integrity culture and the importance of the school's values. Admissions materials might include the code of conduct and might ask students to sign it and to write an integrity-related essay that would be evaluated as part of the admissions package. Sending these materials to a student's home has the advantage of alerting parents that this is an important issue at the institution, perhaps spurring discussion between students and parents on this topic. Some administrators have noted the "problem" of "helicopter parents" who, because of cell phones and other technology, are much more involved in students' lives than they were decades ago. But administrators may be able to use this involvement to their advantage when it comes to enlisting parental support for academic integrity. Also important is that sending these materials home can alert the student to the likely difference between high school and college on academic integrity issues. Given our research on high school cheating, this seems to be really important. In this way, socialization can begin even before a student arrives.

We understand the intentions of various business schools that have recently signed on to use plagiarism detection software to discourage students from plagiarizing all or part of their admissions essays (Bolkan 2011), a practice that appears to be prevalent but one that, we believe, has some problematic aspects. In particular, we are concerned about the level of distrust it may establish between the student and the school in their first formal interaction. Although the use of plagiarism detection software can be one element of a larger selection process that focuses on the integrity of incoming students, in our systems view, it should not be used by itself, if at all, without other cultural efforts. If this is all that a school does, it may "force" students to write their own essays, but it may also "push" them to utilize ghostwriters who write original essays for a fee or to use other less than ethical methods to enhance their applications. In these scenarios, the school has done little to help a student become more ethical or understand the value of being a member of an ethical community. On the other hand, if a focus on integrity begins in the admissions process, is properly positioned and explained to applicants, and is embedded in other cultural systems, applicants will get their first taste of the integrity culture well before they arrive. Some may even choose the school because of it (and others may choose to go elsewhere for the same reason).

Finally, hiring of faculty (and administrators, as noted above) should include questions about their experience with and attitudes toward academic integrity. For example, if unproctored exams are the norm at the institution, prospective faculty members should be willing to participate.

Values, Policies, and Codes

Values play a central role in shaping an ethical culture (Treviño 1990). Values can be thought of as a lens through which organizational members evaluate action—good versus bad, appropriate versus inappropriate, desirable versus undesirable. Values act as a touchstone for students and faculty when there is doubt about the appropriateness of a given policy or behavior. For example, when a student questions why an instructor considers "collaborative cheating" (collaborating on written assignments when the instructor has explicitly asked for individual work) inappropriate, the school's value system can bridge the gap between instructor and student by providing a context for discussion. For instance, if the school's stated values include fairness, trust, and respect, the instructor might initiate a discussion regarding how collaboration by some students is not fair to other students (those who adhere to the rules) and how violating classroom rules erodes respect and trust between students and faculty.

One type of strong value system that can help to guide development of a culture of academic integrity is based in restorative justice (Goodstein and Butterfield 2010; Karp and Allena 2004; Karp and Conrad 2005) and in values such as inclusiveness, humility, reparation, respect, honesty, compassion, patience, open-mindedness, and restoration of damaged relationships (as opposed to simply punishing misconduct) (Pranis 2007). The restorative justice approach traditionally has been used in criminal justice and social welfare systems and is now being used to address student misconduct at an increasing number of colleges and universities, including the University of Michigan, the University of Colorado at Boulder, and Colorado State University. Restorative justice is defined as "a process whereby all the parties with a stake in a particular offense come together to resolve collectively how to deal with the aftermath of the offense and its implications for the future" (Braithwaite 1999, 5).

At the heart of this approach is the restorative justice conference, in which a trained facilitator convenes the affected parties, including the offender (the student who cheated), the victims (e.g., the faculty member who reported the incident, other students), and other key community members (e.g., administrators), for a face-to-face conversation aimed at repairing harm and restoring damaged relationships (Braithwaite 2000). Restorative justice conferences pursue three basic objectives: restoring victims, reintegrating offenders back into the community, and facilitating community healing (Braithwaite 1999). Restoring victims involves receiving an apology or other compensation and offering forgiveness. Offender reintegration involves accepting responsibility and accountability, feeling remorse, earning redemption, offering an apology and/or other amends, and engaging in respectful dialogue with those affected by the wrongdoing. Community healing involves building trust, offering forgiveness to offenders, collective education and learning, rebuilding relationships, and restoring the community's "moral fabric" (Braithwaite 1999; Goodstein and Aquino 2010; Goodstein and Butterfield 2010; Walker 2006). In the context of violations of academic integrity, offenders are encouraged to take responsibility and make amends (e.g., apologize) for their actions. Victims and third parties affected by the incident are encouraged to forgive the offender and begin the process of reintegrating the offender back into the community. An example of the restorative justice (RJ) approach is described on the student affairs website at the University of Colorado (www.colorado.edu/StudentAffairs/judicialaffairs/restjust.html):

> The RJ process brings together in a safe environment the offender and the people harmed or affected by the offender's actions. Also included in the conference or "circle" are a trained RJ facilitator and co-facilitator, and family and/or friends of the offender and the harmed party or parties . . . During the conference, the offender accepts responsibility and talks about what happened; the harmed and affected parties describe how they have been affected; and all parties prepare a "harm-repairing" contract . . . the RJ approach allows participants to focus on understanding the harm that has occurred to relationships and to the community, and to decide how to best repair it.

The restorative justice approach represents an important emerging trend. Although restorative justice practices may not be appropriate for all institutions or for all violations of academic integrity—such as cases involving repeated offenses or rampant and systemic cheating—in instances such as first offenses or minor violations of academic integrity policy, they can be meaningfully integrated into or replace existing campus judiciary processes. We believe that, as educators, we should consider approaches such as these, which have great restorative and educational potential for a student who has crossed the line but can learn from the mistake.

In complete contrast to a restorative justice approach, an institution's values may not support a strong integrity culture at all. Instead, the values can define a "law-and-order" culture. In such environments, students are less trusted, and an emphasis is placed on values such as obedience, the rule of law, and deterrence. Administrators and faculty control policies and procedures and go to great lengths to monitor students' behavior and enforce rules (perhaps through the use of plagiarism detection software, for example, as noted earlier), sending students a strong message that cheaters will be caught and punished severely and that students have little role to play in the system. In our view, such a law-and-order orientation will lead only to a fear-based cheating culture (rather than an aspirational culture of integrity) in which students are motivated only to avoid getting caught.

A campus's integrity culture becomes stronger when aspirational values are widely understood and shared across the campus. One way this can happen is through the adoption of codes and policy statements designed to provide guidance for action and provide ways for members of the culture to enact those values. Codes of academic integrity often begin with broad statements of values such as honesty, integrity, transparency, accountability, responsibility, fairness, trust, and respect. Such values are typical in strong traditional honor code environments, for example. Specific policies and codes are then developed based on these values and should be consistent with them. These policies and codes often develop over time, as an institution's experience with academic integrity grows. Policies and codes can become quite detailed, providing examples of rule violations, for example. Although such examples are obviously necessary and useful, we caution against becoming too rule-oriented and too detailed, because it's impossible to write a rule to cover every situation, and such an approach could lead community members to focus on avoiding breaking specific rules rather than behaving in accordance with the community's values. Institutions must struggle continuously to achieve the right balance between values and rules.

Orientation and Training

Once students and new faculty members arrive on campus, the existing values and policies should be reinforced, and orientation/training should be provided so that both students and faculty understand how the academic integrity culture works and what their responsibilities are. For example, if peer confrontation is an expectation, students should be trained to understand this procedure and how to go about it. We know of at least one institution that currently provides students with training and practice in confronting peers about violations of academic integrity.

Training must also make clear what cheating is. For example, in our experience, many students don't understand the meaning of plagiarism, especially as it applies to online sources. A related issue is that the definition of cheating may be a moving target, unless we can get students and faculty to agree about exactly what it is. Even students who claim to be non-cheaters at institutions with strong honor codes have suggested on recent surveys that behaviors many people would have considered cheating ten or twenty years ago are not cheating in their minds. Just a few comments from our most recent study (conducted in the 2005/2006 academic year) at some of the country's more elite private schools seem to underscore this thinking.

I have participated in "trivial cheating" . . . but I do not participate in "serious cheating" because my parents would be really disappointed.

Cheating has evolved to the point where it is viewed on [a] sliding scale . . . I think that is part of the problem.

My social group accepts minor cheating (rare instances of plagiarism, fabricating some lab data and help on individual homework assignments) but we do not condone outright cheating (cheating on tests, buying papers online, copying/plagiarizing entire works).

The definition of cheating for these students seems relative, dependent not only on the particular act itself, but also on the situation or circumstances surrounding the act (e.g., was the testing fair, was the assignment reasonable and learning oriented?). Although we cannot cite quantitative data to support our view, we believe that students today feel freer to define what is and is not cheating in their own self-interest than did students in 1990/1991, when we started this project. Those earlier students seemed to hold views about cheating that paralleled those of the faculty to a greater degree. Obviously, dialogue is needed, and students, faculty, and administrators need to work together to ensure that everyone agrees about what constitutes cheating and why. Developing a strong culture of academic integrity will be impossible without such basic understanding.

Students and faculty also need to understand how suspected cheating cases are handled through the judiciary system and what their role will be if they are asked to serve on a review board, or if, as a new faculty member, they have to process a complaint of cheating. One of the problems with many existing judicial systems is a failure to effectively orient new faculty on how to handle a suspected case of cheating. As a result, many new faculty members turn to more senior colleagues for advice, as we discussed in chapter 7. Unfortunately, a senior colleague may relay a bad experience (perhaps one that occurred a decade or more ago). For example, a failure to find a student responsible for cheating simply on the faculty member's word that he or she "saw" the student cheating is a system failure in that faculty member's view. Some faculty members feel they should have total authority in this "academic" arena and feel strongly about the intrusion of staff people (especially those from student affairs). Others who have not had bad experiences themselves may pass on horror stories they've heard about how much time it takes to address a violation of academic integrity or how the faculty member becomes the "accused" in an honor board hearing. These stories, often exaggerated, take on the status of urban legends in many schools as they are passed around (as in the old telephone game). Therefore, communication about how the system really works is very important; for example, faculty who have had good experiences and would use the system again can share their stories in orientation sessions. But in spite of such challenges, training can have a big impact on participants, because it begins to bring home the accountability side of the academic integrity culture. Faculty need to be convinced that the system is not designed to put "them" on trial and that it is fair to all involved. Note that turnover among faculty tends to be high at some institutions. And many institutions are hiring adjunct faculty or using doctoral students to teach classes. All of those with responsibility for instruction need to be socialized into the integrity culture, so that they learn about their essential role in maintaining the culture and why it is important for them to do so as a contribution to the larger community of integrity.

We can think about the training and education associated with academic integrity policy as contributing to the creation of a "hidden curriculum" in which students learn about ethics outside any formal ethics courses or classroom training (which we also recommend). This hidden curriculum provides opportunities for students to actively discuss ethical issues and develop moral reasoning capacity through discussion of real-life ethical dilemmas (Treviño and McCabe 1994). This can happen in town hall meetings and other venues designed to get students wrestling with ethical issues related to academic integrity. Students can also learn about ethics outside the classroom by getting involved in designing or changing the campus's academic integrity policies and in educating other students about the importance of academic integrity.

Reward Systems

In work organizations, the "reward system" refers to the system of performance management that includes goal setting and the use of rewards and discipline for job performance. In an academic setting, the sanctions imposed for violations of academic integrity are part of the reward and disciplinary system. For example, some schools, such as Washington and Lee University in Virginia, have a single sanction policy (expulsion) for violation of the honor code. Other schools, such as Bryn Mawr College, have a more rehabilitative orientation. Many schools fall between these two extremes and have recommended sanctions for different types of violations. We are not recommending a particular approach, because we believe schools must choose an approach that fits their institution and its unique culture and traditions. But students (and their parents) need to fully understand the system and how the accountability part of it works.

Reward systems that support academic integrity should apply to all members of the institution, including faculty. Without strong training and incentives, faculty may gloss over academic integrity policies as "boilerplate" parts of the syllabus and look the other way in the face of cheating, believing that the pursuit of such instances will result in lower course ratings—a sentiment we have seen expressed in more than a few of the open-ended comments on our faculty surveys, as we noted in chapter 7. But what if the establishment of a strong environment of academic integrity in the classroom became a part of faculty evaluation? In the Smeal College of Business at Penn State, the dean worked with a faculty advisory committee to add a question about academic integrity to student evaluation forms, completed at the end of each course. Students evaluate faculty on whether they have established a strong environment of academic integrity in the classroom. Because people tend to pay attention to what is measured and rewarded, such a system can focus faculty's attention more on their key role in maintaining the integrity culture. As we suggested in chapter 7, faculty members' role is essential because they are the institutional representatives that students interact with the most. They are on the front lines. Therefore, they must make integrity an important part of their courses, they must talk about it regularly in relation to deliverables, and they must be willing to address violations of academic integrity policy when they occur. Even if their institution does not have a strong culture of academic integrity, individual faculty members can create such an environment in their own classes (Cummings and Romano 2002).

Authority Structure

With regard to the school's authority structure, it is important to think about how students, faculty, and administrators work together to build the culture of integrity. We believe that all must be involved in a system that supports open communication and close working relationships. We talked in chapter 7, and in the discussion above, about the important role of faculty, and we believe that it is absolutely essential to success. But in our experience, the strongest cultures of academic integrity exist at schools that have ceded a lot of authority and responsibility to students, who become the "owners" of the academic integrity system. In earlier work we have noted that student involvement is central to building an ethical community (McCabe and Pavela 2000). With proper guidance, students can play a vital role in designing and enforcing standards of academic integrity, and students' involvement encourages them to take responsibility for their own and their classmates' behavior. When an institution defines ethical behavior as part of the student role, students learn that being part of an ethical community requires them to uphold the rules and actively participate in the enforcement process (McCabe, Treviño, and Butterfield 2001). With this approach, faculty members and administrators play a supporting role, albeit a critical one. They become involved in an ongoing dialogue about academic integrity and how best to promote it at their institution. Once a strong culture of academic integrity becomes established, faculty members are often surprised at how seriously students take their responsibility and how well they carry it out. Once students take on this ownership, it is up to faculty and administrators to work with them, support them, and guide them when they need guidance. Our empirical research has supported the use of ethical community-building techniques, including establishing a dialogue on academic integrity between faculty and students, clearly communicating expectations and responsibilities to students, demonstrating that academic integrity is a clear institutional priority, and involving students in promoting a culture of integrity at the institution (McCabe and Treviño 1993, 2002; McCabe, Treviño, and Butterfield 2002).

One extremely touchy issue is the reporting of violations and whose responsibility that is. In traditional honor code environments, students are often required, or at least encouraged, to report violations of academic integrity, and in some cases they are in violation of the honor code if they don't. This student responsibility goes hand in hand with important freedoms that are generally part of these environments, such as unproctored exams. But the reporting requirement has always been and continues to be the most controversial aspect of traditional honor codes. Today's students appear to be increasingly reluctant to accept a peer reporting requirement, even in institutions with traditionally strong environments of academic integrity. Our research suggests that peer reporting is currently low almost everywhere.

The problem is not restricted to schools. Reporting of unethical conduct is also a huge problem in work organizations, and the underlying psychology is the same. People are reluctant to report misconduct they observe, because, first, they fear retaliation (from peers or leaders) and, second, are concerned that nothing will be done (Milliken and Morrison 2003; Milliken, Morrison, and Hewlin 2003). Why bother sticking one's neck out if nothing is going to come of the report anyway? In response to the first concern, the best work organizations go to great lengths to protect reporters. For example, in one company we know, a secretary reported her boss for lying on his expense reports. To maintain the anonymity of the secretary, the organization launched an investigation into the expense reports of every manager at that level in the company. In that way, no one would be able to trace the tip to the secretary. It may not always be possible to protect the reporter, but an institution that wishes to require (or strongly encourage) reporting must ensure as much protection for the reporter as possible. That might mean that a case will be weaker. But, in our experience, most individuals simply won't risk reporting without anonymity.

The second issue can be tough to address, because—unless a student is expelled—the reporter may never know what happened, due to student privacy protections. Work organizations struggle with this same issue. To help address this concern, some institutions post notices on academic integrity websites that list violations (without identifying the violator) and the associated sanctions, so that students know that some action is being taken, even if they can't know what that action was in a particular instance.

In recent years, at the many campus presentations he has made, McCabe has argued that schools, even those with traditional honor codes, should consider dropping the "requirement" to report peers. His logic is that we know that many violations go unreported even though students know they exist. So if we "require" reporting when we know that most students will ignore the "requirement," we are probably just giving students a rationale to ignore other important aspects of the policy or to be cynical about the entire academic integrity culture. If so, it may be worthwhile not to require (but rather to strongly encourage) reporting, while working on the other issues identified above (protecting reporters and ensuring that students know action is being taken).

In fact, our data suggest that at least some students may be willing to accept responsibility for reporting. For example, more than one-third of the respondents in our 2005/2006 survey of selective institutions said they were likely to report an incident of cheating they observed. This may indicate at least some student willingness to accept responsibility for reporting violations. The difficult task will be discovering what form of responsibility students are comfortable with and what will be required to achieve it.

Our experience at one institution, however, may illustrate how difficult this challenge is. Several years ago, McCabe was involved in a visit to a highly selective school that thought it had done all its homework to garner a yes vote from the three major constituencies on campus—students, faculty, and administration—for adoption of a traditional honor code. Unfortunately, they lost the student vote, and further research revealed that the vote was lost simply because the proposed code included a peer reporting requirement. Students argued that they had no problem signing a pledge that they had done their own work honestly, but they had *strong* objections to pledging that they would report any cheating they observed. Childhood memories seemed to fill their minds at this point, as they indicated that they learned while growing up not to be a "narc," a "tattletale," or a "rat." And they strongly objected to the thought that their school or anyone else had the right to expect them to be. These sentiments seem to support the low level of actual reporting that we see. More than one-quarter of the general student population seem to appreciate that some reasonable level of reporting is essential to maintaining a level of integrity on their campus, and they want to do the "right" thing as defined by their campus integrity policies. We believe that schools need to address this issue more effectively than most have done thus far. And if students want more responsibility for academic integrity on their campus, they need to be willing to hold each other accountable. For example, it is likely to be almost impossible to implement unproctored exams without students' willingness to take on such responsibility. The key question is how we can accomplish this in today's academic environment.

Decision Processes

With decision processes, we include those processes involved in adjudicating honor code violations (discussed above). These need to be worked out in some detail. Questions to be answered include: Who investigates cheating claims, and how are investigations conducted? Who serves on honor boards, and how are these individuals selected? How do honor boards make decisions? How transparent should the processes and decisions be? Developing a system that produces decisions that are trusted by students and faculty is essential. But these processes should not be set in stone. They may need to be altered as the actors involved become more experienced with the types of cases that arise.

We should also ask whether the organization's standard operating procedures take into account ethical considerations. For example, when decisions are being made about curricular changes, are academic integrity issues automatically taken into account? When new faculty and administrators are hired, is their support for the ethical culture considered in the hiring decision? Students seem to be very aware when the school fails to follow ethical procedures and use such instances as an "excuse" or rationale for their own cheating—"If the school doesn't care that much, why should I?"

Informal Systems

The formal systems outlined above can help to fuel establishment of the informal systems that are so crucial to the success of a culture of academic integrity. Bazerman and Tenbrunsel made this very point about the importance of informal systems in work organizations: "Formal ethics and compliance programs represent only the tip of an organization's 'ethical infrastructure.' Underlying formal systems are informal norms and pressures that exert far more influence on [student] behavior than any formal efforts could" (2011, 103). In a variety of ways, informal systems convey to all community members what behavior is *really* expected.

Role Models and Heroes

On the informal side of the academic integrity culture, it's important to ask who the organization's role models and heroes are. Are they individuals of integrity, or does becoming a hero in the campus culture have nothing to do with integrity? Is it possible to be considered a hero for winning in sports, for example, with little concern for how one does it? Or are those who drink excessively the ones who receive the accolades on campus? If so, this signals the existence of an unethical culture. The institution can help by contributing to the creation of heroes and role models. For example, it can develop awards (and perhaps even scholarships) for students who have contributed to academic integrity in the institution. But it will be important to learn whom students identify as their heroes and role models. At many universities, although he or she may be admired, students typically don't name the university president when asked who their cultural hero on campus is. More typically they seem to name an athletic coach. If known for his or her integrity, then that coach can help support a culture of academic integrity on campus.

Informal Norms

As suggested by Bazerman and Tenbrunsel, "informal norms and pressures . . . exert far more influence on [student] behavior than any formal efforts could" (2011, 138). What are the relevant informal norms here? These are the typical behaviors that one sees in the institution, such as the "peer behavior" that, in our studies, has proved to be such an important influence on behavior (McCabe and Treviño 1993, 1997; McCabe, Treviño, and Butterfield 2002). Are students abiding by the academic integrity policies? Or is cheating rampant despite the policies? These norms go a long way toward demonstrating to students how things "really work around here" and how people really behave. As we've learned, it is the perception of what their peers do that is the largest driver of self-reported cheating for students. In a cheating culture, the perception that "everyone is cheating" has powerful negative effects on behavior. By contrast, in a strong culture of academic integrity, peers will look down on students who cheat and will not tolerate cheaters, because cheating is viewed as an insult to the integrity of the institution and to the legitimate efforts and hard work of the other students (McCabe and Treviño 1993; McCabe, Treviño, and Butterfield 2002). In a strong culture of academic integrity, there is a simple, clear message that ethical behavior is the norm.

Rituals

Rituals can also become an important part of a culture of academic integrity. For example, if a school asks every new student to sign an honor code or other form of integrity agreement or statement, this can be accomplished in an orientation session that culminates in a formal initiation ceremony, with the final product being displayed in a central location for all to see. Similarly, integrity rallies, academic integrity case competitions, and other regular events can support integrity as part of the culture.

We would like to offer one anecdote that seems to support the potential power of rituals as part of the broader ethical culture. When we conducted our first study of honor codes in the 1990/1991 academic year, we were struck by certain differences between two all-female campuses in the East, each of which had a long-standing honor code tradition. One campus, as revealed by comments made by juniors and seniors in our survey, had clearly made the decision to cut back on what most would probably describe as an elaborate honor code orientation induction ceremony for new students—evening gowns, candlelight, a formal signing signifying a student's acceptance of the code, and so on. Students at this school generally bemoaned this change and felt it diminished the power of their honor code. Our data tended to back this up, as self-reported cheating on this campus (using Bowers's [1964] 10-item measure) was more than one-quarter higher than at a very similar campus that we also surveyed in 1990/1991. This second women's college was similar in size, comparable in admissions standards, and had a similar mix of majors, strong alumni support, and so on. When we approached the first school and questioned the change in its honor code induction ceremony, it acknowledged that this had taken place primarily because the school felt that students were tiring of the traditional code signing ceremony. But our results on self-reported cheating helped convince the school to return to its tradition. When we surveyed both campuses five years later (in the 1995/1996 academic year), the difference in Bowers's summary measure of cheating between the two campuses was less than 2 percentage points. While there may be other possible explanations, an obvious difference was the reinvigoration of the code signing ceremony.

Myths and Stories

For any school, what are the stories people tell about what it's like to be a part of that institution? If someone were to ask about the school, would a student or faculty member naturally talk about the academic integrity environment as important to the culture, as many students in our qualitative research did when talking about their honor code institutions? For example, almost half of the students (41 of 96) offering a comment about motivations not to cheat at one of the strong honor code schools in our 2005/2006 web-based survey talked, in their open-ended comments, about the peer environment on campus as a major motivation. The following comment was typical:

[The] environment on campus is definitely the most important reason not to cheat. We are held to an honor system that everyone seems to abide by. If I were to cheat I'd be betraying the trust of the community.

Although stories also exist about students who were dismissed for violations of academic integrity, not surprisingly, they seem to be a notable part of the institutional lore only at those schools where expulsion or dismissal for such violations occur with at least some frequency and students are clearly aware of this possibility. And although several schools in our surveys seem to have used stories and myths to help support their code tradition, one campus stands out in particular.

Many years ago, McCabe was invited to speak at Washington and Lee University in Virginia, one of the few single sanction code schools left in the country, where any violation of the honor system's provisions, no matter how small or large, leads to permanent dismissal of the responsible student. McCabe's initial feeling was that it was unlikely that students truly supported such a provision, and he sought, and received, permission from the dean of students to challenge this point in a campus-wide address he was to give that evening. Speaking to a packed house—in spite of several more "enjoyable" events scheduled on campus for the same evening—McCabe was truly taken aback by the reception his challenge received. Speaking freely, almost every student who responded to the challenge spoke strongly in favor of the provision the way it was. Over and over again students said, "Honor knows no measure," a phrase *every* community member at Washington and Lee was familiar with, a phrase attributed to General Lee, whose sarcophagus happened to be positioned next to the dais from which McCabe was speaking, in the college chapel. Clearly, the stories associated with General Lee were having a positive impact on Washington and Lee students more than a century later.

Language

Finally, is ethical language an accepted part of the campus culture? Is it considered not only acceptable but expected to talk about academic integrity as part of the typical conversation? Do faculty members talk about academic integrity regularly in their classrooms as they discuss upcoming deliverables? Do students raise academic integrity issues with faculty and with each other? As suggested above, we know they do at Washington and Lee, and we are aware of several other major institutions where such discussions are common, even after the orientation of first-year students—which seems to be the only discussion that takes place at many schools and often consists of a monologue directed at students by some student affairs personnel. In contrast, at Rice University in Texas, for example, the faculty and administrators have entrusted upperclassmen to orient new students on Rice's pervasive honor system. These students make a point to meet with faculty before this orientation to ensure that they are covering points that the faculty feel are relevant and of which students might not be aware. This kind of working together is another key to success.

Alignment

Essential to the cultural model outlined here is the notion of alignment. Formal and informal systems must be aligned with each other, and all must support academic integrity to produce a strong culture of integrity. In addition, within the formal systems, reward systems must support the values, codes, and policies. If people are rewarded only for achieving grades, and it makes no difference how they achieved them, integrity will be seen as unimportant. If students perceive that their peers cheat and get away with it, that perception alone sends a powerful message that all the words about academic integrity are meaningless. And, between the formal and informal systems, the norms of daily behavior should match the behavior expected in the academic integrity policies. If these don't match, members of the organization get mixed signals about what is really expected and quickly become cynical as a result, thinking that the policy represents just words on a page rather than how one "lives" in the institution every day.

And, as suggested above, one can have a strong cheating culture if the formal and informal systems align to support unethical behavior. In institutions where cheating is rampant, one should ask whether senior administrators and selection systems are silent on academic integrity issues, whether students and faculty are cynical about academic integrity policies (if they even exist), and whether accountability systems are working. One should also ask whether the campus norms support cheating, the heroes are those who get ahead no matter how they get there, and students scoff at the idea that cheating might be controlled. If so, it's clear that the culture is in dire need of intervention.

Failure to follow the ethical culture approach and a lack of alignment among cultural systems is a sure path to failure. One university we know has long used a piecemeal approach to dealing with academic integrity issues. Cheating-related initiatives have been implemented from time to time, but these efforts appear to be driven largely by individual administrator agendas (e.g., to look more like peer institutions) rather than a strong institutional value system. This school has also tried XF grading, a system in which a grade of XF is placed on the student's transcript if cheating is found, with the X denoting that the grade of F was a result of academic misconduct. The X is typically removed if the student has successfully appealed the charge or completed remedial actions such as writing a paper or completing academic integrity training. But students don't seem to be very aware of this grading policy. The school has also seen individual colleges and departments within the university attempt to implement honor codes, but these have generally had little impact. Unfortunately, this school has discovered that, when enacted in isolation (i.e., without the guidance of a strong overarching culture, including a strong value system), such piecemeal changes are often ineffective and can lead to other problems, such as promoting cynicism on the part of students, faculty, and administrators and further eroding attempts to create a culture of academic integrity.

Emphasis on the Aspirational

We have also learned from research in business organizations (Treviño et al. 1999) and from our experience on the ground that people respond best to a culture that is perceived to be primarily aspirational in orientation. Of course, they expect the aspirational message to be backed up by enforcement of the rules and policies, because without such backup the aspirational message would be meaningless. But the general perception among members of the community—in this case, the campus community—must be that the organization is pursuing academic integrity because it cares about honor and that honor and integrity are crucial to the institution's identity. This is obviously a delicate dance (between aspirations and rule compliance). The perceptions of students and faculty should be checked regularly, and the culture tweaked if necessary.

Ongoing Work Is Required

The ethical culture model should also make clear that creating and sustaining a culture of academic integrity is challenging. It requires ongoing attention to and management of *all* of the formal and informal systems simultaneously. It should be abundantly clear that establishing a strong culture of academic integrity takes a lot more work than developing a code of conduct and hanging it on the wall (as a senior administrator said to one of us when his school was planning to institute an honor code "culture"). This may be why some commentators are so pessimistic about the cultural approach. Unfortunately, it seems that few institutions have provided the resources and, more importantly, the ongoing leadership commitment to sustain such an ethical culture over a long period of time. But just because it's hard doesn't mean that it isn't worthwhile or that it isn't the right way to proceed. Those that follow this path can reap huge benefits. And when you talk with students at institutions with strong cultures of academic integrity, you know it's worth it. From our very first survey in the 1990/1991 academic year, students (typically those at traditional honor code institutions) have taught us this lesson, which keeps us in pursuit of what some can only envision as an ideal— not a reality. Although much has changed in the past twenty years, comments from our 2005/2006 survey suggest that the basic feelings of at least some students have not.

> I believe cheating occurs less [here] than at other colleges because of the academic honesty policy which allows students to take self-scheduled exams. Students seem to love this option; and in order for it to continue, students must abide by the honesty code.

> [Our] honor code is a great document and respects students and the integrity they bring to their work. Violation of the honor code should be severe because it is a violation of trust. I do see the code as idealistic, but why not shoot high and expect high caliber students to hold and maintain high standards?

> This college makes the academic dishonesty policy very clear from day one. We operate on the honor system (unlike the college I transferred from where cheating was standard behavior) and I have not witnessed *any* incidences of abusing the honor system. I have complete trust in my fellow classmates that they do not cheat.

> I believe that cheating will happen anywhere, but that it is particularly *un*common [here]. The students, for the most part, respect the honor code.

> [My school's] students really take the honor code seriously—a lot of the violations are self-reported, but serious violations are extremely few & far between. (I only know of 1 in 3 years here.) Everyone trusts us & we respect that trust.

Our honor system works because of the freedoms we enjoy because of it. We recognize that without the honor code we would lose those freedoms, and therefore take it very seriously. I am not aware of anyone I know having cheated.

It is not socially acceptable to cheat.

There is a very clear honor code at [my school] that incoming students must pass a test about during orientation. It is well respected because it gives us freedoms like take home exams and as a consequence I don't think much cheating occurs because the students know & respect this contractual agreement that they are under not to cheat.

Overall, I am very impressed with the Honor Code here . . . It gives students the responsibility and integrity to do what is right.

The Cultural Approach Works

We have emphasized the ethical culture approach to academic integrity as an avenue worth pursuing because we have seen it work, and we believe it is the best option we have to improve students' behavior in a way that may have a *lasting* effect—an essential goal of any educational enterprise. Research has supported the connection between ethical culture and ethical conduct; to the extent that these formal and informal systems work in tandem to support ethical conduct, individual behavior is likely to be more ethical (e.g., Kish-Gephart, Harrison, and Treviño 2010). Our own research on overall organizational culture (Treviño, Butterfield, and McCabe 1998), as well as on individual cultural components such as reward systems (Treviño and Youngblood 1990) and codes of ethics (McCabe and Treviño 1993; McCabe, Treviño, and Butterfield 2002), also supports the culture-conduct connection.

How to Begin?

Anyone who hopes to tackle the academic integrity issue at their school must recognize the commitment it is going to take from multiple stakeholders. Efforts at cultural change are thought to take ten or more years to implement. Those involved must be aggressive, while being, at the same time, patient with the process. So, how would one begin?

It is important, first of all, to assess the campus's current culture of academic integrity, its strengths and weaknesses. This can be accomplished through carefully designed surveys and, more importantly, through focus groups with multiple stakeholder groups. These procedures should be targeted at understanding the current state of all cultural systems from multiple perspectives. What do students and faculty think are the biggest problems, and how would they propose solving them? Are students and faculty open to a change? Once you have a sense of the status quo, involve multiple stakeholders in the development of a plan of attack. We caution administrators not to force a particular approach. Rather, generate an initial level of support for the idea of building a culture of academic integrity among some students and faculty, and give them a key role in the process so that it does not come across as simply administrator-driven—an almost certain death knell in many schools (i.e., the administration's hare-brained idea of the month). We also encourage leaders not to undertake surveys or focus groups until the campus is ready to do something about any problems they might find. Raising the issue of academic integrity and then letting it die is worse than doing nothing at all. Once the campus decides to actually do something, it will be important to involve multiple stakeholders in decision making about what system would best fit the institution and how that system should be designed. Does a traditional honor code approach make sense? Would a modified honor code be a good way to begin, perhaps moving later to a more traditional honor code (which includes unproctored exams and peer reporting)?

We can't tell you what your ultimate goal should be. That should depend on an assessment of your local environment and what you think is possible, now and in the future. But we can say that any effort will require a significant investment of administrative, faculty, and student time. As we suggested earlier, students should be *heavily* involved, preferably the drivers of the process. If students feel they own the system, it has a better chance of success. A technique that has worked in the past is to form an Academic Integrity Advisory Council that consists of a diverse group of student leaders, as well as interested faculty and administrators. The assumption should be that students will play a major role in any system, including the resolution of contested cases. Student leaders can also help to educate their peers and to communicate and reinforce the culture of integrity, especially to incoming students. In the most effective and highly developed cultures, a student can chair the committee that investigates and resolves cheating cases.

Faculty also must play an important role in creating and sustaining a culture of academic integrity. In addition to supporting and guiding student leaders, faculty should assume facilitating roles on advisory councils and adjudication bodies and should be involved in developing fair, prompt, and efficient due process procedures. Faculty also "add teeth" to the system by enforcing penalties. We have found that faculty members react more positively if the system allows them at least some discretion to resolve less serious, first offenses. For example, the system may give faculty members responsibility for academic (grade-related) sanctions for such offenses. If a student agrees to the sanction, the matter is settled, and the faculty member need only file a simple report. If the student does not agree to the sanction, it goes to an honor board for adjudication. Ultimately, faculty play their most important role in their classrooms by addressing academic integrity issues, not just on day one, but regularly in relation to tests and assignments.

Administrators also play a key role. Presidents and deans can be especially important. We have found that student-led initiatives can be a particularly effective way of capturing a president's attention. Administrators must be willing to allocate resources to the ongoing development of the culture, and as noted above, it simply will not work to set something up and then expect it to run on autopilot. It will need to be someone's responsibility to regularly evaluate the culture, attend to multiple ethical culture systems, work with multiple stakeholders to make decisions about change, and then implement those changes.

It is essential that the designers of a new cultural approach to academic integrity recognize that there will be many challenges. First, not all stakeholders will agree about what needs to be done or that anything at all needs to be done. Although everyone can probably agree that honor and integrity are important, that doesn't mean they will all agree on what "honor and integrity" mean in their campus context or the best way to institutionalize those values into the local campus culture. Second, administrators should be ready for the cheating scandals that will probably occur. Such scandals have occurred at traditional honor code institutions over the years and should not necessarily be viewed as a bad thing; they are an indication that the system is making a difference (i.e., someone reported the misconduct). Scandals can also represent a teachable moment that faculty, students, and administrators can use to reaffirm campus commitment to the academic integrity culture. For example, we believe that most people truly familiar with the situations would agree that each time one of the service academies has had a cheating scandal in recent years (e.g., Schmitt 1994), it has strengthened the institution, as students, faculty, and administrators have come together in some way to protect the integrity of the institution and to preserve the student-led honor systems.

Although they haven't had to face such public scandals to test the mettle of their integrity systems, we would remind the reader about the institutions we have described as having especially strong or unique systems. In chapter 2, we mentioned the Haverford School, the Hutchinson School, and Norfolk Academy, among secondary schools. We've mentioned Washington and Lee as a particularly noteworthy example at the college level. Rice University is also a strong example among colleges. And we find the University of Virginia system to be particularly interesting, given its large size and its public (rather than private) character.

So, Where Do We Stand on Honor Codes Now?

Although we have reported research supporting the idea that traditional honor codes "work" (in the sense that cheating is lower at schools that have them), we have also reported on the evidence of some deterioration in the relation between honor codes and cheating between 1990/1991 and 1995/1996 (McCabe, Treviño, and Butterfield 2002). But, even though our data suggest that traditional honor codes may not be working as well as they once did, our experience and our ethical culture perspective lead us to think that this may have more to do with how some honor codes were implemented than with some flaw in the idea behind traditional honor codes.

Research by others has also raised questions about the effectiveness of honor codes. Roig and Marks (2006) examined students' attitudes before and after implementation of a modified honor code and found students' attitudes toward cheating to be largely unchanged by the code. But, as suggested above, these changes don't happen overnight, and modified honor codes have fewer of the traditional honor code elements. To understand whether implementation of an honor code has "worked," one may need to wait years to see whether it has been assimilated into the culture, and one must be sure that the "code" is accompanied by the other essential cultural changes we have described. Otherwise, it may be seen as "window dressing" only. As research in organizational ethics has shown, codes, by themselves, are not effective at changing behavior (Kish-Gephart, Harrison, and Treviño 2010).

Engler, Landau, and Epstein (2008) showed that, although students generally believe that honor codes would reduce the cheating behaviors of their friends and of the average student, many do not believe that honor codes are likely to have much of an effect on their own cheating behavior. We believe that this may be because these students have never actually experienced a strong honor code environment. We have found that even faculty members who have never experienced a strong honor code environment are quite skeptical that such an approach can work. In fact, they can be the most difficult stakeholders to bring on board. Enlisting faculty with strong honor code experiences (either while students or as faculty) can be persuasive with these skeptics.

Perhaps most critical of the traditional honor code approach, authors such as Susan Blum (2009) have argued that approaches focusing on institutional culture, including honor codes, are unlikely to be "universally successful." Bertram-Gallant and Drinan argued this point even more forcefully, referring to "an overemphasis on honor codes" and "the allure of culture" as two "blind alleys" (2006, 856):

> Honor codes cannot serve as the panacea for deficiencies in integrity because integrity cannot be institutionalized by symbolic activity alone. Although the "establishment of an honor code is the clearest statement that a college or university can make that it values and is committed to academic integrity" (Whitley & Keith-Spiegel, 2001, p. 339), most researchers agree that it is not sufficient in and of itself (e.g., Dalton, 1998; Jendrek, 1992; Whitley & Spiegel, 2001). The common practice then advocated has been to create a campus culture or ethos of integrity (Alschuler & Blimling, 1995; Dalton, 1998; Hendershott et al., 2000; Rudolph & Timm, 1998; Whitley & Keith-Spiegel, 2001). This advice may be valid, but it may confound reform. Campuses can be swept up in the design of honor codes and the discussion of culture change. As Kotter (1996) reminds us, culture is "difficult to challenge or even discuss" (p. 151) because a large number of people are unconsciously habituated to its norms and values. Frustrations with the magnitude of the problem, once it has

been diagnosed on a given campus, can lead to regression and cynicism, making progress unlikely. Consciousness of the two "blind alleys" provides a key sensibility in devising sophisticated strategies; there is no "magic bullet" in honor codes, and a preoccupation with campus culture can be so overwhelming or amorphous that paralysis can ensue.

We agree with some of these statements. For example, we agree that traditional honor codes are no panacea or magic bullet, and we have said that they must be part of a broader ethical culture-building effort. We are advocating for honor codes not as *the* solution to the problem but rather as one element of a much broader strategy. Nevertheless, unlike Bertram-Gallant and Drinan, we believe the overall body of evidence continues to support the effectiveness of honor code approaches for reducing academic dishonesty. We remain optimistic that there continues to be a place for honor codes in today's higher education institutions, *as long as* they are part of a broader culture of academic integrity. For us, culture goes well beyond "symbolic activity." And we are not put off by the idea that culture building and change are hard work. In our practical experience, we have learned that effective cultures of academic integrity can be created with systematic development of multiple cultural systems and ongoing nurturing from a broad range of stakeholders that includes students, faculty, and administrators, at a minimum. In some cases, even alumni get involved as they push for a stronger environment of integrity at their alma mater. So, we continue to believe in traditional honor codes to the extent that they follow the broader ethical culture approach.

We are also encouraged by subtle shifts that we detect in students' attitudes and behavior regarding the need to do something about what many perceive as a crisis of academic dishonesty at their institutions. For example, some traditional honor code institutions that sense their code environments are weakening have approached us for help, and in a surprising number of cases, the impetus for attention to the campus environment has come from students who are concerned about cheating in large classes or a public cheating incident of some kind. This may signal something of a pendulum swing, and we hope to convince faculty and administrators that the time is ripe to support student-initiated efforts to improve the state of cultures of academic integrity on their campuses.

Again, a traditional honor code is not the only approach to improving academic integrity; on many campuses it may not even be the best answer. Not surprisingly, it appears that what you do is a lot more important than what you call it. However, we note with interest the growing number of students who view positively the prospect of attending an institution that has some form of "code" as part of the overall culture of academic integrity.

We don't want to be perceived as Pollyannas. We have enough experience to know what the challenges are. But we are cautiously optimistic, because today's students seem ready for a change. As educators, we should enlist this readiness and open the discussion with students to see what they are really ready for. We strongly believe that doing nothing is simply not an option. And spending more time trying to identify the "perfect" solution is simply wasted time, because what will work best is likely to vary from campus to campus. For example, campuses that are large, that have large commuter populations with large numbers of students who are only peripheral members of the campus community, that lack a history of traditions, and so forth, are not strong candidates for a traditional honor code. But that does not mean we should do nothing on those campuses. Individual faculty members at such institutions, who may already be overtaxed with large teaching loads and advising responsibilities, will nonetheless need to carry an extra burden to accomplish this goal. But with the assistance of student affairs personnel, this investment is both critical and doable. And we believe that corporations and other organizations can help mandate such changes by selecting whom they choose to hire—graduates from which schools. Perhaps these "customers" (those who hire our students) can provide the incentive needed for schools to prioritize academic integrity as an institutional goal.

We hope that, in some small way, the work we have done over the past two decades helps convince teachers and administrators to make the move toward building a culture of academic integrity. There is no question that students are the ones doing most of the "cheating," but there is also little question that the "adults"—parents, administrators, and teachers—must *help* students fix the problem in a way that will enhance integrity in society in general, not just reduce cheating or academic dishonesty in our schools. We have called for a broad-based, multipronged, culture-building program that focuses on academic integrity. Doing so should reduce cheating, at a minimum. Our hope is that it will also turn out graduates who are more ethical in general, as we believe our society needs our future leaders to have a strong ethical base.

REFERENCES

CHAPTER ONE: *A Journey and a Commitment to Action*

Bowers, W.J. 1964. *Student Dishonesty and Its Control in College*. New York: Bureau of Applied Social Research, Columbia University.

Callahan, D. 2004. *The Cheating Culture: Why More Americans Are Doing Wrong to Get Ahead*. Boston: Houghton Mifflin Harcourt.

Feldman, K.A., and Newcomb, T.M. 1969. *The Impact of College on Students*. San Francisco: Jossey-Bass.

Frieden, T. 2009. Former Senate aide charged in Abramoff scandal. CNN.com, February 21. www.cnn.com/2009/CRIME/02/21/abramoff.aide.charged/.

Lindsay, J. 2005. Harvard rejects those who saw admissions site. *USA Today*, March 9. www.usatoday.com/tech/news/techpolicy/ethics/2005-03-09-reje cted-applicants_x.htm.

McCabe, D.L., Butterfield, K.D., and Treviño, L.K. 2006. Academic dishonesty in graduate business programs: Prevalence, causes, and proposed action. *Academy of Management Learning & Education* 5: 294–305.

McCabe, D.L., and Treviño, L.K. 1993. Academic dishonesty: Honor codes and other contextual influences. *Journal of Higher Education* 64: 522–538.

———. 1997. Individual and contextual influences on academic dishonesty: A multicampus investigation. *Research in Higher Education* 38: 379–396.

McCabe, D.L., Treviño, L.K., and Butterfield, K.D. 1996. The influence of collegiate and corporate codes of conduct on ethics-related behavior in the workplace. *Business Ethics Quarterly* 6: 461–476.

———. 1999. Academic integrity in honor code and non-honor code environments: A qualitative investigation. *Journal of Higher Education* 70: 211–234.

———. 2002. Honor codes and other contextual influences on academic integrity: A replication and extension to modified honor code settings. *Research in Higher Education* 43: 357–378.

Melendez, B. 1985. *Honor Code Study*. Cambridge, MA: Harvard University.

O'Connell, V. 2009. Test for dwindling retail jobs spawns culture of cheating. *Wall Street Journal*, January 7.

Rest, J.R., and Thoma, S.J. 1986. Educational programs and interventions. In J.R. Rest (ed.), *Moral Development: Advances in Research and Theory*, 38–58. New York: Praeger.

Sanford, N. 1964. Freshman personality: A stage in human development. In N. Sanford (ed.), *College and Character*, 86–90. New York: John Wiley and Sons.

Scannell, K., Bustillo, M., and Perez, E. 2009. SEC accuses Texas financier of "massive" $8 billion fraud. WSJ.com, February 18. http://online.wsj.com/article/SB123489015427300943.html.

Schemo, D.J. 2001. U. of Virginia hit by scandal over cheating. NYTimes.com, May 10. www.nytimes.com/2001/05/10/us/u-of-virginia-hit-by-scandal-over-cheating.html? scp=1andsq=u+of+virginiaandst=nyt.

Sheinin, D., and Hsu, S.S. 2010. Pitching legend Roger Clemens is indicted on charges of lying to a congressional committee. WashingtonPost.com, August 20. www.washingtonpost.com/wp-dyn/content/article/2010/08/19/AR2010081904125.html.

Tomlinson, P. 1974. Some perspectives from academic psychology. In G. Collier, P. Tomlinson, and J. Wilson (eds.), *Values and Moral Development in Higher Education*, 27–39. New York: John Wiley and Sons.

Zambito, T., and Smith, G.B. 2008. Feds say Bernard Madoff's $50 billion Ponzi scheme was worst ever. NYDailyNews.com, December 13. www.nydailynews.com/news/ny_crime/2008N 12/13/2008-12-13_feds_say_bernard_madoffs_50_billion_ponz.html.

CHAPTER TWO: *Where to Begin: Academic Dishonesty among High School Students*

Arum, R., and Roksa, J. 2011. *Academically Adrift: Limited Learning on College Campuses*. Chicago: University of Chicago Press.

Brandes, B. 1986. *Academic Honesty: A Special Study of California Students*. Sacramento: California State Department of Education, Bureau of Publications.

Bruggeman, E.L., and Hart, K.J. 1996. Cheating, lying, and moral reasoning by religious and secular high school students. *Journal of Educational Research* 89: 340–344.

Coles, R., Hunter, J.D., and See, J. 1989. *Girl Scouts Survey on the Beliefs and Moral Values of America's Children*. New York: Girl Scouts of the USA.

Davis, S.F., Grover, C.A., Becker, A.H., and McGregor, L.N. 1992. Academic dishonesty: Prevalence, determinants, techniques, and punishments. *Teaching of Psychology* 19: 16–20.

Evans, E.D., and Craig, D. 1990. Teacher and student perceptions of academic cheating in middle and senior high schools. *Journal of Educational Research* 84: 44–52.

Gould, D., and Roberts, J. 2007. *A Handbook for Developing and Sustaining Honor Systems*. Revised edition. Portland, OR: Council for Spiritual and Ethical Education.

Higher Education Research Institute. 2010. American freshman survey. http://heri.ucla.edu.

Josephson, M., and Mertz, M. 2004. *Honor above All*. Los Angeles, CA: Josephson Institute of Ethics.

Josephson Institute of Ethics. 2011. The ethics of American youth. www.josephsoninstitute.org.

McCabe, D.L. 1992. The influence of situational ethics on cheating among college students. *Sociological Inquiry* 62: 365–374.

———. 1999. Academic dishonesty among high school students. *Adolescence* 34: 681–687.

Murdock, T.B., Beauchamp, A.S., and Hinton, A.M. 2008. Predictors of cheating and cheating attributions: Does classroom context influence cheating and blame for cheating? *European Journal of Psychology and Education* 23: 477–492.

Murdock, T.B., Miller, A., and Kohlhardt, J. 2004. Effects of classroom context variables on high school students' judgments of the acceptability and likelihood of cheating. *Journal of Educational Psychology* 96: 765–777.

Schab, F. 1991. Schooling without learning: Thirty years of cheating in high school. *Adolescence* 26: 839–847.

Sykes, G.M., and Matza, D. 1957. Techniques of neutralization: A theory of delinquency. *American Sociological Review* 22: 664–670.

Writers Center. 2007. Your code of ethics: Schools—high school honor codes. www.yourcodeofethics.com/honorable_words/schools_high_school_honor_codes/.

CHAPTER THREE: *Prevalence, Types, and Methods of Cheating in College*

Ahmad, Z., Simun, M., and Mohammad, J. 2008. Malaysian university students' attitudes to academic dishonesty and business ethics. *Asia Pacific Journal of Education* 28: 149–160.

Baird, J.S. 1980. Current trends in college cheating. *Psychology in the Schools* 17: 515–522.

Bernardi, R.A., Baca, A.V., Landers, K.S., and Witek, M.B. 2008. Methods of cheating and deterrents to classroom cheating: An international study. *Ethics and Behavior* 18: 373–391.

Blum, S.D. 2009. *My Word! Plagiarism and College Culture*. Ithaca, NY: Cornell University Press.

Bouville, M. 2008. Plagiarism: Words and ideas. *Science and Engineering Ethics* 14: 311–322.

Bowers, W.J. 1964. *Student Dishonesty and Its Control in College*. New York: Bureau of Applied Social Research, Columbia University.

Burrus, R.T., McGoldrick, K., and Schuhmann, P.W. 2007. Self-reports of student cheating: Does a definition of cheating matter? *Journal of Economic Education* 38: 3–16.

Christensen-Hughes, J.M., and McCabe, D.L. 2006a. Academic misconduct within higher education in Canada. *Canadian Journal of Higher Education* 36(2): 1–21.

———. 2006b. Understanding academic misconduct. *Canadian Journal of Higher Education* 36(1): 49–63.

Crown, D.F., and Spiller, M.S. 1998. Learning from the literature on collegiate cheating: A review of empirical research. *Journal of Business Ethics* 17: 683–700.

Davis, S.F., Grover, C.A., Becker, A.H., and McGregor, L.N. 1992. Academic dishonesty: Prevalence, determinants, techniques, and punishments. *Teaching of Psychology* 19: 16–20.

Diekhoff, G.M., LaBeff, E.E., Clark, R.E., Williams, L.E., Francis, B., and Haines, V.J. 1996. College cheating: Ten years later. *Research in Higher Education* 37: 487–502.

Diekhoff, G.M., Labeff, E.E., Shinohara, K., and Yasukawa, H. 1999. College cheating in Japan and the United States. *Research in Higher Education* 40: 343–353.

Gardner, W.M., Roper, J.T., Gonzalez, C.C., and Simpson, R.G. 1988. Analysis of cheating on academic assignments. *Psychological Record* 38: 543–555.

Genereux, R.L., and McLeod, B.A. 1995. Circumstances surrounding cheating: A questionnaire study of college students. *Research in Higher Education* 36: 687–704.

Granitz, N., and Loewy, D. 2007. Applying ethical theories: Interpreting and responding to student plagiarism. *Journal of Business Ethics* 72: 293–306.

Hammer, A. 2009. Academic dishonesty—day 2: 100-level courses rife with cheating. *Purdue Exponent*, online edition, November 17. http://archive.purdueexponent.org/?module=article&story_id=18828.

Hrabak, M., Vujaklija, A., Vodopivec, I., Hren, D., Marusic, M., and Marusic, A. 2004. Academic misconduct among medical students in a post-communist country. *Medical Education* 38: 276–285.

Karlins, M., Michaels, C., and Podlogar, S. 1988. An empirical investigation of actual cheating in a large sample of undergraduates. *Research in Higher Education* 29: 359–364.

Ledwith, A., and Risquez, A. 2008. Using anti-plagiarism software to promote academic honesty in the context of peer reviewed assignments. *Studies in Higher Education* 33: 371–384.

Lin, C.H., and Wen, L.Y. 2007. Academic dishonesty in higher education: A nationwide study in Taiwan. *Higher Education* 54: 85–97.

Lupton, R.A., and Chapman, K.J. 2002. Russian and American college students' attitudes, perceptions and tendencies towards cheating. *Educational Research* 44: 17–27.

Marklein, M.B. 2009. Case of the purloined term paper; when work is resold. USA Today.com, November 19; updated November 22. www.usatoday.com/tech/news/2009-11-19-termpapers19_ST_N.htm.

Marsden, H., Carroll, M., and Neill, J.T. 2005. Who cheats at university? A self-report study of dishonest academic behaviours in a sample of Australian university students. *Australian Journal of Psychology* 57: 1–10.

Martin, D.E., Rao, A., and Sloan, L.R. 2009. Plagiarism, integrity, and workplace deviance: A criterion study. *Ethics and Behavior* 19: 36–50.

McCabe, D.L., and Bowers, W.J. 1994. Academic dishonesty among males in college: A thirty year perspective. *Journal of College Student Development* 35: 5–10.

McCabe, D., Feghali, T., and Abdallah, H. 2008. Academic dishonesty in the Middle East: Individual and contextual factors. *Research in Higher Education* 49: 451–467.

McCabe, D.L., and Treviño, L.K. 1993. Academic dishonesty: Honor codes and other contextual influences. *Journal of Higher Education* 64: 522–538.

———. 1997. Individual and contextual influences on academic dishonesty: A multicampus investigation. *Research in Higher Education* 38: 379–396.

McCabe, D.L., Treviño, L.K., and Butterfield, K.D. 2001. Cheating in academic institutions: A decade of research. *Ethics and Behavior* 11: 219–232.

Melendez, B. 1985. *Honor Code Study*. Cambridge, MA: Harvard University.

Rabi, S.M., Patton, L.R., Fjortoft, N., and Zgarrick, D.P. 2006. Characteristics, prevalence, attitudes, and perceptions of academic dishonesty among pharmacy students. *American Journal of Pharmaceutical Education* (online) 70: art. 73.

Rennison, J. 2010. Plagiarism and PhDs: How to deal with copying. Independent.co.uk, April 15. www.independent.co.uk/student /postgraduate /postgraduate-study/plagiarism-and-phds-how-to-deal-with-copying-1942609.html.

Rocha, M.M., da Silva, G.A., Nascimento, L., de Siqueira, J.O., and Otta, E. 2007. Cheating on college examinations. *Psychological Reports* 100: 379–386.

Roig, M. 1997. Can undergraduate students determine whether text has been plagiarized? *Psychological Record* 47: 113–122.

———. 2001. Plagiarism and paraphrasing criteria of college and university professors. *Ethics and Behavior* 11: 307–323.

Roig, M., and Caso, M. 2005. Lying and cheating: Fraudulent excuse making, cheating, and plagiarism. *Journal of Psychology: Interdisciplinary and Applied* 139: 485–494.

Rudd, A. 2009. 49 disciplined for plagiarism. *Otaga Daily Times*, online edition, November 25. www.odt.co.nz/on-campus/university-otago/83309/49 -disciplined-plagiarism.

Simons, A. 2009. Poll: 17 percent of students say they have cheated. *Brown Daily Herald*, November 24. www.browndailyherald.com/poll-17-percent -of-students-say-they-have-cheated-1.2097315.

Singhal, A.C. 1982. Factors in student dishonesty. *Psychological Reports* 51: 775–780.

Spiller, S., and Crown, D.F. 1995. Changes over time in academic dishonesty at the collegiate level. *Psychological Reports* 76: 763–768.

Sykes, G.M., and Matza, D. 1957. Techniques of neutralization: A theory of delinquency. *American Sociological Review* 22: 664–670.

Taylor-Bianco, A., and Deeter-Schmelz, D. 2007. An exploration of gender and cultural differences in MBA students' cheating behavior: Implications for the classroom. *Journal of Teaching in International Business* 18: 81–99.

Teodorescu, D., and Andrei, T. 2009. Faculty and peer influences on academic integrity: College cheating in Romania. *Higher Education* 57: 267–282.

Wajda-Johnston, V.A., Handal, P.J., Brawer, P.A., and Fabricatore, A.N. 2001. Academic dishonesty at the graduate level. *Ethics and Behavior* 11: 287–305.

Wenham, M. 2009. Checks catch thousands of uni students cheating. news. com.au, November 29. www.news.com.au/national/checks-catch-thousands -of-uni-students-cheating/story-e6frfkvr-1225801907376.

Yardley, J., Rodriguez, M.D., Bates, S.C., and Nelson, J. 2009. True confessions? Alumni's retrospective reports on undergraduate cheating behaviors. *Ethics and Behavior* 19: 1–14.

Zopiatis, A.A., and Krambia-Kapardis, M. 2008. Ethical behaviour of tertiary education students in Cyprus. *Journal of Business Ethics* 81: 647–663.

CHAPTER FOUR: *Individual Student Characteristics That Influence Cheating*

Aiken, L.R. 1991. Detecting, understanding, and controlling for cheating on tests. *Research in Higher Education* 32: 725–736.

Antion, D.L., and Michael, W.B. 1983. Short-term predictive validity of demographic, affective, personal, and cognitive variables in relation to two criterion measures of cheating behaviors. *Educational and Psychological Measurement* 43: 467–482.

Baird, J.S., Jr. 1980. Current trends in college cheating. *Psychology in the Schools* 17: 515–522.

Bichler, G., and Tibbetts, S.G. 2003. Conditional covariation of binge drinking with predictors of college students' cheating. *Psychological Reports* 93: 735–749.

Bloodgood, J.M., Turnley, W.H., and Mudrack, P. 2008. The influence of ethics instruction, religiosity, and intelligence on cheating behavior. *Journal of Business Ethics* 82: 557–571.

Bolin, A.U. 2004. Self-control, perceived opportunity, and attitudes as predictors of academic dishonesty. *Journal of Psychology: Interdisciplinary and Applied* 138: 101–114.

Bonjean, C.M., and McGee, R. 1965. Undergraduate scholastic dishonesty: A comparative analysis of deviance and control systems. *Social Science Quarterly* 65: 289–296.

Bowers, W.J. 1964. *Student Dishonesty and Its Control in College.* New York: Bureau of Applied Social Research, Columbia University.

Davis, S.F., Grover, C.A., Becker, A.H., and McGregor, L.N. 1992. Academic dishonesty: Prevalence, determinants, techniques, and punishments. *Teaching of Psychology* 19: 16–20.

Davy, J.A., Kincaid, J.F., Smith, K.J., and Trawick, M.A. 2007. An examination of the role of attitudinal characteristics and motivation on the cheating behavior of business students. *Ethics and Behavior* 17: 281–302.

de Bruin, G.P., and Rudnick, H. 2007. Examining the cheats: The role of conscientiousness and excitement seeking in academic dishonesty. *South African Journal of Psychology* 37: 153–164.

Detert, J.R., Treviño, L.K., and Sweitzer, V.L. 2008. Moral disengagement in ethical decision making: A study of antecedents and outcomes. *Journal of Applied Psychology* 93: 374–391.

Genereux, R.L., and McLeod, B.A. 1995. Circumstances surrounding cheating: A questionnaire study of college students. *Research in Higher Education* 36: 687–704.

Gibson, C.L., Khey, D., and Schreck, C.L. 2008. Gender, internal controls, and academic dishonesty: Investigating mediating and differential effects. *Journal of Criminal Justice Education* 19: 2–18.

Gilligan, C. 1982. *In a Different Voice: Psychological Theory and Women's Development.* Cambridge, MA: Harvard University Press.

Greenberger, E., Lessard, J., Chen, C., and Farruggia, S.P. 2008. Self-entitled college students: Contributions of personality, parenting, and motivational factors. *Journal of Youth and Adolescence* 37: 1193–1204.

Haines, V.J., Diekhoff, G.M., LaBeff, E.E., and Clark, R.E. 1986. College cheating: Immaturity, lack of commitment, and the neutralizing attitude. *Research in Higher Education* 25: 342–354.

Harp, J., and Taietz, P. 1966. Academic integrity and social structure: A study of cheating among college students. *Social Problems* 13: 365–373.

Hendershott, A., Drinan, P.F., and Cross, M. 1999. Gender and academic integrity. *Journal of College Student Development* 40: 345–354.

Hetherington, E.M., and Feldman, S.E. 1964. College cheating as a function of subject and situational variables. *Journal of Educational Psychology* 55: 212–218.

Huelsman, M.A., Piroch, J., and Wasieleski, D. 2006. Relation of religiosity with academic dishonesty in a sample of college students. *Psychological Reports* 99: 739–742.

Jordan, A.E. 2001. College student cheating: The role of motivation, perceived norms, attitudes, and knowledge of institutional policy. *Ethics and Behavior* 11: 233–247.

Kelly, J.A., and Worell, L. 1978. Personality characteristics, parent behaviors, and sex of subject in relation to cheating. *Journal of Research in Personality* 12: 179–188.

Kibler, W.L. 1992. Dealing effectively with cheating. *Chronicle of Higher Education* 39: B10.

Kibler, W.L., and Kibler, P.V. 1993. When students resort to cheating. *Chronicle of Higher Education* 39: B1–2.

Kirkvliet, J. 1994. Cheating by economics students: A comparison of survey results. *Journal of Economic Education* 25: 121–133.

Kisamore, J.L., Stone, T.H., and Jawahar, I.M. 2007. Academic integrity: The relationship between individual and situational factors on misconduct contemplations. *Journal of Business Ethics* 75: 381–394.

Kish-Gephart, J.J., Harrison, D.A., and Treviño, L.K. 2010. Bad apples, bad cases, and bad barrels: Meta-analytic evidence about sources of unethical decisions at work. *Journal of Applied Psychology* 95: 1–31.

Klein, H.A., Levenburg, N.M., McKendall, M., and Mothersell, W. 2007. Cheating during the college years: How do business school students compare? *Journal of Business Ethics* 72: 197–206.

Kohlberg, L. 1969. Stage and sequence: The cognitive-developmental approach to socialization. In D.A. Goslin (ed.), *Handbook of Socialization Theory and Research*, 347–480. Chicago: Rand McNally.

Leming, J.S. 1980. Cheating behavior, subject variables, and components of the internal-external scale under high and low risk conditions. *Journal of Educational Research* 74: 83–87.

Lipson, A., and McGavern, N. 1993. Undergraduate academic dishonesty: A comparison of student, faculty and teaching assistant attitudes and experiences. Paper presented at the annual meeting of the Association for Institutional Research, Chicago. May.

Lucas, G.M., and Friedrich, J. 2005. Individual differences in workplace deviance and integrity as predictors of academic dishonesty. *Ethics and Behavior* 15: 15–35.

Malinowski, C.I., and Smith, C.P. 1985. Moral reasoning and moral conduct: An investigation prompted by Kohlberg's theory. *Journal of Personality and Social Psychology* 49: 1016–1027.

Mazar, N., Amir, O., and Ariely, D. 2008. The dishonesty of honest people: A theory of self-concept maintenance. *Journal of Marketing Research* 45: 633–644.

McCabe, D.L., and Treviño, L.K. 1993. Academic dishonesty: Honor codes and other contextual influences. *Journal of Higher Education* 64: 522–538.

———. 1997. Individual and contextual influences on academic dishonesty: A multicampus investigation. *Research in Higher Education* 38: 379–396.

McCabe, D.L., Treviño, L.K., and Butterfield, K.D. 2001. Cheating in academic institutions: A decade of research. *Ethics and Behavior* 11: 219–232.

Michaels, J.W., and Miethe, T.D. 1989. Applying theories of deviance to academic cheating. *Social Science Quarterly* 70: 870–885.

Murdock, T.B., and Anderman, E.M. 2006. Motivational perspectives on student cheating: Toward an integrated model of academic dishonesty. *Educational Psychologist* 41: 129–145.

Murdock, T., and Stephens, J. 2007. Is cheating wrong? Students' reasoning about academic dishonesty. In E. Anderman and T. Murdock (eds.), *Psychology of Academic Cheating*, 229–254. Burlington, MA: Elsevier Academic Press.

Mustaine, E.E., and Tewksbury, R. 2005. Southern college students' cheating behaviors: An examination of problem behavior correlates. *Deviant Behavior* 26: 439–461.

Nathanson, C., Paulhus, D.L., and Williams, K.M. 2006. Predictors of a behavioral measure of scholastic cheating: Personality and competence but not demographics. *Contemporary Educational Psychology* 31: 97–122.

Niiya, Y., Ballantyne, R., North, M.S., and Crocker, J. 2008. Gender, contingencies of self-worth, and achievement goals as predictors of academic cheating in a controlled laboratory setting. *Basic and Applied Social Psychology* 30: 76–83.

Perry, A.R., Kane, K.M., Bernesser, K.J., and Spicker, P.T. 1990. Type-A behavior, competitive achievement-striving, and cheating among college students. *Psychological Reports* 66: 459–465.

Rest, J.R. 1986. *Moral Development: Advances in Research and Theory*. New York: Praeger.

Rettinger, D.A., and Jordan, A.E. 2005. The relations among religion, motivation, and college cheating: A natural experiment. *Ethics and Behavior* 15: 107–129.

Rettinger, D.A., and Kramer, Y. 2009. Situational and personal causes of student cheating. *Research in Higher Education* 50: 293–313.

Roig, M., and Caso, M. 2005. Lying and cheating: Fraudulent excuse making, cheating, and plagiarism. *Journal of Psychology: Interdisciplinary and Applied* 139: 485–494.

Schlenker, B.R. 2008. Integrity and character: Implications of principled and expedient ethical ideologies. *Journal of Social and Clinical Psychology* 27: 1078–1125.

Singhal, A.C. 1982. Factors in students' dishonesty. *Psychological Reports* 51: 775–780.

Staats, S., Hupp, J.M., and Hagley, A.M. 2008. Honesty and heroes: A positive psychology view of heroism and academic honesty. *Journal of Psychology* 142: 357–372.

Stannard, C.I., and Bowers, W.J. 1970. The college fraternity as an opportunity structure for meeting academic demands. *Social Problems* 17: 371–390.

Storch, E.A., and Storch, J.B. 2002. Fraternities, sororities, and academic dishonesty. *College Student Journal* 36: 247–252.

Taylor-Bianco, A., and Deeter-Schmelz, D. 2007. An exploration of gender and cultural differences in MBA students' cheating behavior: Implications for the classroom. *Journal of Teaching in International Business* 18: 81–99.

Tibbetts, S.G. 1997. Gender differences in students' rational decisions to cheat. *Deviant Behavior* 18: 393–414.

———. 1999. Differences between women and men regarding decisions to commit test cheating. *Research in Higher Education* 40: 323–342.

Ward, D.A. 1986. Self-esteem and dishonest behavior revisited. *Journal of Social Psychology* 126: 709–713.

Ward, D.A., and Beck, W.L., 1990. Gender and dishonesty. *Journal of Social Psychology* 130: 333–339.

Whitley, B.E., Jr. 1998. Factors associated with cheating among college students: A review. *Research in Higher Education* 39: 235–274.

Whitley, B.E., Jr., Nelson, A.B., and Jones, C.J. 1999. Gender differences in cheating attitudes and classroom cheating behavior: A meta-analysis. *Sex Roles* 41: 657–680.

Williams, A.E., and Janosik, S.M. 2007. An examination of academic dishonesty among sorority and nonsorority women. *Journal of College Student Development* 48: 706–714.

Williams, K.M. 2007. The role of psychopathy in scholastic cheating: Self-report and objective measures. Unpublished doctoral dissertation. University of British Columbia.

Wowra, S.A. 2007. Moral identities, social anxiety, and academic dishonesty among American college students. *Ethics and Behavior* 17: 303–321.

Zimny, S.T., Robertson, D.U., and Bartoszek, T. 2008. Academic and personal dishonesty in college students. *North American Journal of Psychology* 10: 291–312.

CHAPTER FIVE: *Institutional Factors That Influence Academic Integrity: The Role of Honor Codes*

Ariely, D. 2008. *Predictably Irrational: The Hidden Forces That Shape Our Decisions*. New York: HarperCollins Publishers.

Bowers, W.J. 1964. *Student Dishonesty and Its Control in College*. New York: Bureau of Applied Social Research, Columbia University.

Dalton, J.C. 1985. *Promoting Values Development in College Students*. Columbus, OH: Teachers College Press.

Desplaces, D.E., Melchar, D.E., Beauvais, L.L., and Bosco, S.M. 2007. The impact of business education on moral judgment competence: An empirical study. *Journal of Business Ethics* 74: 73–87.

Engler, J.N., Landau, J.D., and Epstein, M. 2008. Keeping up with the Joneses: Students' perceptions of academically dishonest behavior. *Teaching of Psychology* 35: 99–102.

Ignelzi, M.G. 1990. Ethical education in a college environment: The just community approach. *NASPA Journal* 27: 192–198.

Jendrek, M.P. 1989. Faculty reactions to academic dishonesty. *Journal of College Student Development* 30: 401–406.

Kish-Gephart, J.J., Harrison, D.A., and Treviño, L.K. 2010. Bad apples, bad cases, and bad barrels: Meta-analytic evidence about sources of unethical decisions at work. *Journal of Applied Psychology* 95: 1–31.

Kohlberg, L. 1969. Stage and sequence: The cognitive-developmental approach to socialization. In D.A. Goslin (ed.), *Handbook of Socialization Theory and Research*, 347–480. Chicago: Rand McNally.

———. 1985. The just community approach to moral education in theory and practice. In M.W. Berkowitz and F. Oser (eds.), *Moral Education: Theory and Practice*, 27–88. Hillsdale, NJ: Erlbaum.

Langone, M. 2007. Promoting integrity among nursing students. *Journal of Nursing Education* 46: 45–47.

Mazar, N., Amir, O., and Ariely, D. 2008. The dishonesty of honest people: A theory of self-concept maintenance. *Journal of Marketing Research* 45: 633–644.

McCabe, D.L. 1993. Faculty responses to academic dishonesty: The influence of student honor codes. *Research in Higher Education* 34: 647–658.

McCabe, D.L., Butterfield, K.D., and Treviño, L.K. 2003. Faculty and academic integrity: The influence of current honor codes and past honor code experiences. *Research in Higher Education* 44: 367–385.

McCabe, D.L., and Pavela, G. 2000. Some good news about academic integrity. *Change* 33: 32–38.

McCabe, D.L., and Treviño, L.K. 1993. Academic dishonesty: Honor codes and other contextual influences. *Journal of Higher Education* 64: 522–538.

———. 1997. Individual and contextual influences on academic dishonesty: A multicampus investigation. *Research in Higher Education* 38: 379–396.

McCabe, D.L., Treviño, L.K., and Butterfield, K.D. 1996. The influence of collegiate and corporate codes of conduct on ethics-related behavior in the workplace. *Business Ethics Quarterly* 64: 461–476.

———. 1999. Academic integrity in honor code and non-honor code environments: A qualitative investigation. *Journal of Higher Education* 70: 211–234.

———. 2001. Dishonesty in academic environments: The influence of peer reporting requirements. *Journal of Higher Education* 72: 29–45.

———. 2002. Honor codes and other contextual influences on academic integrity: A replication and extension to modified honor code settings. *Research in Higher Education* 43: 357–378.

Melendez, B. 1985. *Honor Code Study*. Cambridge, MA: Harvard University.

Nuss, E.M. 1984. Academic integrity: Comparing faculty and student attitudes. *Improving College and University Teaching* 32: 140–143.

Power, F.C., Higgins, A., and Kohlberg, L. 1989. *Lawrence Kohlberg's Approach to Moral Education*. New York: Columbia University Press.

Roig, M., and Marks, A. 2006. Attitudes toward cheating before and after the implementation of a modified honor code: A case study. *Ethics and Behavior* 16: 163–171.

Treviño, L.K., Butterfield, K.D., and McCabe, D.L. 1998. The ethical context in organizations: Influences on employee attitudes and behaviors. *Business Ethics Quarterly* 83: 447–476.

Treviño, L.K., and McCabe, D.L. 1994. Meta-learning about business ethics: Building honorable business school communities. *Journal of Business Ethics* 13: 405–416.

CHAPTER SIX: *Institutional Factors That Influence Academic Integrity: Other Contextual Influences*

Ariely, D. 2008. *Predictably Irrational: The Hidden Forces That Shape Our Decisions*. New York: HarperCollins Publishers.

Bandura, A. 1976. Social learning theory. In J.T. Spence, R.C. Carson, and J.W. Thibaut (eds.), *Behavioral Approaches to Therapy*, 1–46. Morristown, NJ: General Learning Press.

———. 1986. *Social Foundations of Thought and Action*. Englewood Cliffs, NJ: Prentice-Hall.

Bernardi, R.A., Baca, A.V., Landers, K.S., and Witek, M.B. 2008. Methods of cheating and deterrents to classroom cheating: An international study. *Ethics and Behavior* 18: 373–391.

Bisping, T.O., Patron, H., and Roskelley, K. 2008. Modeling academic dishonesty: The role of student perceptions and misconduct type. *Journal of Economic Education* 39: 4–21.

Bonjean, C.M., and McGee, R. 1965. Undergraduate scholastic dishonesty: A comparative analysis of deviance and control systems. *Social Science Quarterly* 65: 289–296.

Bowers, W.J. 1964. *Student Dishonesty and Its Control in College*. New York: Bureau of Applied Social Research, Columbia University.

Broeckelman-Post, M.A. 2008. Faculty and student classroom influences on academic dishonesty. *IEEE Transactions on Education* 51: 206–211.

Carrell, S.E., Malmstrom, F.V., and West, J.E. 2008. Peer effects in academic cheating. *Journal of Human Resources* 43: 173–207.

Evans, N.J., Forney, D.S., and Guido-DiBrito, F. 1998. *Student Development in College*. San Francisco: Jossey-Bass.

Genereux, R.L., and McLeod, B.A. 1995. Circumstances surrounding cheating: A questionnaire study of college students. *Research in Higher Education* 36: 687–704.

Gibbs, J.P. 1975. *Crime, Punishment, and Deterrence*. Amsterdam: Elsevier.

Gire, D.T., and Williams, T.D. 2007. Dissonance and the honor system: Extending the severity of threat phenomenon. *Journal of Social Psychology* 147: 501–509.

Jordan, A.E. 2003. Implications of academic dishonesty for teaching in psychology. *Teaching of Psychology* 30: 216–219.

Kisamore, J.L., Stone, T.H., and Jawahar, I.M. 2007. Academic integrity: The relationship between individual and situational factors on misconduct contemplations. *Journal of Business Ethics* 75: 381–394.

Kohlberg, L. 1969. Stage and sequence: The cognitive-developmental approach to socialization. In D.A. Goslin (ed.), *Handbook of Socialization Theory and Research*, 347–480. Chicago: Rand McNally.

Ledwith, A., and Risquez, A. 2008. Using anti-plagiarism software to promote academic honesty in the context of peer reviewed assignments. *Studies in Higher Education* 33: 371–384.

Leming, J.S. 1980. Cheating behavior, subject variables, and components of the internal-external scale under high and low risk conditions. *Journal of Educational Research* 74: 83–87.

Levy, E.S., and Rakovski, C.C. 2006. Academic dishonesty: A zero tolerance professor and student registration choices. *Research in Higher Education* 47: 735–754.

Liska, A.E. 1978. Deviant involvement, associations and attitudes: Specifying the underlying causal structure. *Sociology and Social Research* 63: 73–88.

McCabe, D.L. 1992. The influence of situational ethics on cheating among college students. *Sociological Inquiry* 62: 365–374.

McCabe, D.L., and Treviño, L.K. 1993. Academic dishonesty: Honor codes and other contextual influences. *Journal of Higher Education* 64: 522–538.

———. 1997. Individual and contextual influences on academic dishonesty: A multicampus investigation. *Research in Higher Education* 38: 379–396.

McCabe, D.L., Treviño, L.K., and Butterfield, K.D. 1999. Academic integrity in honor code and non-honor code environments: A qualitative investigation. *Journal of Higher Education* 70: 211–234.

———. 2001. Cheating in academic institutions: A decade of research. *Ethics and Behavior* 11: 219–232.

———. 2002. Honor codes and other contextual influences on academic integrity: A replication and extension to modified code settings. *Research in Higher Education* 43: 357–378.

Michaels, J.W., and Miethe, T.D. 1989. Applying theories of deviance to academic cheating. *Social Science Quarterly* 70: 870–885.

Murdock, T.B., Miller, A.D., and Goetzinger, A. 2007. Effects of classroom context on university students' judgments about cheating: Mediating and moderating processes. *Social Psychology of Education* 10: 141–169.

Passow, H.J., Mayhew, M.J., Finelli, C.J., Harding, T.S., and Carpenter, D.D. 2006. Factors influencing engineering students' decisions to cheat by type of assessment. *Research in Higher Education* 47: 643–684.

Pulvers, K., and Diekhoff, G.M. 1999. The relationship between academic dishonesty and college classroom environment. *Research in Higher Education* 40: 487–498.

Scanlan, C.L. 2006. Strategies to promote a climate of academic integrity and minimize student cheating and plagiarism. *Journal of Allied Health* 35: 179–185.

Skinner, B.F. 1969. *Contingencies of Reinforcement*. New York: Appleton-Century-Crofts.

Stern, E.B., and Havlicek, L. 1986. Academic misconduct: Results of faculty and undergraduate student surveys. *Journal of Allied Health* 5: 129–142.

Sutherland, E.H., Cressey, D.F., and Luckenbill, D.F. 1992. *Principles of Criminology*. 11th ed. Dix Hills, NY: General Hall.

Tittle, C.R., and Rowe, A.R. 1973. Moral appeal, sanction threat, and deviance: An experimental test. *Social Problems* 20: 488–497.

Treviño, L.K., and McCabe, D.L. 1994. Meta-learning about business ethics: Building honorable business school communities. *Journal of Business Ethics* 13: 405–416.

Vowell, P.R., and Chen, A. 2004. Predicting academic misconduct: A comparative test of four sociological explanations. *Sociological Inquiry* 74: 226–249.

Whitley, B.E. 1998. Factors associated with cheating among college students: A review. *Research in Higher Education* 39: 235–274.

Zimring, F.E., and Hawkins, G.J. 1973. *Deterrence: The Legal Threat in Crime Control*. Chicago: University of Chicago Press.

CHAPTER SEVEN: *The Faculty Role in Creating a Strong Environment of Academic Integrity*

Graham, M.A., Monday, J., O'Brien, K., and Steffen, S. 1994. Cheating at small colleges: An examination of student and faculty attitudes and behaviors. *Journal of College Student Development* 35: 255–260.

Jendrek, M.P. 1989. Faculty reactions to academic dishonesty. *Journal of College Student Development* 30: 401–406.

McCabe, D.L. 1993. Faculty responses to academic dishonesty: The influence of student honor codes. *Research in Higher Education* 34: 647–658.

McCabe, D.L., Butterfield, K.D., and Treviño, L.K. 2003. Faculty and academic integrity: The influence of current honor codes and past honor code experiences. *Research in Higher Education* 44: 367–385.

McCabe, D.L., Treviño, L.K., and Butterfield, K.D. 1999. Academic integrity in honor code and non-honor code environments: A qualitative investigation. *Journal of Higher Education* 70: 211–234.

———. 2004. Academic integrity: How widespread is cheating and plagiarism? In D.R. Karp and T. Allena (eds.), *Restorative Justice on the College Campus: Promoting Student Growth and Responsibility, and Reawakening the Spirit of Campus Community*, 124–135. Springfield, IL: Charles C Thomas.

Nuss, E.M. 1984. Academic integrity: Comparing faculty and student attitudes. *Improving College and University Teaching* 32: 140–143.

Singhal, A.C. 1982. Factors in student dishonesty. *Psychological Reports* 51: 775–780.

Whitley, B.E., Jr., and Keith-Spiegel, P. 2002. *Academic Dishonesty: An Educator's Guide.* Mahwah, NJ: Erlbaum.

Wright, J.C., and Kelly, R. 1974. Cheating: Student/faculty views and responsibilities. *Improving College and University Teaching* 22: 31–34.

CHAPTER EIGHT: *Academic Integrity in Business and Professional Schools*

Anderson, R.E., and Obenshain, S.S. 1994. Cheating by students: Findings, reflections, and remedies. *Academic Medicine* 69: 323–332.

Andrews, K.G., Smith, L.A., Henzi, D., and Demps, E. 2007. Faculty and student perceptions of academic integrity at U.S. and Canadian dental schools. *Journal of Dental Education* 71: 1027–1039.

Austin, Z., Collins, D., Remillard, A., Kelcher, S., and Chui, S. 2006. Influence of attitudes toward curriculum on dishonest academic behavior. *American Journal of Pharmaceutical Education* (online) 70, art. 50.

Baldwin, D.C., Jr., Daugherty, S.R., Rowley, B.D., and Schwarz, M.D. 1996. Cheating in medical school: A survey of second-year students at 31 schools. *Academic Medicine* 71: 267–273.

Bowers, W.J. 1964. *Student Dishonesty and Its Control in College.* New York: Bureau of Applied Social Research, Columbia University.

Chapman, K.J., Davis, R., Toy, D., and Wright, L. 2004. Academic integrity in the business school environment: I'll get by with a little help from my friends. *Journal of Marketing Education* 26: 236–249.

Crissey, M. 1997. Law students at Howard U. complain that cheating isn't punished. *Chronicle of Higher Education*, online edition, October 31. http://chronicle.com/section/Archives/39/.

Davy, J.A., Kincaid, J.F., Smith, K.J., and Trawick, M.A. 2007. An examination of the role of attitudinal characteristics and motivation on the cheating behavior of business students. *Ethics and Behavior* 17: 281–302.

Eastman, K.L., Eastman, J.K., and Iyer, R. 2008. Academic dishonesty: An exploratory study examining whether insurance students are different from other college students. *Risk Management and Insurance Review* 11: 209–226.

Fuller, J.L., and Killip, D.E. 1979. Do dental student cheat? *Journal of Dental Education* 43: 666–670.

Genova, W. 2008. California students sue dental association over exam cheating row. AllHeadlineNews.com, January 24. www.allheadlinenews.com/articles/7009816006.

Ghoshal, S. 2005. Bad management theories are destroying good management practice. *Academy of Management Learning & Education* 41: 75–91.

Harding, T., Finelli, C., and Carpenter, D. 2006. Cheating in college and its influence on ethical behavior in professional engineering practice. In *Proceedings of the 2006 ASEE Annual Conference and Exposition, Chicago, IL.* Washington, DC: American Society for Engineering Education.

Khurana, R., and Nohria, N. 2008. It's time to make management a true profession. *Harvard Business Review* 86: 1–8.

Klein, H.A., Levenburg, N.M., McKendall, M., and Mothersell, W. 2007. Cheating during the college years: How do business school students compare? *Journal of Business Ethics* 72: 197–206.

McCabe, D.L. 1997. Classroom cheating among natural science and engineering majors. *Science and Engineering Ethics* 3: 433–445.

McCabe, D.L., Butterfield, K.D., and Treviño, L.K. 2006. Academic dishonesty in graduate business programs: Prevalence, causes, and proposed action. *Academy of Management Learning & Education* 53: 294–305.

McCabe, D.L., Dukerich, J.M., and Dutton, J.E. 1991. Context, values and moral dilemmas: Comparing the choices of business and law school students. *Journal of Business Ethics* 10: 951–960.

———. 1994. The effects of professional education on values and the resolution of ethical dilemmas: Business school vs. law school students. *Journal of Business Ethics* 13: 693–700.

McCabe, D.L., and Treviño, L.K. 1995. Cheating among business students: A challenge for business leaders and educators. *Journal of Management Education* 19: 205–218.

McCabe, D.L., Treviño, L.K., and Butterfield, K.D. 1996. The influence of collegiate and corporate codes of conduct on ethics-related behavior in the workplace. *Business Ethics Quarterly* 64: 461–476.

Mower, L. 2006. UNLV's handling of dental school cheating applauded. ReviewJournal.com, October 14. www.reviewjournal.com/lvrj_home/2006/Oct-14-Sat-2006/news/10226800.html.

Muhney, K.A., and Campbell, P.R. 2010. Allied dental and dental educators' perceptions of and reporting practices on academic dishonesty. *Journal of Dental Education* 74: 1214–1219.

Passow, H.J., Mayhew, M.J., Finelli, C.J., Harding, T.S., and Carpenter, D.D. 2006. Factors influencing engineering students' decisions to cheat by type of assessment. *Research in Higher Education* 47: 643–684.

Premeaux, S.R. 2005. Undergraduate student perceptions regarding cheating: Tier 1 versus tier 2 AACSB accredited business schools. *Journal of Business Ethics* 62: 407–418.

Rabi, S.M., Patton, L.R., Fjortoft, N., and Zgarrick, D.P. 2006. Characteristics, prevalence, attitudes, and perceptions of academic dishonesty among pharmacy students. *American Journal of Pharmaceutical Education* (online) 70, art. 73.

Rettinger, D.A., and Jordan, A.E. 2005. The relations among religion, motivation, and college cheating: A natural experiment. *Ethics and Behavior* 15: 107–129.

Rubenstein, M.H. 2010. Court affirms dismissal of dental student for cheating. Adjunct Law Prof Blog, December 13. http://lawprofessors.typepad.com/

adjunctprofs/2010/12/court-affirms-dismissal-of-dental-student-for -cheating.html.

Rudavsky, S. 2007. Cheating scandal snares nearly half of IU dental class. *Indianapolis Star*, May 8. www.associatedcontent.com/article/239288/ iu_dental_school_cheating_ring_exposed.html?cat=4.

Ryan, G., Bonanno, H., Krass, I., Scouller, K., and Smith, L. 2009. Undergraduate and postgraduate pharmacy students' perceptions of plagiarism and academic honesty. *American Journal of Pharmacy Education* (online) 73, art. 105.

Sierles, F., Hendrickx, I., and Circle, S. 1980. Cheating in medical school. *Journal of Medical Education* 55: 124–125.

Smyth, M.L., and Davis, J.R. 2004. An examination of student cheating in the two-year college. *Community College Review* 31: 17–33.

Treviño, L.K., Butterfield, K.D., and McCabe, D.L. 1998. The ethical context in organizations: Influences on employee attitudes and behaviors. *Business Ethics Quarterly* 83: 447–476.

Treviño, L.K., and McCabe, D.L. 1994. Meta-learning about business ethics: Building honorable business school communities. *Journal of Business Ethics* 13: 405–416.

CHAPTER NINE: *Creating a Culture of Integrity: Practical Advice for Faculty and Administrators*

Bazerman, M.H., and Tenbrunsel, A.E. 2011. *Blind Spots: Why We Fail to Do What's Right and What to Do about It*. Princeton, NJ: Princeton University Press.

Bertram-Gallant, T. 2008. *Academic Integrity in the Twenty-First Century: A Teaching and Learning Imperative*. San Francisco: Jossey-Bass.

Bertram-Gallant, T., and Drinan, P. 2006. Organizational theory and student cheating: Explanation, responses, and strategies. *Journal of Higher Education* 77: 839–860.

Blum, S.D. 2009. *My Word! Plagiarism and College Culture*. Ithaca, NY: Cornell University Press.

Bolkan, J. 2011. Business schools use software, online groups to combat plagiarism in admissions. CampusTechnology.com, June 15. http://campustech nology.com/articles/2011/06/15/business-schools-use-software-online -groups-to-combat-plagiarism-in-admissions.aspx.

Bowers, W.J. 1964. *Student Dishonesty and Its Control in College*. New York: Bureau of Applied Social Research, Columbia University.

Braithwaite, J. 1999. Restorative justice: Assessing optimistic and pessimistic accounts. *Crime and Justice* 25: 1–127.

———. 2000. Decomposing a holistic vision of restorative justice. *Contemporary Justice Review* 3: 433–440.

Callahan, D. 2004. *The Cheating Culture: Why More Americans Are Doing Wrong to Get Ahead*. New York: Harcourt.

Cummings, K., and Romano, J. 2002. Effect of an honor code on perceptions of university instructor affinity-seeking behavior. *Journal of College Student Development* 43: 862–875.

Dufresne, R.L. 2004. An action learning perspective on effective implementation of academic honor codes. *Group and Organization Management* 29: 201–218.

Engler, J.N., Landau, J.D., and Epstein, M. 2008. Keeping up with the Joneses: Students' perceptions of academically dishonest behavior. *Teaching of Psychology* 35: 99–102.

Feldman, K.A., and Newcomb, T.M. 1969. *The Impact of College on Students.* San Francisco: Jossey-Bass.

Goodstein, J., and Aquino, K. 2010. And restorative justice for all: Redemption, forgiveness, and reintegration in organizations. *Journal of Organizational Behavior* 31: 624–628.

Goodstein, J.D., and Butterfield, K.D. 2010. Extending the horizon of business ethics: Restorative justice and the aftermath of unethical behavior. *Business Ethics Quarterly* 20: 453–480.

Karp, D.R., and Allena, T. (eds.). 2004. *Restorative Justice on the College Campus: Promoting Student Growth and Responsibility, and Reawakening the Spirit of Campus Community.* Springfield, IL: Charles C Thomas.

Karp, D., and Conrad, S. 2005. Restorative justice and college student misconduct. *Public Organization Review: A Global Journal* 5: 315–333.

Kish-Gephart, J.J., Harrison, D.A., and Treviño, L.K. 2010. Bad apples, bad cases, and bad barrels: Meta-analytic evidence about sources of unethical decisions at work. *Journal of Applied Psychology* 95: 1–31.

Kohlberg, L. 1969. Stage and sequence: The cognitive-developmental approach to socialization. In D.A. Goslin (ed.), *Handbook of Socialization Theory and Research,* 347–480. Chicago: Rand McNally.

Lathrop, A., and Foss, K. 2005. *Guiding Students from Cheating and Plagiarism to Honesty and Integrity: Strategies for Change.* Westport, CT: Greenwood.

McCabe, D.L., and Pavela, G. 2000. Some good news about academic integrity. *Change* 33: 32–38.

McCabe, D.L., and Treviño, L.K. 1993. Academic dishonesty: Honor codes and other contextual influences. *Journal of Higher Education* 64: 522–538.

———. 1997. Individual and contextual influences on academic dishonesty: A multicampus investigation. *Research in Higher Education* 38: 379–396.

———. 2002. Honesty and honor codes. *Academe* 88: 37–41.

McCabe, D.L., Treviño, L.K., and Butterfield, K.D. 1996. The influence of collegiate and corporate codes of conduct on ethics-related behavior in the workplace. *Business Ethics Quarterly* 64: 461–476.

———. 2001. Cheating in academic institutions: A decade of research. *Ethics and Behavior* 11: 219–232.

———. 2002. Honor codes and other contextual influences on academic integrity: A replication and extension to modified code settings. *Research in Higher Education* 43: 357–378.

———. 2004. Academic integrity: How widespread is cheating and plagiarism? In D.A. Karp and T. Allena (eds.), *Restorative Justice on the College Campus: Promoting Student Growth and Responsibility, and Reawakening the Spirit of Campus Community.* Springfield, IL: Charles C Thomas.

Milliken, F.J., and Morrison, E.W. 2003. Shades of silence: Emerging themes and future directions for research on silence in organizations. *Journal of Management Studies* 40: 1563–1568.

Milliken, F.J., Morrison, E.W., and Hewlin, P.F. 2003. An exploratory study of employee silence: Issues that employees don't communicate upward and why. *Journal of Management Studies* 40: 1453–1473.

Pranis, K. 2007. Restorative values. In G. Johnstone and D.W. Van Ness (eds.), *Handbook of Restorative Justice,* 59–74. Cullompton, UK: Willan Publishing.

Rest, J.R., and Thoma, S.J. 1986. Educational programs and interventions. In J.R. Rest (ed.), *Moral Development: Advances in Research and Theory,* 38–58. New York: Praeger.

Roig, M., and Marks, A. 2006. Attitudes toward cheating before and after the implementation of a modified honor code: A case study. *Ethics and Behavior* 16: 163–171.

Scanlan, C.L. 2006. Strategies to promote a climate of academic integrity and minimize student cheating and plagiarism. *Journal of Allied Health* 35: 179–185.

Schmitt, E. 1994. An inquiry finds 125 cheated on a Naval Academy exam. *New York Times,* January 13.

Treviño, L.K. 1990. A cultural perspective on changing and developing organizational ethics. *Research in Organizational Change and Development* 4: 195–230.

Treviño, L.K., Butterfield, K.D., and McCabe, D.L. 1998. The ethical context in organizations: Influences on employee attitudes and behaviors. *Business Ethics Quarterly* 8: 447–476.

Treviño, L.K., and McCabe, D.L. 1994. Meta-learning about business ethics: Building honorable business school communities. *Journal of Business Ethics* 13: 405–416.

Treviño, L.K., and Nelson, K.A. 2011. *Managing Business Ethics: Straight Talk about How to Do It Right.* 5th ed. New York: John Wiley and Sons.

Treviño, L.K., Weaver, G., Gibson, D., and Toffler, B. 1999. Managing ethics and legal compliance: What works and what hurts. *California Management Review* 41: 131–151.

Trevino, L.K., and Youngblood, S.A. 1990. Bad apples in bad barrels: A causal analysis of ethical decision-making behavior. *Journal of Applied Psychology* 75: 378–385.

Walker, M.U. 2006. *Moral Repair: Reconstructing Moral Relations after Wrong-doing.* New York: Cambridge University Press.

Whitley, B.E., Jr., and Keith-Spiegel, P. 2001. Academic integrity as an institutional issue. *Ethics and Behavior* 11: 325–342.

Page numbers in italics refer to figures and tables.

85–86; gender, 74–81, *75, 77, 78, 80*; risk taking, 87–88; social class, 87

informal cultural systems, 168–69, *169,* 182–87

institutional factors in cheating, 113–14, 128–29: classroom context, 126–28, 145–46; deterrence, 122–26, 135–36, 143, 174; peer influence, 114–16; policy understanding and acceptance, 114–15, 121–22; rewards, 122–26, 177–78. *See also* honor codes

internal controls, gender, and cheating, 80, 87–88

Internet. *See* cut-and-paste plagiarism

Iyer, R., 156, 157

Janosik, S. M., 85

Jawahar, I. M., 73, 113

Jendrek, M. P., 108, 133

Jones, C. J., 72, 74

Jordan, A. E., 89, 128, 156

Josephson, M., 29

Josephson Institute of Ethics, 17, 25, *25,* 26

junior high students, 19, 20

just communities, 105–6

Karlins, M., 37

Karp, D., 172

Keith-Spiegel, P., 146, 167

Kelly, J. A., 74

Kelly, R., 133

Khey, D., 72, 80

Khurana, R., 159

Kibler, P. V., 89

Kibler, W. L., 72, 89

Killip, D. E., 155

Kirkvliet, J., 86, 87

Kisamore, J. L., 73, 113

Kish-Gephart, J. J., 74, 82, 90, 107, 189, 193

Klein, H. A., 72, 82, 83, 156

Kohlberg, L., 73, 88, 105–6, 123, 165

Kohlhardt, J., 20

Krambia-Kapardis, M., 61

Kramer, Y., 72, 89

Landau, J. D., 102, 193

Langone, M., 110

language, ethical, 185–86

Lathrop, A., 167

law-and-order culture, 174. *See also* deterrence approaches

law students, 148–51, *161,* 162–63

learning theory, 122

Lebanon, 56, 61, 62–63

lecture courses, large, 36–37, 83

Ledwith, A., 61, 127

Leming, J. S., 74, 84, 123

Levy, E. S., 128

Lin, C. H., 61

Lindsay, J., 5

Lipson, A., 74, 82, 83

Liska, A. E., 121

Loewy, D., 59

Lucas, G. M., 88

Luckenbill, D. F., 115, 119

Lupton, R. A., 61

Madoff, Bernard, 8

major, gender, and cheating, *77. See also specific majors*

Malinowski, C. I., 88–89

Malmstrom, F. V., 121

Margolis, John, 51

Marklein, M. B., 36

Marks, A., 110, 192

Marsden, H., 61

Martin, D. E., 37–38

Matza, D., 27, 59

Mazar, N., 89, 102–3, 104

MBA programs, 80–81, 159–62, *161*

McCabe, D. L., 5, 6, 7, 8, 18, 19, 20, 21, 27, 29, 43–47, 51, 56, 61–62, 63, 72, 73, 74, 76, 81, 83–84, 87, 91, 93, 94–96, *95,* 101, 102, 104, 105, 106, 107, 108, 109, 110, 113, 115, 118, 121, 122, 123, 127, 128, 133, 134, 142, 143, 146, 147, 148, 150, 151, 155, 156, 158, 159, 160, 161, 167, 168, 177, 178, 179, 180, 183, 185, 189, 192

McGavern, N., 74, 82, 83

McGee, R., 85–86, 121

McGoldrick, K., 38

McLeod, B. A., 37, 72, 127

media perspective, 36–37, 160. *See also* scandals

medical students, 151–53, *161*

Melendez, Brian, 6, 43, 91

Mertz, M., 29
methodological issues, 37–38, 164
Michael, W. B., 74, 82, 83
Michaels, J. W., 83, 115, 123
Miethe, T. D., 83, 115, 123
Miller, A., 20, 127–28
Milliken, F. J., 179
modified honor codes, 52, *97*, 98–99, 110–11
Mohammad, J., 61
moral development. *See* ethical/moral development
moral obligation of faculty, 165–66
Morrison, E. W., 179
Mower, L., 155
Mudrack, P., 88
Muhney, K. A., 155
Murdock, T. B., 20, 72, 127–28
Mustaine, E. E., 72, 82, 84, 85, 87
myths and stories, 184–85

Nathanson, C., 89
Neill, J. T., 61
Nelson, A. B., 72, 74
Nelson, K. A., 168, 169
neutralization strategies, 59–60, 89, 118
Newcomb, T. M., 5, 165
Ney, Bob, 9
Niiya, Y., 72, 80
Nohria, N., 159
Norfolk Academy, 29, 192
Nuss, E. M., 108, 133

Obenshain, S. S., 152
observations of cheating, *131*, 133
O'Connell, V., 9
offender reintegration, 173
open-ended comments: code and no-code students, 104–5; about cultures of academic integrity, 188–89; explanations for cheating in, 39; of faculty, 136–41; of first-year students, 125; of high school students, 19–20, 25–26, 32
opportunity reduction approaches, 126–27, 128, 146
orientation of students and faculty, 175–77

parents and academic integrity, 32–33, 141, 142, 171
parochial schools, 22, 23, 24, 28, *28*
Passow, H. J., 121, 124
Patron, H., 123–24
Paulhus, D. L., 89
Pavela, G., 98, 110, 178
peer influence, 6–7, 114–16; disapproval as determinant of change, 116–18, *117*; in Lebanon, 63; perceptions of peer behavior, 118–21, *119*, *120*, 183. *See also* honor codes
Penn State, Smeal College of Business, 178
Perez, E., 8
Perry, A. R., 72
pharmacy students, 153–54, 161, *161*
Piroch, J., 72, 81
plagiarism: anti-plagiarism software, 71, 127, 171; definitions of, 38; faculty observations of, 133; among graduate students, 64–65; among high school students, 27–28; media perspective on, 36; among pharmacy students, 154. *See also* cut-and-paste plagiarism
policy: statements of, 174–75; training and orientation about, 175–77; understanding and acceptance of, 114–15, 121–22
Pranis, K., 172
Premeaux, S. R., 157
pre-med students, 153
pre-pharmacy students, 154
pressure to cheat, 6–7, 27, 84
prevalence of cheating, 71; Bowers data, 39–43, *41*, *42*; in broader culture, 164; Center for Academic Integrity survey, 51–52, *53*, 54–55; cross-cultural surveys, 61–63, *62*; cut-and-paste plagiarism, 69, *70*, 71; graduate students, 63–65, *64*; McCabe and Treviño study, 43–47; public universities, 47–50, *48*; two-year vs. four-year colleges, 67–68, *68*; web-based surveys, 55–57, *58*, 59–61
private schools, 21–22, 29–30
professional schools. *See* graduate students

survey research: access to schools for, 21–22; to assess culture of integrity, 190; with Center for Academic Integrity, 51–52, *53*, 54–55; cross-cultural, 61–63, *62*; elimination of first-year students from, 45, 56; first project, 1, 43–47; graduate students, 63–65, *64*; on high school students, 19; honor codes (1995/1996), 94–96, *95*; honor codes (2005/2006), 96–99, *100*; public universities, 46–50, *48*; standard measure of cheating, 2–3; two-year vs. four-year colleges, 67–68, *68*; web-based, 55–57, *58*, 59–61, 96. *See also* response rates

Sutherland, E. H., 115, 119
Sweitzer, V. L., 90
Sykes, G. M., 27, 59

Taietz, P., 86
Taylor-Bianco, A., 61, 72, 80–81
teachers, high school, 19–20, 32–33. *See also* faculty
Tenbrunsel, A. E., 182, 183
tenure, 139–40
Teodorescu, D., 61
test cheating: gender and, *75*, 76; honor codes and, 92–93, *93*; observations of, 60; panic and, 65; prevalence of, *48*, 50, *53*, 54–55, *66*
Tewksbury, R., 72, 82, 84, 85, 87
Thoma, S. J., 5, 165
"throating," 153
Tibbetts, S. G., 72, 81, 88
Tittle, C. R., 123
Tomlinson, P., 5
training of students and faculty, 175–77
Treviño, L. K., 5, 6, 7, 8, 43–47, 72, 73, 74, 76, 81, 82, 83–84, 87, 90, 91, 93, 94–96, *95*, 101, 102, 104, 105, 106, 107, 108, 109, 110, 113, 115, 118, 121, 122, 123, 127, 128, 142, 143, 146, 147, 156, 158, 159, 160, 161, 167, 168, 172, 177, 178, 179, 183, 187, 189, 192
Turnley, W. H., 88
two-year colleges, 67–68, *68*
types of cheating, 40, *40*, *42*, *44*, 44–45. *See also* prevalence of cheating; *specific types*

"understanding of policy" variable, 114–15, 121–22
University of Colorado at Boulder, 172
University of Michigan, 172
University of Virginia, 5, 110, 171, 192
unproctored exams: faculty and, 146, 172; at high school level, 23; just community and, 106; modified honor code and, 52, 98, 110; reporting requirement and, 112, 179, 181; traditional honor code and, 6, 78, 91

values in shaping ethical culture, 172–74
views of cheating: changing definitions and, 38; of college students, 188–89, 195; of faculty, 130–33, *131*, *132*; of high school students, 20, 26, 30–33, *31*; of junior high students, 20; peer behavior and, 118–21, *119*, *120*; of pharmacy students, 154; plagiarism and, 57, 59, 76, 131, 133; self-concept maintenance and, 89, 103; and seriousness, 65, *66*, 67, 130–31, *132*
Vowell, P. R., 115

Wajda-Johnston, V. A., 37
Walker, M. U., 173
Ward, D. A., 72, 74
Washington and Lee University, 177, 185, 192
Wasieleski, D., 72, 81
web-based surveys, 47, 55–57, *58*, 59–61, 96
Wen, L. Y., 61
Wenham, M., 36
West, J. E., 121
Whitley, B. E., 72, 74, 89, 121, 124, 146, 167
Williams, A. E., 85
Williams, K. M., 89
Williams, T. D., 123, 124
women's colleges, honor codes at, 77–79, *78*
Worell, L., 74
workplace codes of conduct, 107–8
Wowra, S. A., 88

Wright, J. C., 133
Writers Center, 23, 24
written work, cheating on: gender and, *75*; at public universities, *48*, 48–49, 50; seriousness and, *66*, 67. *See also* cut-and-paste plagiarism; plagiarism

Yardley, J., 37
Youngblood, S. A., 189

Zambito, T., 8
Zimny, S. T., 87
Zimring, R. E., 123
Zopiatis, A. A., 61